LADAKH'S TRADITIONAL TIES WITH BUDDHIST TIBET

LADAKH'S TRADITIONAL TIES WITH BUDDHIST TIBET

SONAM JOLDAN

KALPAZ

Ladakh's Traditional Ties with Buddhist Tibet

ISBN: 978-81-7835-911-3

Published in 2012 in India by
Kalpaz Publications
C-30, Satyawati Nagar,
Delhi-110052
E-mail: kalpaz@hotmail.com
Phone : 9212729499

Lasser Type Setting : Quick Media, Delhi
Printed at : Chawla Offset Printers, Delhi

Contents

Preface/Acknowledgements

Ladakh is a remote area in the wester Himalaya. In spite of the huge mountains ranges, Ladakh had developed into an active and important religious, cultural and commercial relation with Buddhist Tibet and many other countries. Ladakh along with Sikkim, Bhutan and Mustang in the cis-Himalayan states where Tibetan Buddhism continuous to be practiced, as a living religious, as it has been for thousands years. This study traces the deep historical relationship between Ladakh and Buddhist Tibet. I used here Buddhist Tibet to indicate the time period that is before Chinese invade Tibet.

I would like to express my gratitude for the assistance I have received for the last ten years from various people and institutions researching and writing this book. This book has mainly grown out of a dissertation that I wrote at Jawaharlal Nehru University (JNU), New Delhi. Few articles that I have already published are also included in the book. I have also used some data that I have collected for the undergoing research project at Richen Shah Center for West Himalayan Cultures, Islamic University of Sciences and Technology, (IUST) Awantipora, Kashmir.

In JNU, I am grateful to my supervisor late Professor Dawa Norbu and co-supervisor Professor Mahendra P. Lama. Their richness of references, empathetic understanding, encouragement and support helped me in bringing this study to the final stage. I would like to thank Dr. Meenu Rangunathan and Mr. John Bray, friends and classmates.

In the Government of Jammu and Kashmir, I would like to thank Mr. Nawang Rigzin Jora, Minister for Tourism and Culture and his personal staff. It was a very good experiences working with him as Public Relations Officer.

And in IUST, I would like to thank Professor A.R. Trag, Vice Chancellor, Professor Siddiq Wahid, former Vice Chancellor and Professor Mohmad Amin Masoodi, Register for their continuous support and encouragement that I have received for the last two years. Professor Siddiq Wahid has always encouraged and suggests me to write this book. My thanks also go to my colleagues and friends here in the university.

I would also like to thank Kalpaz Publications and marketing and editorial team for offering to publish the book.

I was benefited immensely through the interviews with all the people especially the monks who have been to monastic centre in Tibet for education and traders. It is difficult to list them all here. I would like thank the staff of the following institutes for providing me the relevant materials: the National Archives, New Delhi, State Archives, Jammu, District Archives, Leh-Ladakh, the library of Tibetan Works and Archives, Dharamsala, and Munshi Aziz Bhat Museum, Kargil. Besides, I have consulted the works of many people here I would like to mentioned some of them especially Professor Luciano Petech, A. Cunningham, A.H. Francke, Austine Waddell, Dr. Janet Rizvi, David Snellgrove, John Crook, Prof. Tsering Shakya, W. Moorcroft, Tashi Rabgais, Thupstan Paldan, Dr. Nawang Tsering, and Nawang Tsering Shakspo.

My thanks also go to my friends in Ladakh. Whenever we get chance, we debate and discussed on many issues and it played an important role in stimulating my thinking. And finally I would like thanks for my wife, son and parents back in Ladakh.

Sonam Joldan

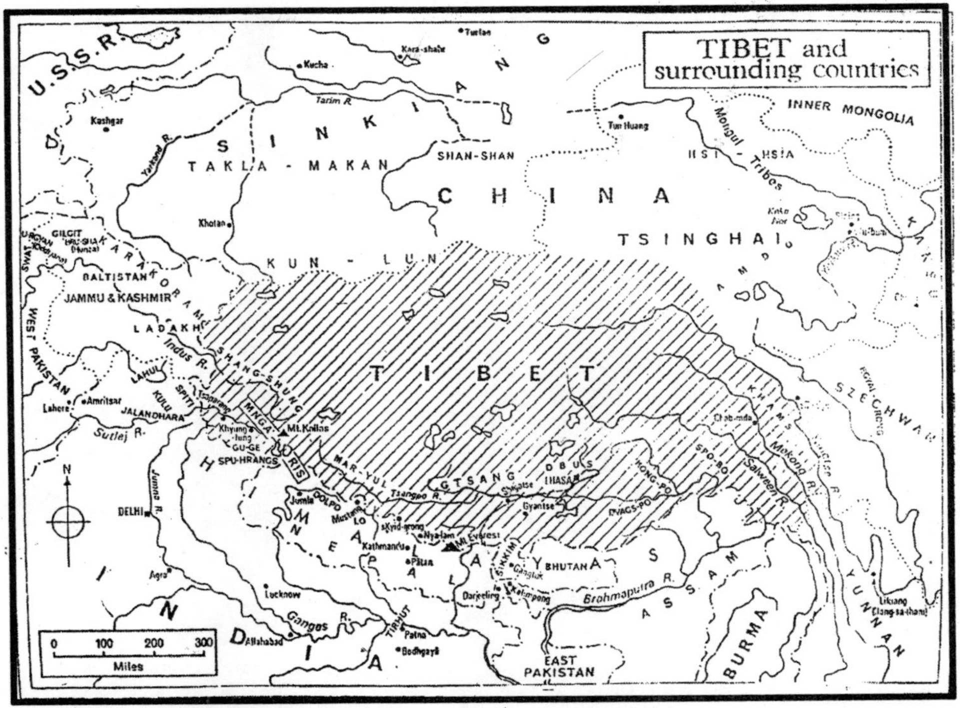

Source: David Snellgrove and Hugh Richardson, *A Cultural History On Tibet*, 1968.

1
Introduction

Geographical Background

Ladakh is the northernmost part of Jammu and Kashmir State, linked with the Kashmir valley by the Zogila pass (3529 meters) and forms a part of the trans-Himalayas.[1] It is one of the most elevated regions of the earth, the altitudes ranging from 3000 meters to 7000 meters.[2] It lies roughly between 32 to 36 North latitudes and 76 to 79 East longitudes.[3]

The chief mountain ranges in Ladakh are the Karakoram, Zanskar and Ladakh. The highest mountain in Ladakh is the Karakoram, situated on the north-east of the Shayok and Nubra valleys.[4] The Ladakh range has no major peak; its average height is a little less than 6,000 meters, and a few of its passes are less than 5,000 meters. The Indus valley is bounded to the south by the Zanskar range.

Ladakh has been referred by many names, the most common being Ladakh, or in Tibetan *La-dvags*, the land of many passes. Formerly, it was also called "dMar-yul" or lowland or Red-land.[5] Ladakh consists of various regions known as Zanskar, Suru valley, Rupshu, Nubra valley and Central Ladakh situated along the different rivers.

Nubra Valley

Nubra valley or the northwestern part of Ladakh is situated along the Shayok and the Nubra rivers.[6] It is separated from Central Ladakh by the Kardongla pass, about 18380 feet high. The road to Nubra valley that was constructed across Kardongla is the highest motorable road in the world. The famous caravan route from Leh to Yarkand passes through Nubra valley. The average altitude of the valley is 10000 feet.

The lower villages of this valley are as warm as the lower portion of Central Ladakh, while the upper villages enjoy a moderate climate.

Central Ladakh

This region is composed of upper, central and lower Ladakh, situated along the Indus River. It stretches along the Indus from South-east to North-west of Ladakh, covering a total area of about 4,000 square miles, and an average altitude of the inhabited portions is about 11,500 feet.[7] It is also called the Indus valley, and is the most populous area of Ladakh. Besides Nubra valley, Central Ladakh forms another fertile track in Ladakh. Historically and culturally it has formed the heartland of Ladakh.

Zanskar

Zanskar lies to the southwest of Leh. It has an area of some 3000 square miles and an average elevation of 13000 feet, and comprises the country lying along the two main tributaries of the Zanskar River.[8] The first one, the Doda, called in Tibetan *dPon-rtse-chu*, has its source at the base of the glacier which descends towards Zanskar near the mountain-pass known as Penzila (dPon-rtse-la), and it then flows along the main valley leading towards Padum, the capital of Zanskar.[9]

The second tributary is formed by two sub- tributaries known as Kurgiakh-chu with its source near the Shingo-La and Tsarap-chu with its source near the Baralacha-La. These two rivers unite below the village of Purne to form the Lingti (Tibetan Lung-nak).[10] The Lung-nak-chu then flows northwestwards along a narrow and precipitous gorge towards the Padum Valley where it unites with the Doda river to form the Zanskar river. The Zanskar river then takes a northeastern course until it joins the Indus river opposite the village of Nimo in Leh.

Zanskar is bounded in the north by Ladakh. To the west and northwest are Kashtawar and Purig. To the south it borders with Lahul and to the east is Rupshu.

Communication with the neighbouring Himalayan areas is maintained crossing mountain passes or along the Zanskar river when it is frozen. The easiest approach leads from Kargil through the Suru Valley and over the Pensila. It is along this track that in 1979 the first and only road in Zanskar was built to connect Padum with the main road from Srinagar into Ladakh. The remoteness of this region also explains why only a few western travelers have visited this area until recent times, the Tibetologist Alexander Csoma de Koros in 1823 being probably one of the first.[11]

Culturally and religiously it has retained close contacts with Ladakh, Guge and Tibet. Its political status depended upon the strengths and weaknesses of her neighbours, especially Ladakh, and in the 17th century it was annexed to Ladakh by king Sen-ge rNamgyal (1616-42) A. D.[12]

Rupshu

Rupshu is an area at the south-east end of Ladakh, lying between the watershed range and the Indus.[13] It the most elevated area in Ladakh.[14] The lowest ground is as much as 13,500 feet above the sea, and the long flat valley is at 15,000 feet, while the mountains that surround it have a height of 20,000 to 21,000 feet.[15] It high altitude and extreme climate render the region unsuitable for agriculture. Pastoralism, practiced in various forms, is the only form of livelihood there. Various animals including yaks and pashmina goat are found in the area. This high altitude and extreme climate make this region a natural habitat of the pashmina goat whose soft wool is known throughout the world.[16] The presence of a salt lake called the Tso-kar or White Lake, and the Tso-Moriri lake are unique features of the area.

Rupshu is bounded on the north by Central Ladakh, on the east by the Tibetan district of Chumusti, and on the south by Lahul Spiti.[17] Historically the region has connected the trade of Ladakh with different countries including Tibet and India.

Suru, Kargil and Dras

These are three areas to the west of Zanskar, on the high road between Kashmir and Leh.[18] Dras is the most westerly among them. According to A. Cunningham "its Tibetan name of hem-babs (snowfed or snow descended) is descriptive of its most striking peculiarity, as the most snowing districts of Ladakh."[19] Kargil and Suru valley are situated along with Suru River. Historically Kargil was also one of the important trade and transit center.

Spiti and Lahul

The two form the southern districts of Ladakh.[20] "Spiti comprises the whole valley of the Spiti river, from its source to the junction of the para,"[21] comprising about 1,900 square miles. Lahul comprises the valleys of the Chandra and Bhaga rivers, as well as that of the Chandra and Bhaga (united stream) following upto Treloknath, where the Chenab river enters Chamba.[22] It is about sixty-eight miles in length and thirty-four miles in breadth,[23] which gives an area of 2,312 square miles.

In 1846, when Gulab Singh became the Maharaja of Jammu, Kashmir and Ladakh, the British India government detached Spiti and Lahul from Ladakh and added it to the Kulu sub-division of Kangra district of Punjab under their control.[24] Thus, these areas are the natural divisions of Ladakh and formed administrative units under the native rulers.[25]

Today, Ladakh comprises of two districts, namely Leh and Kargil. For its administrative bifurcation in 1979, Kargil was carved out comprising two tehsils, namely Kargil and Zanskar having 129 villages and a geographical area of about 14,000 square kilometers.[26] At the time of the 1971 census there were 238 villages in the entire district of Ladakh having a geographical area of 95,876 square kilometers including the areas of Ladakh occupied by China and Pakistan).[27] According to the 2004 census the population of Ladakh was 2, 32, 864, divided almost equally between Buddhist and Muslims. There is also small percentage of Hindus, Christians and Sikhs.

The present day population of Ladakh is a mixed race, the chief of which are the Tibetan (Mongoloid) and the Dardic (Indo-Iranian).[28] Ladakh is known not only for its strategic location but also for its culture. Ladakh, along with Sikkim, Bhutan and Mustang are some of the places in the cis-Himalayan states where Mahayana Buddhism continues to be practiced as a living religion, as it has been for a thousand years. These cis-Himalayan states have had a long and consistent cultural relation with Buddhist Tibet. This study takes Ladakh as a case study to demonstrate to examining its deep traditional relations with Buddhist Tibet.

Sources

This study is based on various sources. The unpublished records are available with the National Archives of India, New Delhi, State Archives, Jammu and District Archives, Leh. These records deal mostly with the trade of Ladakh from 1867 onwards. Oral sources are the interviews with the monks, from Lamayuru, Rigzong, Likir, Spituk (dPe-t'up), Thiksay and Disket monasteries in Ladakh and traders. There are ninety-six monks in these monasteries who had been to Tibet for their higher monastic education. The details information about the monks have been mentioned in chapter two. It was fortunate that when we visited these monasteries in the summer 2004, monks were assembled for the Mandala prayers in most of the monasteries. Besides, the La-dvags rgyal-rabs, the Chronicle of Ladakh, the Tibetan texts published in A. H. Francke (1926), and few other Tibetan Texts are also used. For the names and translations of the Tibetan texts into the Roman alphabets, we tried to use those forms adopted in the modern books in western language. Written Tibetan has a number of unpronounced prefixes, and thus the radical consonant of any syllable may be the second or even third litter, e.g. dPe-t'up is pronounced as Pe-t'up. Also the travelogues and books in western language on the religion, culture and history of Ladakh and Tibet are consulted.

Methodology

This is an exercise in cultural history and trans-border cultural diffusion. Though the study of early cultural history of Mahayana Buddhism in Tibet in its formative state we came to understand early receptive tools and nature of Mahayana Buddhism. To study not only the nature of Mahayana Buddhism in Tibet but also how this region adopted itself in the Himalayas state Ladakh. Mahayana Buddhism gets it this Himalayan character, transported and transferred in the Himalayan conditions. The nature of Mahayana Buddhism is not only depends on Mahayana Buddhism but also on the nature of Himalayan conditions. Methods used in cultural studies, history and anthropology are judiciously borrowed to shed light on this subject. This research work is based on both primary and secondary sources. The primary sources are consisted of interviews with two groups of people and archival materials. These two groups include those local traders of Ladakh who used to go for the trade and the monks who have been to Tibet for higher education.

Historical Background

The term 'cultural relation' can be interpreted to include a number of aspects like paintings, sculpture, dance, music, films, theatre, literature, and so on. But here I am emphasizing the religious and spiritual ties, not the political, either implicit or deduced.

The Tibetan polity and its culture have been decisively shaped by Buddhism, which having originated in India assumed particular characteristics in the Tibetan setting, both in its doctrine and its practice. Gautama Buddha founded Buddhism around 2500 years ago. The changes and developments within Indian Buddhism in its long history were enormous. It was during this long period that it gradually became the religion of most of Asia. Buddhism disappeared from India at the end of the 12th century. By that time Buddhism was already well established in Tibet.

Tibet becomes Mahayana Buddhist Centre

Buddhism was first introduced to Tibet in the 5th century, but for the first two hundred years its impact was not so strong. In the 7th century, King Songtsen Gampo gave firmer footing to Buddhism. He married two princesses, one who was from Nepal and the other who was from China. The two princesses played a major role in influencing the king to take an interest in Buddhism and he in turn used his influence to spread Buddhism in Tibet.

Another famous king, Tisong Detsen ruled over Tibet during the latter half of the 8th century. It was during his reign that Santrakshita and Guru Padmasambhava, masters of Buddhism, were invited to Tibet from India. Padmasambhava, better known in Tibet, as Guru Rinpochey was a tantric master. He built the first Buddhist Monastery around 766-767 A.D. in Tibet. The great debate on whether the Tibetan king should choose the Indian form of Buddhism or the Chinese form took place during King Tisong Detsen's time. The Indian Buddhist master won the debate and the king decided for the Indian version of Buddhism.

The translation of Buddhist Sanskrit texts into Tibetan began under King Ralpachen (814-836 A.D). The king invited many Indian masters to Tibet who engaged in the translation of Buddhist texts along with Tibetan collaborations. The above three kings, Sontgsen Gampo, Tisong Detsen and Ralpachen, were the outstanding figures, both in war and peace, among the kings of Tibet. They are known to Tibetans as, 'The three religious kings, and men of power'.

Then came the 9th century and King Lang Dharma who was anti Buddhist. He persecuted the Buddhist Sanga and destroyed many temples. After Lang Dharma, Tibet disintegrated into a number of principalities and the central power of Tibet also disappeared. Central Tibet was hardest hit by the following Dark Age. But in Western Tibet, particularly in Guge and Purang, the political fragmentation and the decline of Buddhism were not so long lived. It was in

Western Tibet that Buddhism was rekindled and less than two centuries after the anti Buddhist persecution by Lang Dharma, Buddhism was revived in Tibet. The moving spirit behind this Buddhist renaissance, which started in western Tibet, was to be found in two holy men, Rinchen Zangpo, the translator (958-1055 A.D)[29], and the great Indian Buddhist saint Atisa (982-1052 A.D). These two were the initiators of what Buddhist historians call the second spread of Buddhism in Tibet.

All the formation of the four major sects of Mahayana Buddhism, the rNin-ma-pa sect, the bKa-gyud-pa sect, the Sa-skya-pa sect and the Ge-lug-pa sect took place in the 12th century in terms of doctrine, practice and the monastic organizations. Soon Tibet became a centre of Mahayana Buddhism. Buddhism brought tremendous changes in the Tibetan society. As Prof. Norbu said, "it changed from warrior nation to a peaceful community, from warrior kings to Lama rulers, from Bonpo magic to Buddhist rationality and from violence to compassion."[30] Mahayana Buddhism spread from Tibet to the Himalayan States of Ladakh, Mustang, Sikkim and Bhutan.

Cultural Relations between Ladakh and Buddhist Tibet

Buddhism in Ladakh first came from Kashmir and some of its remains can still be seen in Ladakh but the real influence came from Mahayana Buddhism from Tibet. Ladakh appears to have come into contact with Tibet in the 7th and 8th centuries, when the latter not only conquered western Tibet but also dictated terms to China.

With the establishment of the Ladakhi kingdom in the 10th century, Ladakh shared with Tibet the development of some Lamaic institutions. Tibetan cultural influence has been simply uniform. From the point of view of language, it has provided Ladakh with the western Tibetan dialect which is still generally spoken to this day by Ladakhi Muslims as much as Buddhists. As far as literature is concerned, the regular style of literary Tibetan has remained current in Ladakh from

10th century onwards. Tibetan influence can also be seen on the Ladakhi dress, customs, food and drink. The Ladakhi dress 'goncha' is an adaptation of the Tibetan 'chuba'. Both Ladakh and Tibet have the same staple food, 'tsampa' or barley flour and 'chang', a mildly alcoholic drink made of fermented barley. As regards religion, the major sects and the several sub-sects like the Bri-gung-pa and Brug-pa of Mahayana Buddhism were developed in Ladakh. Besides, Tibetan influence can also be seen on the Ladakhi architecture, astrology and paintings. Ladakh's religious and spiritual ties with Buddhist Tibet were very close for centuries. In terms of historical developments and evolution, Ladakh earned the present-day reputation as a peaceful Buddhist community.

The aims and objectives of this research is to study the diffusion of Mahayana Buddhism in Ladakh, the nature of relationship between Buddhist Tibet and Ladakh, the medium through which Mahayana Buddhism spread to Ladakh and the nature of Mahayana Buddhism in Ladakh today.

There were three most important tools through which Mahayana Buddhism from Tibet spread to Ladakh. They were the lama missionaries, monastic education of the Ladakhi monks in Tibet and pilgrimage and trade.

Lama Missionaries

Sending missionaries is not a new concept in Buddhism. In fact, it goes back to the time of King Ashoka, who sent missionaries to different countries. In the case of Ladakh and the Buddhist Tibet relationship also, lama missionaries played a major role in terms of monastic education, construction of monasteries and the spread of Mahayana Buddhism in Ladakh as a whole. Following are some of the important lamas who visited Ladakh mostly from Tibet and played a vital role in the teaching and spread of Mahayana Buddhism there.

Guru Padmasambhava was the first to come to Ladakh and he is believed to have visited Ladakh in the 8th century A.D. Caves where he is believed to have meditated are still found in Ladakh. Then came the famous Lotswa Rin-chen Zangpo, and the spread of Mahayana Buddhism in Ladakh is closely connected with him. He founded many monasteries in Ladakh, Lahul Spiti and Guge. Several monasteries of his time have been preserved in Ladakh, the most important among them being Nyarma, Alchi, Mangyu and Sumdo in Zanskar.

In the 15th century, another famous lama Chos-rje Gdan-ma was invited by the king of Ladakh, probably from Tibet. He built the present Phyang monastery. Phyang along with Lamayuru monastery are the important monasteries of Bri-gung-pa, a sub-sect of the bKa-gyud-pa sect of Mahayana Buddhism. The 15th century saw the growth of influence of the Ge-lug-pa or the Yellow sect in Ladakh. The king of Ladakh, Grags-bam Ide had received an envoy from the reformer Tsong Kha-pa, and in order to commemorate the event he is said to have built the dPe-t'up monastery for the new sect. According to Luciano Petech the monastery had been actually founded in the 11th century and the king must have assisted in a thorough restoration and to the transference to the Yellow sect.[31] The Ge-lug-pa sect in Ladakh developed rapidly and many monasteries were built, like Thiksey, Likir and Disket in Nubra, and Bardan in Zanskar. Stag-tsan-Ras-pa was another great lama who was invited from Tibet and was responsible for the development of the Brug-pa, a sub-sect of the bKa-gyud-pa sect in Ladakh. The great lama founded many monasteries of the Brug-pa sub-sect in Ladakh, including the famous Hemis monastery. Brug-pa sub-sect ascendance in Ladakh was fully established by Stag-tsan-Ras-pa.

Thus, the development of many sects, sub-sects and their monasteries in Ladakh was with the help of close contacts and encouragement from the main centre of the sects in Tibet. Though all the four major sects and several sub-sects of Mahayana Buddhism had developed in Ladakh, only three Lamaist sects played a major role in Ladakhi history. They were in chronological order, the Bri-gung-pa, sub-sect of the bKa-gyud-pa sect, the Ge-lug-pa sect and the Brug-pa, another sub-sect of the bKa-gyud-pa sect. The other remaining sects were the rNin-ma-pa and Sa-skya-pa, neither of which ever played a major influence in Ladakhi history. The existence of the lay monarchy, an overall authority independent of the Church did not allow a complete ascendance by one sect. However, the head Lamas had considerable influence on the royal house and the social and daily life of the people.

Monastic Education

Monastic education of Ladakhi monks in Tibet was another important medium through which Mahayana Buddhism from Tibet came to Ladakh. Tibet became an important center for monastic education and many lamas from Ladakh went to the different monasteries in Tibet for studies. There were no records of how many lamas went to Tibet for education except those sent by the royal house, who were mentioned and recorded. After getting educated in different monastic centres in Tibet, many lamas returned to their native places and played a major role in spreading Mahayana Buddhism in Ladakh. Many royal princes became monks and went for higher studies to Tibet. After coming back from Tibet, they became heads of important monasteries and played an important role in the spread of monastic education in Ladakh. For example, King Del-dan rNamgyal's second son named Lobsang Nawang Puntsog studied at the university of Brans-spun and after nine years study, he obtained the high degree of dge-bses-rab-byams-pa. After coming back from Tibet, he was appointed the abbot of Thiksey monastery, which heads seven monasteries in Ladakh.[32] The supremacy of Thiksey abbots over the other Ge-lug-pa monasteries in Ladakh did not last long; at an unknown date a royal prince became abbot of dPe-t'up and made that monastery independent of Thiksey.[33] The hallmark of Ladakhi lamas was their perusing a comprehensive study in various branches of Buddhist studies in some renowned monastic institution in Tibet, and for the lamas a visit to Lhasa, their spiritual home, was a cherished dream.

There are two important reasons why the cis-Himalayan people looked upon Tibet as the centre of Mahayana Buddhism. First of all, Mahayana Buddhism came directly from Tibet to the Himalayan areas and secondly, Tibet in due course of time became a centre of Mahayana Buddhism and the residence of leading Lamas who taught Mahayana Buddhism.

Pilgrimage and Trade

The Capital of Ladakh, Leh, due to its strategic location had developed into an active and important centre for commercial intercourse with Tibet, Persia, Yarkand and China. Though the majority of the Ladakhi lived by subsistence agriculture, yet trade played a vital role in the development of its economy and culture.

The trade relation between Ladakh and Buddhist Tibet is an old one. It is quite possible that the inhabitants of Ladakh felt the Tibetan influence as early as mid-seventh century, for the nomadic Tibetans of Changthang (Western Tibet) would have good reasons to have contact with the sedentary Mon and Dard, exchanging grains for the animal products. Then come the two missions 'Lapchak' and the 'Cha-pa' between Ladakh and Buddhist Tibet, which were setup as the result of the Tinmosgang Treaty.[34] This treaty brought to an end the three-corner conflict between Ladakh, Tibet and the Moghul Empire, and established the border between Ladakh and Tibet, and some trade regulation especially about wool and pashm. The Lapchak mission went from Leh to Lhasa once in every three years. The king of Ladakh was to send offerings to Buddhist Tibet for the Smon-lam festival and for the blessing of the Dalai Lama. In return, the Tibetan government sent an annual trade caravan from Lhasa to Leh, popularly known as the Cha-pa mission or tea man as the mission used to come with loads of tea. This mission gave rise to a number of lesser missions. The major monasteries sent half religious and half commercial missions to Tibet. The participants ranged from the big merchants to ordinary peasants, from bigger monasteries to lama entrepreneurs.

The effect of the traditional relationships, which continued for hundreds of years between Ladakh and Buddhist Tibet were felt in nearly every village in Ladakh. It disappeared after the Chinese occupation of Tibet when the borders were closed. Of late, India and China have made progress in boosting economic ties, prompting both sides to look at opening up new routes to encourage cross-border trade. In June 2003, India and China agreed to open the border trade along the eastern stretch of the rugged Himalayan border between Sikkim and Tibet. In this changed environment, the people of Ladakh are optimistic about the opening of the old trade route through Demchok on the Ladakhi side and Tashigang on the Tibetan side. Trade and subsistence agriculture have been the Ladakhis only livelihood through the ages. At the moment there is no border trade, but there is smuggling and goods selling in the streets of Leh. There is no reason why this old trade route should not be reopened. Besides economic benefits, reopening of this old route will promote pilgrimage to the Kailash Mansarovar Lake and other holy places in Tibet. The Kailash Mansarovar Lake can be reached in a relatively shorter time than the present hazardous fifteen-day trek from further South. One of the important advantages of the route through Ladakh is that there is a motorable road on both sides of the border; one can drive all the way up to Kailash. This is ideal for older people and women. The hope for Ladakhis is the restoration of normal border trading and cultural relations between them and Tibet. The re-opening of the old trade routes will not only help trade in the region but also promote pilgrimages and tourism.

Chapterisation

This study is organized in the following manner. Chapter Two of my thesis is about monastic organization and education. There are many monasteries that have been founded in Ladakh. The foundations of these monasteries are associated with the effort of active lama missionaries and encouragement, guidance and support from Buddhist Tibet. Chapter Three and Four trace Ladakh's deep historical relations with Buddhist Tibet. Chapter three covers the Ladakhi history and its cultural relations with Buddhist Tibet from 10th century, when the first kingdom in Ladakh was established, to the beginning of the rNamgyal dynasty. In the 10th and 11th centuries, the cultural influences on Ladakh came from both Kashmir and Guge and Puran, provinces in western Tibet. Alchi monastery and its paintings are the best example of both Kashmiri and Tibetan influences during the period. In these two provinces of western Tibet, the Buddhist renaissance took place after central Tibet disintegrated. And from western Tibet Buddhism was not only spread to cis-Himalayan states but most importantly re-introduced in Tibet. From the 12th century onwards the cultural influence in Ladakh was mainly from Tibet. This is shown by the fact that several important monks from Tibet visited Ladakh and built monasteries during the period. Chapter Four covers the Ladakhi history and its cultural ties with Buddhist Tibet during the 16th to 19th centuries. The cultural influences from Tibet during this period were consistent and close. Most of the present monasteries in Ladakh were built during this period. Chapter Five deals with trade and pilgrimage. Trade and pilgrimage is played also an important role in the development of close relationship between Ladakh and Tibet. The Sixth chapter is the concluding part where the analytical conclusions reached in each of the chapters are elaborated.

Many people have written on the history and culture of Ladakh but nobody has worked on cultural relations with Buddhist Tibet. This study will cover Ladakh's traditional relations with Buddhist Tibet from 10th Century till Chinese occupation of Tibet. There has been a consistence cultural relationship between Buddhist Tibet and Ladakh. The advent of Mahayana Buddhism in the Himalayan States where the people were having faith in primitive religions did not create any serious conflict, as they were peaceful 'diffusions'. Tibetan

Buddhist ideas and values, which came into contact with the indigenous culture, ecology and psyche of the Himalayan people added to the Himalayan Character. The dynamic and living principles of Mahayana Buddhism gradually transformed the history and religion of the Himalayan States. In the past there have been tendencies to state that the cultural ties between Buddhist Tibet and the Himalayan States have political significance in that the cis-Himalayan States were somewhat subordinate to Tibet. I, however, beg to differ. This is in keeping with the contemporary views of Ladakhi people. The fact is that there have been considerable developments in the Lamaist culture areas in the cis-Himalayas since the early traditional relation between the Himalayan states and Tibet. First of all there is a steady growth of local identities in the Lamaist culture areas in the Himalayas. This is a new social fact, which we have to recognize and take into consideration when studying the relations between Buddhist Tibet and the Himalayan states. Secondly, there have been unprecedented modern historical developments, which have transformed South Asia into an engine of change. Economic growth, education, science and technology have influenced indirectly and invisibly but very effectively the Lamaist culture areas in the cis-Himalayan region, which looked upon Buddhist Tibet as the 'epicenter' of their faith towards South Asia.

REFERENCES

1. *Census of India- Series 8-Jammu and Kashmir*, 1981, p. 12.
2. *Ibid.*, p. 12.
3. *Ibid.*, p. 12.
4. Janet Rizvi, *Ladakh: Crossroad of High Asia*, (Delhi: Oxford University Press, 1983), p. 20.
5. A. Cunningham, *Ladakh, Physical, Statistical and Historical*, (London: W. H. Allen, 1854, Reprinted, New Delhi: Sagar Publication, 1970), pp. 18-19.
6. *Ibid.* p. 21.
7. *Census of India-Series 8-Jammu and Kashmir*, 1981, p. 8.

8. David L. Snellgrove and Tadeusz Skorupski, *The Cultural Heritage of Ladakh Vol. II* : Zanskar and the Cave Temples of Ladakh (New Delhi: Vikas Publishing House, 1980), p. 3.
9. *Ibid.* p. 3.
10. *Ibid.* p. 3.
11. W. Moorcroft and George Trebeck, *Travels in the Himalayan Provinces of Hindustan and Punjab; in Ladakh and Kashmir; in Pashawar, Kabul, Kunduz and Bokhara, from 1819-182, Vol. 1* (New Delhi: Sagar Publications, 1971), p. 338.
12. David L. Snellgrove and Tadeusz Skorupski, op. cit. 8, p. 11.
13. Frederic Drew, *Northern Barrier of India* (Jammu: Light and Life Publishers, 1973), p. 296.
14. A. Cunningham, op. cit. 5, p. 22.
15. Frederic Drew, op. cit. 13, p. 296.
16. Foreign Department, Political. A. Branch, Nos. 21-24, Consultation September 1875.
17. A. Cunningham, op. cit. 5, p. 21.
18. *Ibid.* p. 22.
19. *Ibid.* pp. 22-23.
20. C. L. Datta, *Ladakh and Western Himalayan Politics, 1819-1948*, (New Delhi: Munshiram Manoharlal Publishers Pvt. Ltd. 1973), p. 4.
21. A. Cunningham, op. cit. 5, p. 24.
22. *Ibid.* p. 24.
23. *Ibid.* p. 24.
24. C. L. Datta, op. cit. 20, p. 5.
25. *Ibid.* p. 2.
26. *Census of India- series 8-Jammu and Kashmir*, 1981, pp. 3 & 8.
27. *Ibid.* p. 8
28. Luciano Petech, *The Kingdom of Ladakh, C. 950-1842 A.D* (Roma: *Istituto Italiano Per IL Medio Ed Estremo Orient*, 1977), p. 6.
29. David Snellgrove and Tadeusz Skorupski, *The Cultural Heritage of Ladakh Vol. One* (England: Aris & Phillps Ltd., 1977), p. 5.
30. Dawa Norbu, "Indo-Tibetan Cultural Relations Through The Ages," *Tibet House Bulletin*, May 1998, p. 3.
31. Luciano Petech, op. cit. 28, p. 22.
32. *Ibid.* p. 85.
33. *Ibid.* p. 85.

34. A. H. Francke, *Antiquities of Indian Tibet, The Chronicles of Ladakh and Minor Chronicles, Texts Translation, with Notes and Maps, Part II* (New Delhi: S. Chand and Co., 1926), p. 42. See also Luciano Petech, op. cit. 28, p. 74.

2

Monastic Organization and Monastic Education as a Sustaining Factor

The name for a Buddhist monastery in both Tibetan and Ladakhi is Gonpa (dGon-pa), a solitary place or hermitage. According to Robert James Miller "any unit where in there is a resident body of monks will be called Monastery".[1]

The Buddhist monastery is a central feature of the Buddhist tradition and has been so since the early development of Buddhism. The origin of the monastery goes back to the time when the Buddhist monks wandered around for knowledge and food. There is a problem with spending the whole year wandering in India. During the rainy season for about four months the roads and tracks are covered with water and it is simply very difficult to move around the country. There is also a moral question, which has been raised at times, that wandering around in water/floods may cause harm to living beings. Due to this it seems that already in the time of Buddha there was a tradition of staying in one place for the rainy season. So, it likely that in many ways the origins of the Buddhist monastic tradition goes back to these rainy season retreat dwellings. Royal patronage especially after the king Ashoka, radically transformed the monastic structure.

Tibetan Buddhist monasteries were the cornerstones of Tibetan religion, culture, education and knowledge. For centuries, great monasteries with their renowned universities become famous across Tibet and in neighboring countries where Mahayana Buddhism from Tibet took deep roots. Many monks from different countries used to go to Tibet for higher studies. Many monks from Ladakh also went to different monasteries in Tibet. There were no records how many Lamas from Ladakh went to Tibet for education except those sent by the royal house, who were mentioned and recorded. As with Tibet, when Tibetans went to study in India, there were no records except the sixteen Tibetans who were sent to India with Thonmi Sambhota[2] by the royal court. As we are going to see in the third and the fourth chapters there was a close and consistent cultural relationship between Ladakh and Buddhist Tibet for centuries and this resulted in the development of many monasteries in Ladakh.

Monasteries in Ladakh can be categorized into three levels. These are the village level monasteries, medium monasteries and the main monasteries. Every Buddhist village in Ladakh has a village level monastery (mini Lhakang), and a few such monasteries are attached to medium monasteries and are in turn linked with a major monastery. The cases of Lamayuru monastery and Spituk (dPe-t'up) monastery very well illustrate the system of hierarchy in each monastery complex in Ladakh. The Spituk Monastery manages several medium monasteries like Sanker and Sabu. and each of these manages a large number of village-level monasteries. In the case of Lamayuru monastery also, it is connected with several medium level monasteries like Skurbuchan, each of which manage a large number of village-level monasteries.

Monastic Locations

There are about thirty-seven monasteries in Ladakh including Zanskar. This figure does not include the small village-level monasteries. In the eastern part of Ladakh, there are some four monasteries including the Korzok monastery, at an altitude of about 4200 meters from sea level, situated about 170 kilometers east of Leh. In Central Ladakh, i.e. from Hemis to Phyang, there are about nine monasteries belonging to different sects and sub-sects of Tibetan Buddhism. In the northern part of Ladakh, i. e. in Nubra valley, there are some four monasteries at the average altitude of 3300 meters from sea level. In the western part of Ladakh, i. e. from Nimo to Shargola[3], there are some nine monasteries. In the Zanskar valley of Ladakh, there are some twelve monasteries[4].

Besides, there are some small nunneries, run on the same lines as the monasteries. Each nunnery has attached to it a small estate, usually worked by the nuns themselves. The nunnery at Rigzong, about eighty kilometers west of Leh is called Chomoling and at present there are some twenty nuns living there.

Like in Tibet, wood is also scarce in Ladakh and most of the monasteries in Ladakh are built of stone or sun-dried bricks. The design and style are the same as those in Tibet. The monasteries are often quite imposing buildings, several stories in height, with large courtyards in which the Lamas perform the yearly monastic festival. The ground floor is with smaller windows and is generally used as a storehouse. Other floors house different deities. In terms of size, the monasteries in Ladakh are smaller than the Tibetan monasteries. The size of Tibetan monasteries sometimes is immense, several containing thousands of monks.[5]

Monastic Hierarchy and Administration

There are several stages of monkhood. The first stage is when a boy enters the monastery as a drapa (grava-pa)[6]. Then he enters the next stage called Getsul (Ge-ts-ul), the commencing of monkhood but not quite fully ordained monk.[7] He is expected to participate in the daily prayers and to perform duties of the monasteries. The Getsul may continue to study under a senior monk of the monastery. At Rigzong monastery in Ladakh, August 2004, there were twenty drapas and Getuls, all young boys, aged between seven years to twenty-two years. There is a monastic school for these young boys, where besides the monastic teaching, there are subjects like Mathematics, English and Hindi languages are also teaching. In the same monastery there are some twenty senior monks. The name of the oldest monk is Tsultim Angdus, eighty-six years old. He had been to Tibet for higher studies in 1948. He comes from the village Balam near Spituk in Leh District. He studies in Dre-pung monastery in Tibet from three years.

After the completion of Getsul, the monk will be eligible for entering the rank of the full monk, the Gelong (Ge-long). The Gelong takes his vows in the presence of the entire monastic community in the main temple. The parents of the monk celebrate the success of their son by inviting all the monks of the monastery as well as villagers for lunch. I have seen several such celebrations. The last one was in July 2004, we were with a tourists group, and went to visit the Hemis monastery. It was around lunchtime when we reached there, and the temples were closed as a family from the same village invited all monks whose son became a Gelong in the same monastery. After some time, the monk in charge of the main assembly hall came back and opened the temples for the tourists.

The Gelong is the fully ordained monk. As such, he is entitled to be called Lama, although the title is used in courtesy for almost all monks in Ladakh. He is eligible for the various offices and services in which he contributes to the administration of the monastery as a whole. The highest degree of the monastic education is the dge-bshes, equivalent to the doctorate degree of the modern education system. In addition to the above categories, there are some other sacred specialists. Like Lamas, the nuns (chomos) have also been categorized. A novice Chomo is termed as Geyenma. On the next promotion, she becomes Gesulma and then Gelongma.

The appointment of Gelong to the various offices of mastery is a remarkably democratic system. The governing body of the monastery is in-fact the collective assembly of monks, which meets regularly to discuss questions of the day, to make policy and to appoint officers. The opinion of older monks are given due weight in the major decisions of the entire monkhood. Usually the officers are appointed for a period of two or three years, depending on the monastery. One can also be re-elected to the same post for more years and also get elected to various other posts in the monastery. Thus, every senior monk has a wide experience of the main offices and monastic affairs. According to John Crook and

Tsering Shakya, "the system drives from the code of governance in the Vinaya: the earliest regulation of a community."[8]

There is a well-organized administrative system in every monastery in Ladakh. In most of the major monasteries there, an incarnate lama, called in Ladakhi and Tibetan 'Rinpochey', occupies the highest post. To take the case of Phyang and Thiksay monasteries in Central Ladakh, Togdan Rinpochey heads the Phyang and Thiksay Rinpochey heads Thiksay monastery. The Rinpochey takes part only in the important decisions of the monastery, whereas the elected officers carry out the normal activities and administration in the monastery. The monastic administrative ranks in Ladakh are as follows:

I Khenpo (mKan-po) = Abbot

II. Lobon (slob-dPon) = Teacher

III. Umzat (dBu-mDzad) = Director of Ceremonies

IV. Uchung (dBu-Chung) = Junior Umzat

V. Gesko (dGe-bsko) = Disciplinarian

VI. Chagzot (Phang-mDod) = Treasurer

The officers carry out the daily activities of the monastery and implement the decisions taken by the entire monkhood. Although each office has fixed duration, the incumbent may resign or sometimes get an extension, subject to the general approval of the assembly of monks of the monastery. The first five positions in the administration hierarchy usually manage the religious and spiritual work of the monastery. But the Chagzot organizes and manages all the secular tasks of the monastery, especially the economic tasks. He collects revenue, lends money, keeps accounts and conducts all other economic affairs of the monastery.

When the monks assemble for the performance of liturgies, each monk sits in his own position according to educational qualifications and right of office. At Thiksay monastery in central Ladakh, all the monks of the monastery assemble every morning in the main assembly hall for prayer and each monk sits in his position. There are four rows of seating arrangement in this hall and the monks occupy their position in these rows as per their qualifications and seniority. At the end of each row sit the younger monks and all except the Gesko (disciplinarian) face inwards towards the opposing rank that faces them. The Gesko sits near the entrance facing the shrine, and can thus observe everybody.

Monastic Function and the Monastery—Village Relationship

Each of the major monasteries in Ladakh is supported by nearby villages. Some of the monasteries also have villages very far from the monastery affiliated to it. For example Hemis monastery has the support of many villages in all parts of Ladakh. The number of villages that support a monastery is largely dependent on the size of the monastery. The bigger monasteries like Lamayuru, Spituk and Hemis have the support of many villages than the smaller monasteries.

Monasteries are essentially religious establishments catering to the religious and spiritual needs of the people. Besides their contribution in the field of education, their role in cultural and social needs of the people is no less significant. The monasteries receive boys as novices from the families. Most families send a son, normally the younger one, who lives usually with an older relative of a monk's house. The older monk has the job of instructing his junior in reading, writing and reciting the liturgical texts, as well as in the formal discipline of the monastery.

The Lamas play an important role as linkages between the monastery and the villages. The monks carry out all functions of the monastery. Quite a few events in Ladakhi Buddhist life are based on the achievement of religious merit, and the importance of religious merit is transmitted through the monks and nuns. The existence of monkhood enables the laity to acquire merit (bSod-nams) ensuring a satisfactory or improved rebirth in the next life. A villager can add to his stock of merit through services to the monastery in the form of donation, work and the sponsorship of rituals.

The monks provide religious services to the village and additionally produce religious objects. Most of the village houses are filled with Buddhist religious objects and symbols. A family chapel can be found in most houses. It is often the most elaborate and expensive part of the house and filled with religious texts, rugs, thangkas and other treasures passed on from generation to generation.

The monks and nuns are invited by individual families and also to villages for village ceremonies and the recitation of important Buddhist texts. Usually a family invites monks and nuns and even laymen[9], to recite the 'Bum' the Prajnaparamita in 100,000 lines, the Heart Sutra.[10] This text consists of sixteen volumes and most families can afford the recitation of this text by the clergy. The monks get food and money for their services. The recitation of Kanjur (collection of Buddhist texts), consisting of one hundred and eight volumes, takes place at the village level.

The major monasteries in Ladakh have the annual cycle of ceremonies, comprising a series of small and large festivals. Following are some of the ceremonies performed annually by major monasteries in Ladakh.

I. Recitation of important Buddhist texts like the Bum, the Kanjur, etc.

II. Monlam- the recital of progress expressing the aspiration for enlightment.

III. Ritual celebrating the life of Tsong-kha-pa.

IV. Evocation of Dharmapalas or protectors.

V. Monastic festival with religious dances.

Among these, the biggest annual event of the monastery is the monastic festival. The monastic festivals are annual events of the major monasteries, which the local people eagerly look forward to attending, both for attaining religious merit and as a means of social entertainment. These are generally held to commemorate the establishment of a particular monastery, the birth anniversary of its patron saint or some major events in the history and evolution of Tibetan Buddhism. For example the Hemis festival is celebrated to commemorate the birth anniversary of Guru Padmasambhava. Except few festivals like the Hemis, Phyang and Lamayuru most of the monastic festivals in Ladakh are held in winter. People turn out in thousands to attend these festivals in their colouful best, making every event a carnival of colours.

The core event of the monastic festival is a highly choreographed ritual dance-drama known as 'chams' directed by the 'cham-spon', the dance master of the monastery. The dances are performed not only to dramatize the esoteric philosophy of the event for the benefit of the lay devotees, but also by way of ritual offerings to the tutelary deities of the monastery and the guardians of the faith. A select group of resident lamas of the monastery, dressed in brightly patterned brocade robes, perform these dances in the courtyard of the monastery. They also wear masks representing various divinities. The dancers hold ritual instruments in their hands, which along with hand gestures or *mudras* of the dancers symbolize different aspects of the dance.

The 'Rimpochey' or head lama of the monastery conducts the rites and ceremonies of the festival. The Lamas of the monastery and the Lama musicians in their full ceremonial attire sit on carpet-covered cushions on either side of the throne in the festival ground, according to their hierarchy. For the lay devotees, however, seeing the masked dancers serve to familiarize themselves with the kind of deities they are to encounter during the transition period between death and rebirth in one of the six forms of existence, depending upon one's *karmic* existence. The event is also essentially a pilgrimage to the monastery and its various temples.

For each of these ceremonies, villagers supply food and services. To ensure a regular supply a few families are appointed for each of these ceremonies. The appointed families are called (gNyer-pa), who are responsible for ensuring the availability of foodstuff in the form of teas (mang-ja) and meals for the community of monks and also the materials essential for the ritual, mainly 'tsampa' roasted barley flour, the staple food of Ladakh and butter for gTor-ma[11] and butter for oil lamps.

The monastery not only plays an important role in the religious and spiritual life of the people in Ladakh but also in their social functions. Lama interaction is important in every major Buddhist social function in Ladakh. On the occasions of birth, marriage and death, monks are consulted and invited to perform worship. When a child is born, the parents visit with the child the head Lama and request him to suggest a name for their child. An auspicious day for a marriage is suggested by the local astrologer (onpo) or by a monk. On the occasion of the marriage, monks perform worship at both the bride and groom's houses. In the event of death in a family, the monk gives the sermon of 'Phoa' before anyone else touches the dead body. The sermon is believed to pave the way for a smooth heavenly journey, and for a better rebirth. Monks are invited for cremation, and after the cremation is over, monks continue to perform worship for more days in the house of the dead.

The monastic organization has a strong bearing to individual and public health. The Lamas lead and guide for the betterment of life, using a variety of devices and practices. Tibetan medicine is well developed in Ladakh and those who are experts in this practice are known locally as 'Amchies'. Though most of the people who learn this traditional medicine are laymen but there are also several monk 'Amchies' taking care of the health of the people especially in the remote areas of Ladakh.

As far as the economic function goes, the role of the monastery in the economy of Ladakh is still significant. Monasteries own fertile lands in villages and, to a large extent, control and operate the economy of the territory through ownership of land and through exploitation of its resources. Monasteries have received donation of land from rulers and village families over many generations. So the land belonging to the monastery is widely scattered in many localities or villages. The dwellers of these localities or villages work on the land either as tenants or as agricultural labourers. The tenants pay some percentage of the produce to the monastery. According to Harjit Singh, "the tenants pay 1/5 to 1/2 of the produce to the monastery as rent"[12]. The monastery being economically sound and having a surplus advances loans to the needy people. Generally, the loan is in kind in the form of wheat, barley, etc. These articles are borrowed for a specific period and they are then returned with some addition to the borrowed quantity. According to Tsering Shakya, "Loans are made to farmers against interest which can be considerable. In the past, in Tibet and in the Himalaya generally, such debts have been crippling but there has been a steady reduction in this burden on villagers".[13] The sources of the monastery are:

I. Interest from the money and articles lending operation.

II. Donations collected for particular liturgical events by the Nyerpa (gNyer-pa) assigned to event specific responsibilities.[14]

III. Donations and offerings made by the general population.

IV. Trade carried out by major monasteries.[15]

Much of these incomes are provided in the form of wheat, barley, barley flour and butter. There is also a cash reserve, but monetary transactions rather than barter are probably of recent origin. Since Ladakh opened for tourists in 1974, tourists fees have begun to generate a useful income in cash for the monasteries. The income of the monastery is utilized to support the religious community especially during the important performance of monastic rituals. A reserve is kept for the repair of the communal halls.

Apart from the above functions, monasteries provide traditional monastic education; young monks are taught not only "Buddhist subjects" such as philosophy, study of canonical texts, Buddhist ethics, etc., but also the Tibetan language, logic, and the fundamentals of Tibetan medicine and astrology. The traditional education implies the fivefold sciences of Buddhist knowledge; medicine, fine arts, logic, language and religion.[16] In ancient times many Tibetan students visited India with the aim of receiving first-hand knowledge of these sciences. There were no records as to how many students went to India for education except the 16 Tibetans who were sent to India with Thonmi Sambhota, the person who invented the Tibetan alphabet, by the royal court. Many perished on the way before they could even reach the land of the Buddha.

The Tibetan quest of knowledge continued between the 7th–12th centuries. By the time Buddhism disappeared from India at the end of the 12th century, Tibet had already received the complete works of Indian Buddhist sciences. Tibetan along with Indian Buddhist scholars played an important role in spreading these Buddhist teachings in Tibet. Tibetans were intelligent students. They were able to not only bring the complete works of Buddhist teaching to Tibet but also invented their own alphabet. Thonmi Sambhota, who along with others were sent to India by the royal court to study in India in the 7th century, invented the Tibetan alphabet with thirty consonants. All Buddhists texts, which were brought from India, were translated into the Tibetan language. Without deviating from the original Buddhist thinking, Tibetan scholars devised a comprehensive system of teaching Buddhist knowledge more effectively.[17] Gradually, Mahayana Buddhism spread to all parts of Tibet. Many monasteries were founded. Samye (bSam-yas) was the first monastery in Tibet, founded by King Thi-Sron Detsan in 749 A.D.[18] Before 1959, there were many monasteries in Tibet with hundreds of monks and nuns.

Some of the Important Monasteries in Tibet

Tibet became an important Mahayana Buddhist centre. Great monasteries with their renowned universities became famous across Tibet and neighboring countries where the Tibetan Culture and Tibetan Buddhism took deep roots. Many monks from the cis-Himalayan region used to go to different monasteries in Tibet for their higher monastic education. Following are some of the important monasteries in Tibet where many monks from Ladakh used to go to for higher education.

Samyas (bSam-yas)

bSam-yas the oldest monastery in Tibet, was founded in 749 A.D by Guru Padmasambhave[19], who visited Tibet around that period. Tibetans were trained as monks for the first time in this monastery.[20] It was constructed as a great complex of buildings arranged around a central temple said to be modeled after the Indian Qdantapuri of Magadha[21] in Bihar. A great debate was held at bSam-yas about 792 A.D., as to whether the Indian version of teachings or the Chinese version should be followed.[22] The scholar Kamasala led the Indian side and Hoshang led the Chinese side. According to David Snellgrove and Hugh Richardson:

> "The Indian side, as represented in the debate, argued the conventional Mahayana teaching connected with the theory of the gradual course of a 'would-be Buddha' (bodhistsatva), towards buddhahood. The basis of these teaching was necessary to accumulate vast quantities of knowledge and merit throughout innumerable ages, if one wished to progress towards the final goal of buddhahood; this was now proclaimed according to Mahayana as the only true goal for the real followers of Sakyamuni, in that it benefited all other sentient beings as well as oneself. The Chinese case concentrated upon

the absolute nature of buddhahood, which could be realized by any practitioner who established himself in the state of complete repose."[23]

The Indian Buddhist monks won the debate and the king followed the Indian version of Buddhism in Tibet.

Lhasa

Lhasa, "God's place"[24], which gives its name to the place, is the religious, commercial and political centre of Tibet. In the heart of Lhasa is the temple called the Jokhang (Jo-wo K'an), built by King Songtsen Gampo.[25] He built it for the preservation of the images of Buddha brought to him by his two wives. The Buddha image still stands inside the temple. Also in Lhasa is the Norbulinka, the summer palace of the Dalai Lama. Lhasa's most famous shrine is the Potala palace, built by Ngawang Lobsang Gyatso (1617-1682), the fifth Dalai Lama. It served as the winter palace of the Dalai Lamas.

Reting (Rva-sgreng)

Reting monastery, situated in the Rong Chu valley of central Tibet, was founded in 1056 A.D.[26] The monastery was initially associated with the Indian scholar Atisa, a watershed figure in the revival of Buddhism in Tibet, and later had important ties with the Dalai Lama and the Ge-lug-pa sect. It contains a main assembly hall with murals of venerable Lamas and tantric gods, and the much-revered gold statue of 'Guhyasumaja', usually defined as the personal tantric deity of Atisa. Many monks used to study in this monastery. The most famous student among them was Tsong kha-pa, who later introduced the Ge-lug-pa sect in Tibet. At the age of forty he joined the Rva-sgreng monastery, sanctified by Atisa.[27] While at Rva-sgreng, Tsong kha-pa wrote some of his most important works.

Sakya (Sa-skya)

Sa-skya "Tawny-Soil" is located at an altitude of about 4200 meters above sea level in the province of Tsang. It was founded in 1071 A.D.[28] by dKon-mchog-rgyal-po of the 'Khon family'.[29] This monastery gives its name to the Sa-skya-pa sect, which has played an important role in the history of Tibet. It became famous as a seat of learning.

It contains many temples, including a spacious assembly hall known as 'the White Hall of Worship'.[30] The monastery is still famous for its magnificent library, containing numerous unique treasures of Sanskrit and Tibetan literature. According to Austine L. Waddell, the hall of the great temple, called P'rul-phi lha-k'an, has four enormous wooden pillars brought from different areas and the fourth pillar, which is black, from Ladakh.[31]

Bri-gung (Di-kung)

Bri-gung was founded by Jig-rten-mGon- po.[32] He was also the founder of Bri-gung-pa, sub-sect of the bka-rgyud-pa sect of Tibetan Buddhism. This monastery is situated about one hundred miles northeast of Lhasa.[33] According to David Snellgrove, "within only few years of its foundation there were 800 monks at Bri-gung monastery."[34] Many monks from Ladakh especially of the Bri-gung-pa sub-sect used to go there for their studies. At present, there are still about thirty monks in Lamayuru monastery in Ladakh who studied in Bri-gung monastery in Tibet.

Gandan (dGa-ldan)

Gandan, 'place of joy,' is situated about thirty miles east of Lhasa.[35] It was founded by Tsong-kha-pa in 1409 A. D.[36] It is one of the four great Ge-lug-pa monasteries in Tibet, the others being Dre-pung, Sera and Tashi Lhunpo. Its full name is dGa-Idan rNam-par Gyal-whi gling,[37] or the continent of completely victorious happiness. Unlike the other larger Ge-lug-pa monasteries, the headship of Gandan is not based on hereditary incarnation but he is chosen by a conclave from the most scholarly of the monks of Sera, Dre-pung and Gandan monasteries.[38]

Gandan with its 3300 monks is divided into two colleges, namely Byan-rtse and S'ar-tse.[39] These colleges have a number of houses or K'am ts'an. The House or K'am ts'an was the basic unit. If one wanted to become a monk, one had to apply to the chief teacher of the K'am ts'an.

Many monks from different regions come to study in this monastery. Eashey Wangchok[40], who studied in Gandan monastery for six years in the 1950s, mentioned that there were about fifteen monks from Ladakh in the monastery. He had to come back Ladakh after the Chinese invaded Tibet. He remembered how the Chinese army treated the local people there. Many monks including him were put into prison. After two years in prison the Chinese army sent back many monks from Ladakh, Sikkim, Lahul Spiti and Bhutan to their respective countries.

Dre-pung (Bras-spung)

Dre-pung monastery is situated about three miles west of Lhasa. It was founded in 1416 A.D.[41] Its founder was Paldan Jamyang Choje, a close disciple of the revered Tsong-kha-pa. Bras-spung means 'the rice heap' and it was so named because it was said to have resembled the great Indian tantric monastery of 'The rice heap' in Kalinga and identified with the Kalachakra doctrine.[42] Dre-pung monastery is one of the most populous and powerful of all the monasteries in Tibet. It contains about 7700 monks.[43] Many monks from Ladakh studied in this monastery. There are still about fifty-two monks in different monasteries [44] in Ladakh, who had studied in the Dre-pung monastery in Tibet. This figure has been collected during my field study from the month of May-August 2004 in Ladakh. Most of these monks had to return to Ladakh after the Chinese army occupied Tibet.

Dre-pung monastery with its thousands of monks, is divided into four great colleges (grwa-ts'an), namely: bLo-gsal-gling; sGo-man; bde-yans; and sNags-pa.[45] The sGo-man, the largest of its four colleges, has 3300 monks. Each college consisted of a number of houses or K'am ts'an; for instance, the largest college of Dre-pung had twenty-three houses or K'am ts'ans.[46] The monks were accommodated according to their nationalities and provinces in these K'am ts'ans. As Tsering Stobgais[47], who studied in Dre-pung monastery for about eleven years, stated that all the monks from Ladakh who studied in Dre-pung monastery stayed in Spituk K'am ts'an. These houses or K'am ts'ans were also of varying size, some with as many as 700 monks and some with only 150.[48]

Sera

Sera or "The Merciful Hail" is situated about a mile and a half to the north of Lhasa, on the lower slopes of a range of barren hills name Ta-ti-pu.[49] Sakya Yeshe, one of the disciples of Tsong-kha-pa, founded it in 1419 A.D.[50] According to tradition, Tsong-kha-pa, the founder of the Ge-lug-pa School, composed his commentary on Nagarjuna's Root Verses on the Middle Way, entitled The Ocean of Reasoning (rings pa'i rgya mtsho), in a small hermitage called Sera Choding (Sera chos Iding) in the foothills just above Sera around the year 1409 A.D. In the midst of writing this work, one of the folios of the text flew into the air in a gust of wind. It began to emit "A" letters (the symbol of the perfection of wisdom) in the colour of molten gold. Some of the letters dissolved into a stone at the base of the hill and permanently imprinted themselves on it. Witnessing this, Tsong-kha-pa prophesied that this would be the future site of a great center of Buddhist learning. A decade later, one of his disciples founded Sera monastery at this very site.

Sera monastery, with its 5500 monks, maintained three colleges of instruction. These colleges were Bye-wa, sNags-pa and, sMad-pa.[51] The Bye-wa and sMad-pa colleges were colleges of philosophy (mtshan nyid grwa tshang), with long years of studies culminating in the prestigious Geshe (dge bshes) degree, like a doctoral degree (Ph.D: Doctor of Philosophy) in the modern educational system. The sNags-pa college was an institution dedicated to the practice of tantric ritual (sku rim grwa tshang). Like in the Dre-pung monastery, each college of Sera also has a number of K'am ts'an. The K'am ts'ans were organized chiefly along geographical lines, and monks from different regions of the country entered the house that corresponded to their specific region. K'am ts'an buildings take up the largest part of the monastery. Sera monastery has four major temple complexes: one belonging to each of the three colleges, and then the Sera Tsogchen (tshogs chen) or Great Assembly Hall, where the monks from all of the colleges would meet together.

Tashi-Lhunpo (bKra-sis Lhun-po)

bKra-sis Lhun-po or the "Heap of Glory" is situated near the south bank of the Tsang-po, at the junction of the Nying river.[52] It was founded by dGe-dun-grub, who is said to have been Tsongkha-pa's nephew.[53] This great monastery along with Sera, Gandan and Dre-pung belong to the Ge-lug-pa sect of Mahayana Buddhism. This monastery is the seat of the Panchen Lamas.[54]

The number of monks generally in residence at Tashi-Lhunpo is said to be 3800.[55] There are four colleges attached to the monastery, all of which receive students from every part of Tibet and also from neighbouring countries. Many monks from Ladakh have studied in this monastery. There are still about forty-three monks in various monasteries in Ladakh[56], who had studied in Tashi Lhunpo monastery in Tibet. Most of them stayed in the Stakmo K'am ts-an in the monastery. There were many K'am ts-an in this monastery. According Sarat Chandra Das,[57] Tashi-Lhunpo monastery is divided into forty k'am ts-ans, which are placed under the jurisdiction of the three great Ta-tshang or theological colleges. These K'am ts-ans are:

(a) "Thoisamling college exercises control over the following K'am ts-an:-

1. Gya K'am ts-an
2. Tiso K'am ts-an
3. Hamdong " "
4. Chawa " "

5. Tang K'am ts-an
6. Tang-moc'he " "
7. Tinke " "
8. Chunee " "
9. Lhum-bu-tse " "
10. Ser-ling " "
11. Je-pa " "
12. Chang-pa " "
13. Leg-thug " "
14. Norpugandan, the first house built when the monastery was established.
15. Srepa (Hrepa) K'am ts-an
16. Pa-so K'am ts-an
17. Don-tse " "

(b) The following belong to Shar-tse Ta-tshang:-

1. Thon-pa K'am ts-an
2. Gyal-tse-tse K'am ts-an
3. Shine " "
4. Lhopa " "
5. Latoi (Ladakh) " "
6. Chang-pa " "
7. Potog-pa " "
8. Nenin " "
9. Tom-khaling " "
10. Deyang-pa " "
11. Samlo " "
12. Neninng-po " "

(c) The following are under Kyil-khang:-

1. Khogye K'am ts-an
2. Tangmo K'am ts-an
3. Rog-tsho " "
4. Lakha " "
5. Dodan " "
6. Piling " "
7. Khalka " "
8. Darpa " "
9. Lhundup-tse " "
10. "Tsa-oo K'am ts-an, also called Tsa-oo para".[58]

Different nationalities and provinces have houses or K'am ts-an in the monastery. The monks were accommodated according to their nationalities and provinces in these K'am ts'ans. Lobsang Phuntsog from Thiksay monastery, who studied in Tashi Lhunpo monastery for about eight years stayed in Stakmo K'am ts-an.

Ladakhi Monks Education in Tibet

It is difficult to say exactly when the Ladakhi lamas first started to go to Tibet for their monastic education. According to the Chronicles of Ladakh; it started during the reign of King dNos-grub-mgon (1300-1325).[59] As the Chronicle has mentioned:

> "Lha chen dNos-grub dei dus su rab du jung wa dBus, gTsan du iGro wai srol bTugs."[60]

It means that during the reign of king Lha chen Lha chen dNos-grub, the tradition of sending monks for their study in the dBus and gTsan region of Tibet has began.

Later, they started to go to various monasteries in other areas of Tibet. There are two important reasons why the cis-Himalayan people looked upon Tibet as the centre of Mahayana Buddhism. Firstly Mahayana Buddhism came directly from Tibet to the Himalayan areas and secondly, Tibet in due course of time became a centre of Mahayana Buddhism and the residence of leading Lamas who taught Mahayana Buddhism.

While several Ladakhi monks made Tibet their home, many others after getting education in different monastic centres in Tibet came back to their native place and played a major role in spreading Mahayana Buddhism in Ladakh. A few royal princes became monks and went to Tibet for higher studies; after coming back from Tibet, they became heads of important monasteries and played an important role in spreading monastic education in Ladakh. For example, King Deldan rNamgyal's second son, named Lobsang Puntsog, became a monk and went to study in Tibet. He studied at the university of Bras-pun (Dre-pung).[61] After nine years of study in the slo-gsay-glin college at Dre-pung, he obtained the high degree of dge-bses-rab-byams-pa.[62] Upon his return from Tibet, he was appointed the abbot of Thiksay monastery, which headed seven Ge-lug-pa monasteries in Ladakh at that time.[63]

Ladakhi monks were intelligent and several monks were able to achieve higher degrees in Tibet. As Nawang Tsering mentioned:

> "A few Ladakhi monks were able to obtain the degrees of Lha-rams-pa or bka-chen in Tibetan monasteries. The Five-fold philosophical subjects: the Pramanasatra, Madhyamikasastra, Prajnaparamitra-satra, Abhidharma and Vinaya, were difficult to master. Sras Rinpoche of Ridzong monastery, and bka-chen bZod-pa of Thiksay, are few who have achieved thorough knowledge of these philosophical subjects in Tibet."[64]

Monks in Ladakh who Studied in Tibet

There are still many monks in most of the monasteries in Ladakh who had studied in various monasteries in Tibet. During my field survey in the month of May-August 2004 in seven monasteries in Ladakh, i interviewed about ninety-six monks who have been to Tibet. The seven monasteries are Lamayuru, Rigzong, Likir, Phyang, Spituk, Thiksay and Disket. In the case of Phyang monastery, i could interview only one monk, though there are many monks there who have been to Tibet. I could not go to other monasteries in central Ladakh and Zanskar. Several monks told me that there are also many monks in various monasteries in Zanskar who had been to Tibet.

Out of ninety-six monks, the longest stay in Tibet was Lobsang Tomba, who stayed about twenty-two years in Dre-pung and Tashi Lhunpo monasteries. He comes from village Shara in Leh- Ladakh. He is about eighty years old and still regularly participates in the major ceremonies in the Thiksay monastery in Ladakh. On the other hand, Konchok Rigzen and Tashi Punchok of Lamayuru monastery could stay only two years in Tibet. They have to come back after two years of study in Bri-gung monastery because of the Chinese army occupation of Tibet.

Out of the total ninety-six monks, forty-two monks studied in Tashi lhunpo monastery, thirty stayed in Bri-gung, twenty stayed in Dre-pung and two monks stayed in Gandan monastery. All the thirty monks who stayed in Bri-gung monastery are from Lamayuru monastery in Ladakh and belong to the Bri-gungpa sub-sect. When asked is it compulsory to go to the same sect monasteries in Tibet for their education? All of them answered in negatives. "It is not compulsory for the monks to go to the same sect monastery in Tibet for their study" said Konchok Namgail, who is from Phyang monastery. Although the monastery belongs to the Bri-gung-pa, sub- sect of the bka-bgyud-pa sect, he studied in Dre-pung monastery in Tibet which belongs to Gylupa sect. When asked why they wanted to go to Tibet for their education; they all had the same answers: that it is because the best monastic education is available in the great monastic institutions in Tibet. Ladakhi monks who were fortunate enough to study in Tibet remember those times with nostalgia.

Yeshe Jamyang from Nurla who studied in Bri-gung monastery in Tibet said: "I love the monastery where we studied in Tibet and never thought of coming back. I was interested in rituals and started learning from my Tibetan teacher and I became an expert in making ritual objects, especially butter painting etc. and I was one of the famous students in the monastery." He had to come back against his wish in 1959, when the Chinese occupied Tibet. After coming back from Tibet he became the dance teacher (Cham-spon) for a few years and was very active in teaching dances to young monks at Lamayuru monastery in Ladakh. Besides, he contributed many other monasteries in Ladakh[65], painting various religious objects like masks, Thangkas etc. At present he is painting the Dalai Lama's Photang (temple) at Bod-Karbu.[66] Like Yeshe Jamyang, there are many monks who had played important role in teaching of monastic education to novices, development of monastic organization and spreading of Mahayana Buddhism in Ladakh after they returned from Tibet. On being asked, why did none of the monks who returned to Ladakh with this incredibly long and testing period of education behind them, and with presumably highly trained intellects, set up centres of learning like Tibet, in Ladakh? Majority of them gave economic reasons that Ladakh cannot effort to support such centres then. I have discussed this question with several other people. Janet Rizvi said that "clearly there was a centralizing tendency in Tibetan Buddhism, & the religious authorities weren't keen that independent centres should come up on the peripheries"[67].

Routes Taken by Ladakhi Monks to Tibet

The monks whom interviewed have stated that they have been to Tibet through three different ways. Most of the older monks among them went to Tibet through the Southern-Eastern road, locally known as (dzung-lam) or middle route. From Leh it followed the course of the Indus upstream till Karu, and then to Sakti over the Chang-la to Tangtse, Chushul, and cut over to the Indus Valley via the Tsak-la and then to Demchok. From there, they would go to Gartok, a trading centre in Tibet. This is one of the trading routes between

Ladakh and Tibet. All the monks who followed this route were accompanied by trading groups. Lobsang Tonba, from Thiksay monastery who went to Tibet through the above route mentioned, " We went to Tibet with the trading party from lower Ladakh (Shamma), and after walking for many days reached a trading centre, the Ladakhi traders were going back from there and they requested their Tibetan counterparts to take us along with them to Tibet. So we went with the Tibetan traders and they were also very nice people, they not only guided us on those difficult and long tracks but also gave us food." This route is the hardest among the three routes because it takes months to reach and has to be walked the whole way mostly on the high altitude desert of Changthang. Many of the Ladakhi folk songs especially Chos-Lhu, religious songs were composed by the monks during their long travel to Tibet. Only those monks who can effort can go to Tibet for their higher education.

The second route was walking from Leh to Kargil and then to Kashmir, and from there, till Sikkim by bus and train, and then again walking till Lhasa. The majority of monks followed this road. And the last route, which was followed by few monks, is from Leh to Lahul-Spiti to Shimla and then to Delhi. Delhi to Sikkim by train, and then again walking to Lhasa.

The tradition of going to Tibet for education, which continued for hundreds of years, was suddenly stopped when the Chinese occupied Tibet. Most of the monks from Ladakh had to come back. This abrupt end would have had a major impact on the standard of monastic educational level in Ladakh. But luckily three important developments have worked in the favour. First of all, the monks who came back to Ladakh after the Chinese occupation of Tibet played a major role in teaching the young monks in Ladakh, and soon a Buddhist institute named the Central Institute of Buddhist Studies was established in 1959 at Leh, where initially novices from different monasteries in Ladakh came for their education. Later the major monasteries in Ladakh set up their own schools in their monasteries. With the establishment of the Tibetan government in exile, in India and the establishment of some monastic institutions in India, many monks from Ladakh go to these institutions for higher education. Some of these institutions are in Karnataka and few other places in India, where many well-known teachers from Tibet are teaching.

At present all the major monasteries in Ladakh have their own schools. In these schools, besides the monastic education, they teach subjects like Mathematics, Social sciences and Hindi and English languages are teaching. Many novices are studying in these schools and after the completion of their courses they go for higher studies in southern India and few other places in India.

Following are the list of monks from seven monasteries in Ladakh, who have been to various monasteries in Tibet for higher education:

Tabnle 2.1. There are some nine monks in Thiksay monastery who have been to Tibet

Name	*Present Age*	*Name of the House/ Village*	*No. of Years in Tibet*	*Place of study/ Monastery in Tibet*
Lobsang Gyalson	77	Stakmo/Thiksay	18	Tasshi-Lhunpo Monastery
Lobsang Paljor	74	Nyarchubg/do	12	do
Lobsang Phuntsog	77	Chushot	8	do
Lobsang Tonba	80	Shara	22	do and Dre-pung Monastery
Lobsang Stanba	67	Shey	3	do
Lobsang Namgyal	60	Shernos	2	Tashi-Lhunpo Monastery
Lobsang Shesrab	79	Kilbuk/Thiksay	15	Dre-pung Monastery
Lobsang Chotak	62	Thiksay	7	Tashi-Lhunpo Monastery
Lobsang Gyalson	60	Stakmo/Thiksay	3	do

Sources: Information/data collected by author from 15/6/2004 -17/6/2004.

Table 2.22. There is only one monk in the Rigzong monastery who has been to Tibet

Name	*Present Age*	*Name of the House/ Village*	*No. of Years in Tibet*	*Place of study/ Monastery in Tibet*
Tsutim Angdu	86	Togapa Balam/Spituk	3	Dre-pung Monastery

Sources: Information/data collected by author on 5/6/2004.

Table 2.3. Following are some monks of the Spituk monastery who have been to various monasteries in Tibet for their education

Name	*Present Age*	*Name of the House/ Village*	*No. of Years in Tibet*	*Place of study/ Monastery in Tibet*
Thupstan Shesrieu	64	Tsogsal/ Choklamsr	4	Dre-pung Monastery
Lobsang Tundup	73	Rumbak	6	do
Eshey wangchuk	69	Choklamsar	9	Dre-pung and Gandan
Tsering Stobgais	88	Nimoo	11	Dre-pung
Lobsang Tunpstan	63	Stok	5	Tashi-Lhunpo
Lobsang Norbu	73	Leh	10	Dre-pung
Lhundup Rabstan	71	Nimoo	—	Dre-pung
Chamba Takpa	85	Rumbak	10	Do not Tashi-Lhunpo
Lobsang Tsering	65	—	4	Tashi-Lhunpo
Chanba Norbu	84	Nimoo	4	Dre-pung
Lobsang Thakmet	66	Nomoo	7	do
Lobsang Gyalson	69	Spituk	6	do
Angdu	74	Phey	6	Tashi-Lhunpo
Lobsang Thinlas	76	Stok	11	do
Eashey Shesrab	66	Stok	5	Dre-pung
Nawang Rinchen	65	Stok	5	Tashi-Lhunpo

Thupstan Joldan	67	Stok	6	Dre-pung
Nawang Tsering	60	Saboo	3	Tashi-Lhunpo
Nawang Lobyang	68	Chushot	4	Do

Sources: Information/data collected by author from 15/6/2004 &17/7/2004.

Table 2.4. There are some thirty monks in the Lamayuru monastery who studied in various monasteries in Tibet. Most of them returned when the Chinese occupied Tibet

Name	*Present Age*	*Name of the House/ Village*	*No. of Years in Tibet*	*Place of study/ Monastery in Tibet*
Konchok Chokdrop	65	Timosgang	12	Bri-gung, Dre-pung, Sera
Tashi Phuntsog	77	Timosgang	5	Bri-gung
Konchok Wangyal	68	Gongmapa/Nurla	7	Bri-gung
Rabgyas	82	Timosgang	12	Bri-gung
Konchok Norbu	77	Gomgmapa/Nurla	6 8	Drepun and Bri-gung
Konchok Tharpa	64	Drikopa/Timosgang	6	Bri-gung
Konchok Tagspa	68	Pharkeythang/Nurla	7	Bri-gung
Tsering Morup	69	Thuthing/Wanla	3	Bri-gung
Padma Jugskyob	68	Tongthilpa/Wanla	3	Bri-gung
Tunndup	80	Mikir/Bodh Kharbu	7	Bri-gung
Konchok Rigzin	60	Lampa/Bodh Kharbu	2	Bri-gung
Rigzin	68	Monding/do	3	Bri-gung
Sonam Jorphel	65	Gongmapa/do	7	Bri-gung
Dorje Phuntsog	70	Choktsepa/do	7	Bri-gung
Tsewang	78	Ribyapa/Kanji	8	Bri-gung
Konchok Tsering	60	Khosal/Kanji	5	Bri-gung
Konchok Stanzin	66	Shali/Kanji	3	Bri-gung
Phuntsog Rabtan	82	Dakchan/Henasku	12	Bri-gung
Konchok Tsultim	77	Shingkhan/do	5	Bri-gung
Tashi Phuntsog	68	Kyalbapa/Yuru	2	Bri-gung
Phuntsog Namgyal	80	Yultak/Takmachik	5	Bri-gung
Tashi Wangyal	75	Yultak/Takmachik	5	Bri-gung
Konchok Samstan	64	Thitkyangpa/do	4	Bri-gung

Konchok Stanzin	65	Manipa/do	3	Bri-gung
Tashi Norbu	65	Domkhar Gongma	5	Bri-gung
Konchok Stanzin	64	Domkhar Barma	5	Bri-gung
Konchok Smanla	73	Chongzi/Kuksho	-	Bri-gung
Konchok Rabzang	70	Stara/Khalatse	4	Bri-gung
Konchok Tsewang	60	Spangpa/Skyindiyang	3	Bri-gung
Yeshe Jamyang	72	Paley/Nurla	11	Bri-gung

Sources: Information/data collected by author from 7/8/2004 & 8/8/2004.

Table 2.5. There are some twenty-two monks in the Likir Monastery who studied in various monasteries in Tibet

Name	*Present Age*	*Name of the House/ Village*	*Place of study/ Monastery in Tibet*
Nawang Gelek	85	Larjepa/Likir	Tashi-Lhunpo
Nawang Stonba	79	Sarpopa/Timosgang	Tashi-Lhunpo
Lobsang Tharchin	78	Hemis Shukpachan	Tashi-Lhunpo
Lobsang Dorje	79	Gochakpa/Timosgang	Dre-pung
Chamba Migo	80	Towapa/Wakha	Dre-pung
Lobsang Stobgyas	77	Laldanpa/Likir	Tashi-Lhunpo
Lobsang Stanzin	79	Tangsponpa/Alchi	Tashi-Lhunpo
Lobsang Jodpa	71	Skidjor/Timosgang	Tashi-Lhunpo
Yeshe Chamba	75	Gashoo/Timosgang	Dre-pung
Chamba Tsultim	74	Sgangzor/Himis Shukpachan	Dre-pung
Yeshe Thinlas	76	Mogol/Likir	Gandan
Lobsang Rabgyas	64	Lingstidpa/Likir	Dre-pung
Lobsang Rinchan	75	Saspotse	Tashi-Lhunpo
Nawang Jundnas	72	Sarapa/Saspol	Dre-pung
Nawang Samstan	72	Rinchanpa/Saspol	Tashi-Lhunpo
Lobsang Norbu	70	Makponpa/Ney	Dre-pung
Lobsang Chotak	69	Chaskyangpa/Shargol	Tashi-Lhunpo
Lobsang Namtak	76	Pangkhor/Ney	Dre-pung
Lobsang Choklang	70	Pandan/Wakha	Tashi-Lhunpo
Lobsang Chinba	65	Yokmapa/Timosgang	Tashi Lhunpo
Lobsang Norbu	67	Rutpa/Timosgang	Tashi-Lhunpo
Lobsang Chosgyal	69	Palde/Timosgang	Tashi-Lhunpo

Sources: Information/data collected by author on 5/8/2004, when monks were assembled for the Mandala prayer at the monastery.

Table 2.6. There are some fourteen monks in Disket monastery in Nubra valley who have been to various monasteries in Tibet for their education

Name	*Present Age*	*Name of the House/ Village*	*No. of Years in Tibet*	*Place of study/ Monastery in Tibet*
Rabsang Norbu	81	Charsa	18	Tashi-Lhunpo
Lobsabg Rigzin	76	Disket	9	Tashi-Lhunpo
Lobsang Rigzin	75	Pinchimit	11	Tashi-Lhunpo
Lobsang Tharchin	76	-	7	Tashi-Lhunpo
Lobsang Tundup	72	Hunder	7	Tashi-Lhunpo
Lobsang Tenzin	67	Panamik	7	Tashi-Lhunpo
Lobsang Tsundus	65	Kuri	7	Tashi-Lhunpo
Tundup Palzang	76	Chamshin	10	Tashi-Lhunpo
Lobsang Phuntsog	72	Hunder	7	Tashi-Lhunpo
Lobsang Samtan	69	Laksang	7	Tashi-Lhunpo
Lobsang Tsultim	75	Charsa	8	Tashi-Lhunpo
Lobsang Namgyal	71	Kuri	7	Tashi-Lhunpo
Tsewang Namgyal	72	-	6	Tashi-Lhunpo
Lobsang Phuntsog	65	Chamshin	6	Tashi-Lhunpo

Sources: Information/data collected by author on 13/8/2003 &14/8/ 2004.

Table 2.7. Though there are many monks in the Phayang monastery who have been to various monasteries in Tibet for their education. I could interview only one of them

Name	*Present Age*	*Name of the House/ Village*	*No. of Years in Tibet*	*Place of study/ Monastery in Tibet*
Konchok Namgyal	54	Nyaro/Phying	7	Dre-pung Monastery

Sources: Information/data collected by author on 11/6/2004.

Conclusion

Thus, the tradition of the Ladakhi monks to go for higher studies in various monastic institutions in Tibet has continued for hundreds of years and resulted in the development of many monasteries in Ladakh. The monastic organizations and monastic education of Ladakhi monks in Tibet have played an important role in the development of a close cultural relationship between Ladakh and Buddhist Tibet.

The hallmark of Ladakhi lamas were their pursuing a comprehensive course of study in various branches of Buddhist studies in some renowned monastic institution in Tibet, and for the Lamas, a visit to Lhasa, their spiritual home was a cherished dream. The hope for the Ladakhi is to open up the borders it will not only revive the pilgrimage and cultural ties but also promote tourism.

REFERENCES

1. Robert James Miller, *Monasteries and Culture Changes in Inner Mongolia* (Wiesbaden: Otto Harrassonwitz, 1959), p. 12.
2. He invented Tibetan alphabets.
3. The name of the village as well as the monastery, on the way to Kargil District of Ladakh.
4. John Crook and Tsering Shakya, "Monastic Communities In Zanskar: Location, Function and Oraganisation" in Crook, J. H and Henry, A. Osmaston (eds.), *Himalayan Buddhist Village: Enviroment, Resources, Society and Religion Life in Zanskar- Ladakh* (Bristol and New Delhi: Motilal Banarasidass, 1994), p. 561.
5. Austine L. Waddell, *The Buddhism of Tibet or Lamaism* (First Published: 1899 and reprinted New Delhi: Asian Educational Service, 1959), p. 260.
6. John Crook and Tsering Shakya, op. cit. 4, p. 580.
7. Austine L.Waddell, op. cit. 5, p. 171.
8. John Crook and Tsering Shakya, op. cit. 4, p. 581.
9. Those laymen who can recite the texts.
10. John Crook and Tsering Shakya, op. cit. 4, p. 588.
11. A Tantric Ritual.
12. Harjit Singh "Territorial Organization of Gonpas in Ladakh", Collogues Internationaux du C. N. R. S, No. 268- Ecologie Et Geologie De Himalaya (Paris, 7-10 December, 1976), p. 355.

13. Tsering Shakya, Tashi Rabgias and John Crook, "Monastic Economics in Zanslar, 1980" in Crook, J. H and Henry, A. Osmaston (eds.), *Himalayan Buddhist Village: Enviroment, Resources, Society and Religion Life in Zanskar- Ladakh* (Bristol and New Delhi: Motilal Banarasidass, 1994), p. 602.
14. *Ibid.* p. 602.
15. Bigger monasteries in Ladakh used to send religious and trade missions to Buddhist Tibet.
16. Nawang Tsering, "The fate of traditional Education in Ladakh", *in* Osmasten, Henry, and Philip Denwood, (eds.) *Recent research of Ladakh 4 & 5. Proceedings of the fourth and fifth International Colloquiam on Ladakh*, (Bristol, 1989, and London: SOAS Studies, 1992). p. 209.
17. *Ibid.* p. 209.
18. David Snellgrove and Hugh Richardson, *A Cultural History of Tibet* (London: Trinity Press, 1968), p. 78.
19. Michael Harris Goodman, *The Last Dalai Lama* (New Delhi: Rupa and co., 1986), p. 78.
20. David Snellgrove and Hugh Richardson, op cit. 18, p. 78.
21. Austin Waddell, op. cit. 5, p. 28.
22. David Snellgrove and Hugh Richardson, op. cit. 18, p. 79.
23. *Ibid.* p. 79.
24. Austine Waddell, op. cit. 5, p. 301.
25. *Ibid.* p. 301.
26. David Snellgrove and Hugh Richardson, op. cit. 18, p. 131.
27. *Ibid.* p. 181.
28. Austine Waddell, p. cit. 5, p. 69.
29. David Snellgrove and Hugh Richardson, op. cit. 18, p. 132.
30. Austine Waddell, op. cit. 5, p. 274.
31. *Ibid.* p. 274.
32. David Snellgrove and Hugh Richardson, op. cit. 18, p. 137.
33. Austine Waddell, op. cit. 5, p. 276.
34. David Snellgrove and Hugh Richardson, op. cit. 18, p. 140.
35. Michael Harris Goodman, op. cit. 19, p. 74.
36. Austine Waddell, op. cit. 5, p. 61.
37. *Ibid.* p. 268.

38. *Ibid*. p. 268.
39. *Ibid*. p. 189.
40. A monk from Spituk monastery in Ladakh
41. David Snellgrove and Hugh Richardson, op. cit. 18, p. 182.
42. Austine Waddell, op. cit. 5, pp. 268-69.
43. Tom Grunfeld, *The Making of Modern Tibet* (Bombay: Oxford University Press India, 1987), p. 29.
44. Monasteries are Lamayuru, Rigzong, Likir, Phying, Spituk, Thiksay and Disket in Nubra valley.
45. Austine Waddell, op. cit. 6, p. 188.
46. David Snellgrove and Hugh Richardson, op. cit. 18, p. 238.
47. A monk from Spituk monastery in Ladakh.
48. David Snellgrove and Hugh Richardson, op. cit. 18, p. 238.
49. Austine Waddell, op. cit. 5, p. 269.
50. David Snellgrove and Hugh Richardson, op. cit. 18, p. 182.
51. Austine Waddell, op. cit. 5, p. 189.
52. *Ibid*. p. 270.
53. Michael Harris Goodman, op. cit. 19, p. 74
54. Panchen Lama is the second most senior Lama in the hierarchy of Tibetan Buddhism, the first being the Dalai Lama.
55. Austine Waddell, op. cit. 5, p. 272.
56. These monasteries are Lamayuru, Rigzong, Likir, Spituk, Thiksay and Disket in Nubra valley.
57. Cited in Austine Waddell, op.cit.5, p. 189
58. *Ibid*. p. 189.
59. A. H. Francke, *Antiquities of Indian Tibet, The Chronicles of Ladakh and Minor Chronicles, Part II* (New Delhi: Chand and Co., 1926), p. 36.
60. *Ibid*. p. 36.
61. Luciano Petech, *The Kingdom of Ladakh, C. 950-1842 A.D* (Roma: *Istituto Italiano Per IL Medio Ed Estremo Orient*, 1977), p. 84.
62. Ibid. p. 85.
63. *Ibid*. p. 85.
64. Nawang Tsering, op.cit. *16*, p. 210.

65. These monasteries are Lamayuru, Phying, Gonpa soma, Leh, Shashikul, Spituk, Ayang Gonpa Balakupi in Karnataka, Timosgang in Ladakh.
66. A village between Leh and Kargil on the way to Kashmir.
67. Email exchanged on 14 Feb. 2011.

3

Early History of Ladakh and its Cultural Ties with Buddhist Tibet

The history of Ladakh prior to the birth of the kingdom in the 10th century is limited. This is partly because the period has not received the attention of scholars, except few and most notable among them is Luciano Petech.

The present-day population of Ladakh is composed of mixed races. The main among them are the Indo-Iranic race, the Tibetan race and the Mongoloid race. According to the Ladakhi Chronicles and some other sources, the earliest inhabitants of Ladakh were composed of the Mons and the Dards.[1] They migrated to Ladakh at an early time, but it is difficult to fix an exact date. According to Petech the earliest population of Ladakh was composed of the Dardis.[2] According to A.H. Francke the Mons came from India.[3] As far as the Dards are concerned, they migrated to Ladakh from Gilgit.[4] The remains of contemporary Dardis are still found in Dha-Hanu, Darchik and Garkon in Lower Ladakh. The Dards are believed to belong to the Aryans race. The last ethnic group mainly Mongols of Tibetan origin came in the 8th and 9th centuries, and which is the dominant ethnic group in Ladakh at present.

It is believed that Buddhism was first introduced to Ladakh from Kashmir during the reign of the emperor Ashoka. The great Ashoka who adopted Buddhism as his state religion, zealously spread it throughout not only his own empire but also sent missionaries to neighboring countries. It is believed that Ashoka also sent missionaries to Ladakh.[5] When the third Buddhist council was held by king Ashoka (272-232 B.C.), it was resolved to send Buddhist missionaries to Yarkand,

Kashmir and many other countries. Buddhism got such a firm foothold in Kashmir that the fourth Buddhist council, under the King Kanishka (125-152.A.D.), is said have to been held in Kashmir. According to Francke, either after the third or the fourth council, Buddhism must have been carried to western Tibet, situated between Kashmir and Yarkand.[6] The remains of the Kashmiri influence can still be seen in Ladakh. The Kanishka Stupa at Sani and the ancient sculpture at Padum in Zanskar are believed to be from that period. The statue of Maitreya Buddha at Mulbek, which is about 40 km before Kargil, is another monument of Kashmiri influence.

In the 7th and 8th centuries, the Tibetan cultural influence took place in Ladakh. "This is shown by the fact that Chinese Chronicles of those years refer to the areas east of Baltistan as Tibet; and Ladakh is what exists east of Baltistan".[7] In fact it is quite possible that the inhabitants of Ladakh felt the Tibetan influence even earlier, for the nomadic Tibetans of Changthang would have good reason to have contacts with the Mon and Dard, exchanging grain for animal products. The Tibetan nomads occupied the higher pasture ground for their animals and the Aryan tribes (Mons and Dards) irrigated in the lower plains. At any rate, by the mid-seventh century, during the reign of the King Songstan Gampo in Central Tibet, Ladakh became increasingly aware of her eastern neighbour. During this period the Tibetan nomads of Changthang probably inter-married with the Mon and Dard population and allowed a trading or bartering system to develop between the two groups of people. According to Francke, the products of the fields were as welcome to the Tibetans as were the produce of the flocks to the Dard peasants.[8] But the real Tibetan influence in Ladakh started with the origin of the first Ladakhi Kingdom. Its origin is connected with the decline and fall of the Tibetan monarchy. The King Glan-der-ma who had openly persecuted Buddhism in Tibet was killed by a Buddhist monk. After his murder in 842 A.D. Tibet disintegrated into a number of principalities. The central power of Tibet disappeared and the old aristocracy plunged into a struggle for power. Under such circumstances, Skid-ide Ni-ma-mgon, a royal prince migrated to western Tibet.[9] Western Tibet in those days called Naris (mNgari). There is a popular tale in the Chronicle of Ladakh why the Ladakhi king used a giant napkin. On his way to western Tibet, Skid-ide Ni-ma- mgon was once in such straitened circumstances that he had nothing to eat but fish and eggs. His servant brought him this dish covered with a large napkin and ever since it has been used by the Ladakhi king. Within a short period of time Skid-ide Ni-ma-mgon conquered the whole of western Tibet and thus laid the foundation of the first (Ladakhi) Lha-Chen dynasty.

Before the origin of the first Ladakhi dynasty in the 10th century by Skid ide Ni-ma-mgon, it is said that Upper Ladakh was under the descendents of Gesar and Lower Ladakh was divided into small principalities. According to the Chronicles of Ladakh, Skid-ide Ni-ma-mgon had three sons, dPal-gyi-ide-mgon, bKra-sis-mgon and *D*e-gtsug-mgon, called collectively "the three STOD-mgon". The kingdom was divided among three the princes. The first son got Ladakh; the second son got Guge and Pu-ran and the third son got Zanskar and Spiti. As the Chronicles mentioned:

Che-wa dPal- gyi- mgon la mNgaris Maryul,
bar- pa bKar-sis mgon-la Guge, Pur-ran,
chung-wa De-gtsug –mgon la Zans-dkar Spiti.[10]

Its translation means, eldest son, dPal-gyi-mgon got Ladakh, middle son, bKar-sis mgon got Guge and Pur-ran and the youngest son, De-gtsug –mgon got Znaskar (Zans-dkar) and Spiti. The actual conquest was affected by dPal-gyi-mgon himself. He was the real founder and organizer of the Ladakhi Kingdom and the Chronicle gives a sketching description of its boundaries.

The most important role played during this period to spread Mahayana Buddhism in Ladakh was by Lotswa Rin-cen bzang-po (958-1055 A. D.)[11]. But long before that, Guru Padmasambhava is believed to have visited Ladakh in the 8th century A.D.[12] Caves where he is believed to have meditated are still found in Ladakh. The most famous one is Brag-tog Gonpa or monastery, which is about 45 km towards northeast of Leh. The Cave in this monastery is the oldest part of the monastery. This monastery belongs to the rNin-ma-pa sect of Tibetan Buddhism in Ladakh. This sect is known as the oldest sect of Mahayana Buddhism.

Coming back to the period of Lotswa Rin-cen-bzang-po, whose contribution to Ladakh in spreading Tibetan Buddhism was enormous. Not only in Ladakh had he played a vital role in terms of spreading Mahayana Buddhism but also in other areas including Guge and Lahul Spiti. In fact, he along with Atisa, were the main persons who were responsible for the reintroduction of Buddhism in Tibet what Buddhist historian called as second spread Buddhism in Tibet. In his lifetime Lotswa Rin-cen-bzang-po had built 108 monasteries in Western Tibet. In Ladakh, he built about three monasteries. The most famous of them is Alchi, which is about 75 km west of Leh. This monastery is famous for it's painting, which is the mixture of Tibetan and Kashmiri influences. It is said that Lotswa Rin-cen-bzang-po invited many artists from Kashmir. The other monastery is Mangyu monastery. This monastery is about three hours walk from Sgera village, which is about five miles below Alchi along the Indus river.

With the opening of Ladakh for tourists in 1974, Alchi monastery has been visited by many tourists. One of the most important benefits of such visits is that many people have studied and written about it, and it also created awareness among the local people about the importance to preserve the monastery in particular and Ladakhi culture in general. The Alchi monastery is looked after by the Likir (Lhu-k-yil) monastery and it now belongs to Ge-lug-pa sect of Mahayana Buddhism. There were two monks in-charge of the Alchi monastery in August 2003. These monks are from Likir monastery and every one or two years a new in-charge takes over. As far as Mangyu is concerned, not much study has been done on this monastery. One of the reasons may be that it is far from the main jeep road, and secondly, it has not been highlighted, unlike Alchi. In August 2003 the Maitreya Temple of the monastery has been badly damaged. It is a very nice walk up along the stream. The size of the monastery is smaller than Alchi but the paintings are similar in age and style.

Another old monastery in Ladakh is Lamayuru or gYun-drun-dgon-pa.[13] This monastery is about 120 km west of Leh, on the way to Kargil road. It is believed that its site is said to have been selected by Naropa (956-1040 A.D.), the famous teacher of Marpa, who drained away a lake to make it accessible. The cave where Naropa is believed to have meditated is still found in the main assembly hall of the monastery. This cave is probably one of the oldest parts of the monastery. The Sen-ge-lha-khang, a small room below the main building of the monastery, is another oldest part of the monastery.

According to the Chronicles of Ladakh and Luciano Petech, about sixteen kings succeeded dPal-gyi-mgon, till the end of the first Ladakhi dynasty i.e. till Lha-cen-grags-bum-ide. The information about these kings seems to be remembered in folklore. But it is certain that during this period the cultural influences in Ladakh were coming mainly from Tibet.

dPal-gyi-mgon had two sons, named Drogon and Chosgon.[14] Nothing has been mentioned in the Chronicle of Ladakh about these two princes. It seems that Drogon had succeeded his father as the king of Ladakh. His son Lha-chen-dragspa-ide succeeded him. The next king who came to throne was Lha-chen Jang Chub Semspa who succeeded his father Lha-chen dragspa-ide (1075-1100 A. D.).[15] According to Tashi Rabgias, during the reign of this king, the dKa-dam-pa sub-sect of Mahayana Buddhism developed in Ladakh. As he mentioned:

> Gyalpo Lha Chen Jang-chup Sems pa, dei
> skaps su La-dvags su dKa-dam-pai chos lugs
> tar wai gang yin. Sapol gi nyi Zla phug, dzhan

yang gYun-drun chi wan gi Lha-Khang Ning-pa
dPe-t'up kyi drag kung kha bo chey sogs mDor
na lotswa Rin-c'en-bzan-poi Lha-kan Nrams
dKa-dams pas dak skyin dZad pa yin.[16]

It means that during this period, the Cave temple at Saspol, the old temple of Yan-drun or Lamayuru monastery and the Cave temple locally known as 'drag kung kha-bo chey' of Spituk (dPe-t'up) monastery belong to dKa-dam-pa sect of Mahayana Buddhism. This sect is the first reformed sect in Mahayana Buddhism in Tibet.

The reformation of Mahayana Buddhism was started by the Indian monk Atisa, who visited Tibet in 1038 A.D.[17] Atisa started the reform by emphasizing strict monastic discipline. He also began to enforce celibacy and high morality. So, this new sect is called bKa-dam-pa or "those bound by orders (commands).

The chief disciple of Atisa was Dom-ton, who was from Tibet. He succeeded after his master as the head of the bKa-dam-pa sect. He built the Ra-Deng monastery in 1058 A.D.[18] This monastery, which is situated to the northeast of Lhasa was the first monastery of the dKa-dam-pa sect. The monastery of T'o-din in Pu-rang, built in 1025 A.D. is considered to have become a dKa-dam-pa institution by Atisa's residence therein. Following this sect, many sects and sub-sects of Mahayana Buddhism developed over time in Tibet.

The next Ladakhi king who succeeded his father Lha-chen drags-pa was Lha-chen Gyal-po (1100-1125 A.D.).[19] The most important work during his period in terms of religion and culture was the founding of the Likir monastery at Likir village. According to the Chronicles:

Lha-cen Gyal-po adiyi dus su klu-k'yil gi
dgon-pa btab nas dgen adun gi sdey btsugs.[20]

It means the king Lha-cen Gyal-po founded the monastery and encouraged a brotherhood of Lamas to settle down there.

This monastery is about 50 km to the west of Leh. In earlier times Likir village was connected with the trade route between Leh and villages below Likir. Also, the local route connecting different villages like Hemis Shukpachan and Timosgang goes through Likir village.

The next ruler was Lha-Chen-Utpala (1125-1150 A.D.).[21] He succeeded his father Lha Chen Gyalpo. He brought Purang, Purig, Kulu (which included Lahul-Spiti also) under his dominance.[22] According to Luciano Petech, Ladakh was for a short time the greatest power in the western Himalayas during Lha-Chen-Utpala's reign.[23] Lha-Chen-Naglug (1150-1175 A. D.)[24] succeeded his father Lha-Chen-Utpala. This king is credited with the construction of palaces at Wamle and Khalatse. According to the Chronicles of Ladakh, the Palace at Wamle was built in the Tiger year and the Palace of Khalatse in the Dragon year.[25] During his reign, there was the building of the bridge across the Indus at Khalatse.[26] He further added that the reason for building the bridge was to promote trade and thus to collect the taxes.[27] This bridge connects central and the areas in the west and southwest of Ladakh to Kashmir. Thus, it means during this period, the trade among different areas in Ladakh and also with her neighbours was quite developed.

The next king was Lha-Chen dGe-bhe.[28] He succeeded his father Lha-Chen Naglug in 1175-1200 A.D.[29] Lha-Chen Jo-ldor succeeded his father Lha-Chen dGe-bhe (1220-1225 A.D.).[30] According to Francke, he succeeded in 1200 A.D.[31] The next king who succeeded Lha-Chen Jo-ldor was his son Lha-Chen bKra-is-mgon. Not much has been written about the above three kings. Lhargyal was the next king to follow. He was the son of bKra-sis-mgon.[32] Lhargyal ruled Ladakh around 1250-1275 A.D.[33] The name of this king has been preserved on a sculpture near the village of Taru. Vajrapani was the favourite deity of this king. Besides this, he ordered two voluminous Lamaist works to be written in gold. As Tashi Rabgias mentioned that:

> Gyalpo dyi skor la Taru drong gSyb ki mTsams na dao-wa bKros pai yig cha tang Sky adra yod. Gyalpo di Chang-dor la mos shay ying. Chag-dor gyi gryud dser yig la bZha-yings. gZa-n yang Sung rab mang po dser yig la bZha-ngs.[34]

It means that the name of this king has been preserved on a sculpture near the village Taru and his favourite deity was Vajrapani; besides this, he ordered two voluminous religious books to be written in gold. According to Francke, during the reign of this king, there was the first recording of the introduction of religious literature into western Tibet.[35]

The next king who came to the throne was Lha-Chen Chosphel, who succeeded his father Lhargyal and he ruled around 1275-1300 A.D.[36] He was known to have promulgated religious edicts as well as defined the socio-administrative laws and ensured their perfect implementation. In a popular song the happy days under this king are described:

> "Under this king people become so rich that they wore hats of gold and their mouth never empty of tea and beer. Masters and servants alike spent their days in frolic and merriment."[37]

Lha-Chen dNos-grub (1300-1325 A.D.), ascended the throne after the death of his father, Lha-Chen Chosphel. During his reign, the custom of sending novices from Ladakh to various monastic centers of learning in dBus and the dTsang provinces of Central Tibet was introduced.[38] According to Luciano Petech:

> "This custom had a baneful of effect in the long run. It meant absolute spiritual dependence from central Tibet, it hindered the rise of an original philosophic and literary life in Ladakh."[39]

Most of the monks who had been to Tibet have answered that the introduction of this custom provided the opportunities to get the best monastic education, as Tibet became the leading Mahayana Buddhist Centre and the residence of leading Lamas who taught Mahayana Buddhism.

King dNos-grub's other contributions in the field of cultural developments in Ladakh included the repair and renovation of the monasteries that his ancestors had built. He also ordered two sets of the bKa-gyur (the words of Buddha), probably from Tibet. One set of the bKa-gyur consists of 108 volumes. Not only this, according to the Chronicles of Ladakh, King dNos-grub also acted as patron to C'os-kyi-rje 'Jig-rten gsum-gyi-mgon-po.[40] This is C'os-rje 'Jig-rten-mgon-po, alias Dharmasvamin or Rinc'n-dpal, who was the founder of the monastery of Bri-gung and the sub-sect of that name in Tibet.[41]

dNos-grub son was Lha-Chen Gyalbu Rinchen. Not much has been written about him. Unlike others he did not succeed his father, and the exact reason has not been mentioned anywhere. According to Francke, Gyalbu Rinchen left for Kashmir after a son had been born to his wife, and embraced Islam, and he came to be known as Rinchen Shah.[42] Walter R. Lawrence mentioned that Rinchen Shah came as an adventurer to the valley of Kashmir after having quarreled with his father.[43] According to Wazir Hashmatullah Khan, Rinchen Shah could not become king in Ladakh due to some political conflicts with his king father and he was compelled to migrate to Kashmir in the beginning of the 14th century along with some Ladakhi traders.[44] The Rajatarangini of Jonaraja mentioned that he came to Kashmir via Zojila and settled down somewhere in north Kashmir.[45] Whatever the reasons Rinchen Shah was an ambitious and very far sighted prince. He came to Kashmir along with his friends including Ladakhi traders and became the first Muslim king of Kashmir.

The next king was Lha-Chen Shesrab or Ses-rab. He was the son of Lha-Chen Gyalbu Rinchen. He is known to have built a castle on the top of the Han-rtse-mo in Sabu village, known as Sen-ge-sgan.[46] This village is about seven kilometers southeast of Leh. His son Lha-Chen Khri-gtsug-ide (1375-1400 A. D.)[47], succeeded to the throne. He built a row of 108 chortens (stupas) at Leh, and two rows of 108 chortens at Sabu to earn religious merit.[48] Many people settled there at

Sabu. During this period, a disciple of Zur-Phug-pa called Bharva, a well educated lama from Tibet, made a visit to Zanskar and blessed the site of the present Bardan Gonpa (monastery), predicting that a Gonpa would be built there.[49]

Lha-Chen Khri-gtsug-ide had two sons, Grags-pa-bum-ide and Grags-pa 'bum. The two brothers were of different characters. Grags-pa-bum-ide was of mild and merciful disposition and was religiously inclined. Whereas the younger brother, Grags-pa-bum was fierce and did not care in the least about his future state. The elder son, Grags-pa-bum-ide (1400-1440 A.D.)[50], succeeded his father. He was a great builder of temples and images. He first built the 'Red Temple' on the rNamgyal-semo hill at Leh and on the same hill, the statue of Maitreya or future Buddha escorted by Manjushri and Vajrapani.[51]

During his reign, two monks as envoys from rGyal-ba Tson-k'a-pa (1357-1419 A.D.), the founder of Ge-lug-pa sect in Tibet, came to Ladakh.[52] According to the Chronicles, Tsong-kha-pa sent with the two monks an image of the Buddha with the instruction that it should be handed over to the king of Ladakh. As the monks reached Nubra, the northern region of Ladakh, they met with the younger brother of the king. The two monks offered the scared image to him. He, however, did not care even to look at it and the two monks then went to the king at Leh. The King treated them courteously and received the sacred image with outmost reverence. In order to commemorate the event the King is said to have built the monastery of dPe-t'up for the Ge-lug-pa sect.[53] The monastery had been actually founded in the 11th Century[54]. The King must have assisted in a thorough restoration and to the transference to the Ge-lug-pa School. The king also built two Maitreya Statues, one at Timosgang, and the Maitreya of Byams-pa-dmar-po next to the palace at Leh.[55] These two images along with the one that was built on Tsemo hill were popularly known as "Byams-ba-rnam-gsum", the three Maitreya statues. Besides, this king is also said to have built four Byang-Chub Chortens at Timosgang, each one for the four points on the compass on the Lion-shaped mountain. He also built what locally is called as "Tiseru or Te 'u gser-po.[56] It looks like a stupa from outside but it said that it had 108 chapels inside. Ruins of that structure may be seen about three kilometers above Leh. Recently, the Archeological Survey of India has started to reconstruct this monument.

Meanwhile, Grags-pa-bum-ide's younger brother, Dragspa was ruling in the lower valley of Ladakh. According to Francke, his principal seats were Basgo and Timosgang in lower Ladakh.[57] He is called the builder of the royal city of Tomosgang and also made it his Capital.[58] He is also said to have improved the fortification at Basgo, to make it a stronghold of the first rank. In the meantime, the conversion of Kashmir to Islam created a new element of instability in the western Himalayas. There were several invasions of Ladakh by Kashmir. The first Muslim force from Kashmir to cross the Zoji-la (pass) and to invade the country beyond the pass was led by Rai Madari,[59] in the reign of Skinder (1394-1416 A.D.).

The next king who comes to the throne was Blo-gros-mc'og-idan. He succeeded his father Grags-pa-bum-ide in 1440 A.D and reigned until 1470 A.D. He sent presents to the first rGyal-ba (Dalai-Lama) dGe-dun-grup (1391-1474)[60]. According to the Chronicles, he conquered mNagris rKor-gsum and from there he brought to Ladakh turquoises, saddles, horses, swords etc.[61] Blo-gros-mc'og Iden was the last king of the first dynasty of Ladakh. His reign ended disastrously. According to Luciano Petech, he was deposed and imprisoned by a prince descending from a side branch of the family.[62] It was the end of the first Ladakhi dynasty.

The Important Monasteries Built during the First Dynasty

As I mentioned earlier in my first chapter, the Tibetan polity and culture have been decisively shaped by Buddhism. The monasteries are the most important aspect of Buddhism. Following are some of the important monasteries that have built during the first dynastic rule in Ladakh, and which had direct encouragement, guidance and support from Tibet.

Lamayuru Monastery

Lamayuru monastery[63] is one of the oldest in Ladakh. It is also known as gyun-drun (Swastika). As the legend goes, Lamayuru was a lake. It was blessed by a Lama after which the water of the lake reduced, leaving place for the monastery. It was founded in the 10th century. Its age is indicated by one small temple, from whose iconography the period may be placed in the time of Rin-cen-bzang-po.[64]

The main assembly hall or Du-khang has been repainted. In the same hall there is small cave known as Naropa's cave. It contains his statue along with those of Marpa and Mi-la Raspa. Naropa is believed to have meditated in this cave and the cave is one of the oldest parts of the monastery. Connected to the same assembly hall is a small room, dedicated to the protecting divinities. Sen-ge-sgang is another oldest part of the monastery. The main image in this temple is Vairocana, seated on his lion throne.

This monastery belongs to the Bri-gung-pa a branch of the bKa-gyud-pa sect.[65] The Bri-gung-pa sub-sect is named after the monastery of 'Bri-gung', which was founded by Jig-rtan mGon-po[66] in Tibet. According to Snellgrove and Skorupski, Bri-gung monastery played a very important role in the political life of Tibet.[67] In the 13th century it was the main contender against the Sa-skya monastery for the favour of their Mongol overlords.

In Ladakh, Lamayuru and Phyang are the main monasteries of the Bri-gung-pa sub-sect.

Alchi Monastery

The monastery of Alchi is also one of the oldest and most famous in Ladakh. It is called A-lci-chos-khor or 'religious enclave'. It is believed that Rin-cen bzang-po built many monasteries in Ladakh including Alchi.[68] The other monasteries are Nyar-ma, now a ruin some twenty kilometers up the Indus beyond Leh, Mangyu and Sumda.

The monastery of Alchi is about 75 kilometers west of Leh. Built over the banks of the Indus, it has many rooms containing beautiful paintings. These paintings are a mixture of Kashmiri and Tibetan influences. There are four main rooms in this monastery. The first one is the Assembly Hall or Du-Khang. In this Du-Khang the Buddhist monks assemble for the performance of ceremonies. According to Snellgrove and Skorpuski, architecturally the Alchi assembly hall resembles that of Nyar-ma (now ruined), and that of Tabo and other temples attributed to Rin-cen-bzang-po.[69] The main statue in the assembly hall is Vairocana enthroned in the Sanctuary. The paintings are still very well preserved.

The next room is called Sum-Tsek or gSum-brtseg (three-tier temple). This temple contains three impressive images, well decorated with painting on it. The first image is of Avalokitesvara or Chanrazig (Buddha of Compassion) on the left, then Maitreya (future Buddha) opposite the entrance and finally Manjusri (Buddha of Wisdom). These three stand for peace and prosperity. The style of the paintings especially on the lower part of these images shows the Kashmiri influence.

The Lotswa Lhakhang is another room where one can see a small image of Lotswa Rin-cen bzang-po.On his left side is the image of Buddha Sakyamuni in the earth-witness posture, and on his right side is the image of Avalokitesvara. Next to the Lotswa Lhakhang is the Manjusri temple. Inside are the fourfold images of Manjusri, each aspect facing one of the quarters and painted in the appropriate directional colour; blue, yellow, red and dark green.

Alchi Chos-khor is one of the wonders of the Buddhist world. One hopes that some means will be found to ensure its continued preservation.

Mangyu and Sumda

Mangyu and Sumda are the other monasteries that have

built during Rin-cen bzang-po's period. Mangyu monastery has been described earlier in this chapter.

As far as Sumda is concerned, it is a small one and comprises of three temples. The main temple is the assembly hall or Du-khang. The image of Vairocana in this hall is well decorated and preserved. The other two temples, which are smaller than the assembly hall, are the temples of Maitreya and Avalokitesvara. The style of paintings in this monastery is similar to that of Alchi monastery.

Likir Monastery

This monastery was founded during the reign of King Kha-chen Gyal-po (1100-1125).[70] This monastery has been described in detail earlier in this chapter. To add little more, this monastery was initially associated with the dKa-dam-pa sect and in the 15th century it was taken over by the Ge-lug-pa establishment.[71] The present monastery dates back to the eighteenth century, as its earlier structure was destroyed in fire. The head of this monastery is a brother of the Dalai Lama. The present monastery is quite big. In Du-khang or the assembly hall, there are seats for about seventy monks. The images of Buddha Sakyamuni and Maiterya are in this hall. It also contains on either side on wooden racks the volumes of the Buddhist holy books. There is another smaller Du-khang, which has the image of Avalokitesvara. Upstairs is the private apartments of the head Lama. The Gon-khang is on the same floor, and this temple is dedicated to the protector divinities. These images are normally covered and opened only during the time of the monastery festivals. This monastery has its festivals in winter. The Museum is on the top floor. It has an interesting collection of old thankas from Tibet, old religious and domestic costumes, some official letters, different coins and implements.

Phugtal Monastery

Phugtal monastery is the most picturesque in the whole of Zanskar[72] and perhaps also the most isolated in the region.

It is accessible from the Padum-Darcha (Manali) tracking route through a seven kilometers long trail that branches off from the Purney Bridge on the main trail. We got an opportunity to visit this beautiful monastery a few years ago with a trekking group. According to Snellgrove and Skorupski, Phugtal monastery was founded by a Zanskar translator named Phags-pa Shes-rab.[73] The date of the Zanskar translator was more or less contemporary with Mi-la-ras-pa (1040-1123 A.D.).[74]

There are many interesting temples in the monastery. The assembly hall or Du-khang is decorated with murals of Sakyamuni and Tsong-kha-pa. Another room called the sTon-pa Lha-khang contains interesting murals from several periods. The oldest is probably from the time of Rin-cen-bzang-po and it resembles those at Tabo (rTa-po)[75] monastery. Tabo monastery is in Lahul Spiti and is believed to have been built by Rin-cen bzang-po. The use of stucco in the images in Phugtal monastery resembles those at Alchi and Sumda,[76] suggesting an earlier period. The next sets of murals are probably from the sixteenth century.[77] The Gon-khang has the images of the protector divinities and collections of old weapons. There is also a fine library in Ka-gyur lha-khang. About forty monks inhabit this beautiful monastic establishment.

Important Lamas who Visited Ladakh during this Period

Many important Lamas had visited Ladakh from Tibet and other places. Following are some of the important early Lama missionaries who visited Ladakh and they played an important role in establishing Mahayana Buddhism in Ladakh.

Padmasambhava

Padmasambhava is believed to have visited Ladakh in the 8th century.[78] According to Tashi Rabgias, besides Central Ladakh, Padmasambhava visited Baltistan, from where he went to Phokar rZong, a place to the west of Leh and then to Zanskar.[79]

Rin-chen bzang-po

Lotswa Rin-cen bzang-po[80] played a vital role in laying a firm foundation for Mahayana Buddhism in Ladakh. At the age of eighteen in the year of the Pig (i.e. 975 A.D), Rin-cen bzang-po visited Kashmir.[81] After studying many years in Kashmir, he visited many places in western Tibet including Ladakh. Many temples attributed to him are still found in Ladakh.

Zanskar Lotswa

Zanskar Lotswa was one of the great learned men from Zanskar. His name was Phas-pa Shes-rab,[82] and he was born in Zanskar. He left his native place to go to western Tibet, probably to Guge for higher studies. It is difficult to fix his exact dates. According to Snellgrove and Skorupski, he was more or less contemporary with Mi-la Raspa (1040-1123 A. D.).[83] He studied and worked with several Tibetan, Indian and Kashmiri teachers.

Phags-pa Shes-rab translated many books from Sanskrit into Tibetan including part of the bstan-gyur, the Tibetan Canon.[84] His reputation as a translator and teacher gained him a considerable following not only in Ladakh but also in Tibet. He came to be called as Zanskar Lotswa, the translator from Zanskar.[85] He played an important role in establishing the Mahayana Buddhism not only in his native place but also contributed to the mainstream religion tradition in Tibet. He was also well known as a teacher and his students were from many areas including Baltistan. One of his students was from Skardo, known as Balti Lotswa.[86]

rGod-tsang-pa

rGod-tsang-pa mGon-bo dPal (1189-1258 A. D.) was another Lama who visited Ladakh.[87] He received instructions both at Rva-Lung and 'Brug Monastery in Tibet and took ordination from his teacher.[88] His teacher was rTzang-pa rGya-ras who was a prominent master of the Brug-pa sub-sect of Tibetan Buddhism.[89]

sGod-tsang-pa traveled many places in the west Himalayan region including Ladakh. His visit had resulted in the propagation of 'Brug-pa tenets and tradition in these West Himalayan regions. He stayed and meditated in several places in Central Ladakh. First he resided in the upper Igu. From there he is said to have 'flown' to Martselang and finally went to upper Hemis, popularly known as sGod-stang.[90] Even now caves and hermitages named after him are found in Central Ladakh.

Conclusion

This chapter has surveyed the Ladakhi history from early years to the end of the first dynasty rule in Ladakh. It is certain that before the Tibetan influence, the cultural influence on Ladakh was from Kashmir but far too little remains except some rock-carvings.

The first important and widespread cultural influences came from Tibet came with the establishment of the first Ladakhi dynasty rule in the tenth century. During this period emphasis was on the patronage and support of construction of monasteries and stupas in Ladakh. Besides, the Kingdom's patronage of Tibetan Buddhism, Lama Missionaries also played an important role in the spread of Mahayana Buddhism. The influences were two ways affair. Ladakhis made their own contributions to the mainstream religion tradition of Tibet. One example of such contributions was Zanskar Lotswa's translation works mentioned above.

Ladakh's religious and spiritual ties with Buddhist Tibet during this period were close and consistent.

REFERENCES

1. A. H. Francke. Ladakh: The Mysterious Land, *A History of Western Tibet* (London: n/a, 1907and reprinted, New Delhi: Cosmo Publication, 1978), p. 19.
2. Lucuano Petech, *The Kingdom of Ladakh, C. 950-1842 A.D* (Roma: *Istituto Italiano Per IL Medio Ed Estremo* Orient, 1977), p. 5.
3. A. H. Francke, op. cit. 1, p. 50.

4. *Ibid*. p. 31.
5. Austine. L.Waddell. *The Buddhism of Tibet or Lamaism* (First Published: 1899 and reprinted New Delhi: Asian Educational Service, 1959), p. 43. Also see Alexander Cunningham, *Ladakh: Physical, Statistical and Historical* (London: W. H. Allen, 1854 and Reprinted, New Delhi: Sagar publication, 1970), p. 317.
6. A. H. Francke. op. cit, 1, p. 20.
7. Siddiq Wahid and Keneth R. Storm, *Ladakh between earth and Sky* (New Delhi: B.I Publications, 1981), p. 15.
8. A. H. Francke. op. cit, 1, p. 47.
9. A. H. Francke. Antiquities *of Indian Tibet, The Chronicles of Ladakh and Minor Chronicles, Part II* (New Delhi: Chand and Co., 1926), p. 35.
10. *Ibid*, Also see Tashi Rabgias. *Maryul La dvags Kyi Snon Rabs Kun gsal melong Zhes bya ba zugso: History of Ladakh Called the Mirror which Illuminates* All (Delhi: Jayyed Press, 1984), p. 59.
11. David Snellgrove. L and Tadeusz Skorupdki, *The Cultural Heritage of Ladakh, Volume One* (England: Aris & Phillips Ltd., 1977), p. 5.
12. Tashi Rabgias, op. cit. 10, pp. 50-51.
13. Thupstan Paldan, The guide to the Buddhist Monasteries and Royal Castles of Ladakh (Delhi: n/d, 1997), p. 8.
14. Tashi Rabgias, op.cit. 10, p. 67
15. A. H. Francke, op.cit. 1, p. 63
16. Tashi Rabgias, op.cit. 10, pp. 86-87.
17. Austine Waddell, op. cit. 5, p. 54.
18. *Ibid*, p. 56.
19. A. H. Francke, op.cit. 1, p. 63.
20. A. H. Francke, op. cit. 9, p. 35.
21. A. H. Francke, op.cit. 1, p. 64
22. O. C Handa, *Buddhist Western Himalaya- part-I* (New Delhi: Indus Publishing Company, 2001), p. 130.
23. Lucuano Petech, op. cit. 2, p. 18.
24. Tashi Rabgias, op.cit. 10, p. 93.
25. A. H. Francke, op. cit. 9, p.36.
26. Tashi Rabgias, op. cit. 10, p. 93.
27. *Ibid*. p. 93.

28. Luciano Petech, op. cit. 2, p. 17.
29. A. H. Francke, op. cit. 1, p. 66.
30. Tashi Rabgias, op. cit. 10, p. 95.
31. A. H. Francke, op. cit. 1, p. 66.
32. A. H. Francke, op. cit. 9, p. 36.
33. A. H. Francke, op.cit. 1, p. 67.
34. Tashi Rabgias, op. cit.10, p. 105.
35. A. H. Francke, op. cit. 1, p. 67.
36. Nawang Tsering Shakspo, *An Insight into Ladakh*, Francesca Mirritt (eds.) (Sabu-Leh: Ayu-Changchug, 1993), p. 17.
37. A. H. Francke, op. cit. 1, p. 67.
38. A. H. Francke, op. cit. 9, p. 36.
39. Luciano Petech, op. cit. 2, p. 166.
40. A. H. Francke, op. cit. 9, p. 36.
41. Luciano Petech, op. cit. 2, p. 19. Also see Austine Waddell, op. cit. 5, p. 69.
42. A. H. Francke, op. cit. 9, p. 70.
43. Walter R. Lawrence, The Valley of Kashmir, (Srinagar: Gulshan Books, 2007), p. 189
44. Cited in Zain-ul-Aabedin Aabedi, Emergence of Islam in Ladakh, (New Delhi: Atlantic Publishers & Distributers (P) Ltd., 2009), p. 1
45. Jogesh Chunder Dutt, The Rajatarangini of Jonaraja, (Delhi: Gyan Publishing House, 1986), p. 17.
46. A. H. Francke, op. cit. 9, p. 36.
47. Tashi Rabgias, op. cit. 10, p. 119.
48. A. H. Francke, op. cit. 1, p. 72.
49. Nawang Tsering Shakspo, op. cit. 36, p. 18.
50. *Ibid*. p. 18. Luciano Petech, suggested (1410-1435), op. cit. 2, p. 22.
51. A. H. Francke, op. cit. 1, p. 75.
52. D. L. Snellgrove and Skorupski, op. cit. 11, p. 82.
53. A. H. Francke, op. cit. 9, p. 37.
54. Luciano Petech, op. cit. 2, p. 18.
55. Nawang Tsering Shakspo, op. cit. 36. p. 18.
56. D. L. Snellgrove and Skorupski, op. cit. 11, p. 82.

57. A. H. Francke, op. cit. 1, p. 80.
58. Luciano Petech, op. cit 2, p. 25.
59. *Ibid*. p. 22.
60. *Ibid*. p. 23.
61. A. H. Francke, op. cit. 9, p. 37.
62. Luciano Petech op. cit. 2, p. 24.
63. Thupstan Paldan, op. cit. 13, p. 9.
64. D. L. Snellgraove and Skorupski, op. cit. 11, p. 21.
65. *Ibid*. p. 20.
66. Luciano Petech, op. cit. 2, p. 18.
67. D. L. Snellgrove and Skorupski, op. cit. 11, p. 21.
68. Thupstan Paldan, op. cit. 13, pp. 7-8.
69. D. L. Snellgrove and Skorupski, op.cit. 11, p. 30.
70. A. H. Francke, op. cit. 1, p. 63.
71. Janet Rizvi, Ladakh: *Crossroad of High Asia* (New Delhi: Oxford University Press, 1983), p. 185.
72. A region in the South of Leh.
73. David, L Snellgrove and Tadeusz Skorupski, *The Cultural Heritage of Ladakh, Vol. 2* (New Delhi: Vikas Publishing House, 1980), p. 42.
74. *Ibid*. p. 38.
75. John Crook, and Tsering Shakya, "Monastic Communities In Zanskar: Location, Function and Organization" in Crook, J. H and Henry, A. Osmaston (eds.), *Himalayan Buddhist Village: Enviroment, Resources, Society and Religious Life in Zanskar- Ladakh* (Bristol and New Delhi: Motilal Banarasidass, 1994), pp. 559-99.
76. D. L. Snellgrove and Skorupski, op. cit. 73, p. 53.
77. *Ibid*. p. 53.
78. Tashi Rabgias, op. cit, 10, pp. 50-51.
79. *Ibid*. pp. 50 & 51.
80. D.L. Snellgrove and Skorupski, op. cit. 11, p. 5.
81. Gangnegi Hira Paul, *Lo Tsa Ba Rin Chen Bza Po and Sarma School*, An unpublished thesis, submitted to the department of Buddhist Studies, University of Delhi, 1994, p. 73.
82. Tashi Rabgias, op. cit. 10, p. 87.

83. D.L. Snellgrove and Skorupski, op. cit. 73, p. 38.
84. Tashi Rabgias, op. cit. 10, p. 87.
85. Nawang Tsering Shakspo, op. cit. 36, p. 15.
86. Tashi Rabgias, op. cit. 10, pp. 88-89.
87. Nawang Tsering Shakspo, op. cit. 36, p. 16.
88. Nawang Tsering, *Buddhism in Ladakh: A study of the life and works of the eighteenth century Ladakh Saint Scholar* (New Delhi: Sterling publishers, 1979), p. 25.
89. *Ibid*. p. 25.
90. Tashi Rabgias, op. cit. 10, pp. 99-100.

4

Ladakh's Cultural Ties with Buddhist Tibet during the 16th to 19th Centuries

The second dynasty of Ladakh is called rNamgyal dynasty, the last dynasty to rule Ladakh when Ladakh became a part of Jammu and Kashmir, India.

Lha-chen Bhagan is regarded as the founder of the rNnamgyal dynasty.[1] According to Tashi Rabgias, Lha-Chen Bhagan's real name was Rin-chen-rNamgyal and his bad reputation had earned him the nickname of Bhagan or Old Bull.[2] He is believed to have reunited the two medieval kingdoms in Ladakh, which were divided between two brothers during the reign of Grags-bum-ide.[3] The two kingdoms were the one with its centre at Leh or Shey, and the other one of Basgo or Tingmosgang. Bhagan was a grandson of King Basgo.[4] After having reunited the two kingdoms, succeeding kings of second dynasty took the surname of rNamgyal, which means victorious.

The king Bhagan had two sons, Lha-dbang rNamgyal and bKra-sis rNamgyal.[5] The two sons were different personalities. Lha-dbang rNamgyal had great physical strength and was clever at many royal sports. But his younger brother, bKra-sis rNamgyal was very crafty.[6] To attain his aim, bKra-sis rNamgyal caused his elder brother's eyes to be blinded and usurped the throne.[7] Then he sent his blind brother to Lingshed on the borders of Zanskar.

bKra-sis rNamgyal seems have been an energetic and able ruler. He conquered the neighboring areas under his rule. bKra-sis rNamgyal is described in the Chronicle of Ladakh as a deeply religious person despite the crime committed by him to his elder brother. He carried out many religious activities, which included the offerings to various monasteries in Tibet, and building new monasteries in Ladakh. According to the Chronicles, the king made many offerings to Bri-gung, Sa-skya, Gandan (dGa-idan) and Samyas (bSam-yas). Besides, he also brought the bKa-gyur Canon from Tibet.[8] The king invited C'os-rje iDan-ma, a great Lama of Bri-gung-pa sub-sect in Tibet to Ladakh. With the advice of the Lama, the king founded the sGan-Snon bKra-sis-cos-adzong or Phyang monastery.[9] bKra-sis-rNamgyal also built the Castle, now in ruins on top of the rNamgyal-rtse-mo hill behind Leh and the Gon-khang; a temple, below it.[10] He also founded the hamlet of Chubi at the foot of the western declivity of the rNamgyal-rtse-mo.

In the field of monastic education, the king introduced an important custom. Every family having more than one male child had to give up one son, not necessarily the eldest, to become a monk.[11] Thus, the reign of bKra-sis-rNamgyal marked a partial renewal of the Bri-gun-pa sub-sect of bKa-gyud-pa influence in Ladakh.

Around this time, the Central Asian adventurer, Mirza Haider Dulat invaded Ladakh.[12] In his campaign in 1532, Mirza Haider encountered resistance first in the Nubra valley. He, however, overcame this resistance. But in Central Ladakh, he met stiff resistance from the king, bKra-sis-rNamgyal. In this battle, Mirza Haider lost many soldiers and their bodies were buried on the rNamgyal-rtse-mo hill.[13] Then the king built the Gon-kang[14], housing the statue of the protector deity above the corpses of the soldiers. The invaders returned with heavy losses. However, Mirza Haider, after becoming the ruler of Kashmir, invaded Ladakh a couple of more times. He raided Ladakh again in 1545 and 1548[15], but with no lasting consequences.

bKra-sis-rNamgyal died childless. After his death, his elder brother Lha-dbang-rNamgyal, whom he blinded, and his family found release from Lingshed. Lha-dbang-rNamgyal had three sons, Ts'e-dbang-rNamgyal, rNamgyal-mgon-po and Jam-dbyans-rNamgyal. The eldest son, Ts'e-dbang-rNamgyal (1530-1560 A. D.), succeeded his uncle, bKra-sis-rNamgyal. He emerged as a wise and a great conqueror. The Kingdom witnessed significant expansion under him. He conquered in the south Nun-ti (Kulu), and in the west Si-dkar in Baltistan.[16] He wanted to attack the Khan of Yarkand in the north but the Nubra people advised the king against it as it would seriously damage the trade through the passes, which was of vital importance to Nubra. Guge and Rudok remained separate kingdoms but had to pay tribute to Ladakh.[17]

Besides, Ts'e-dbang-rNamgyal carried out many religious activities. He built Mani walls and stupas in many places in Ladakh. He also maintained and added many statues and monasteries, which were built by his ancestors. His reign was marked by a continuation of Bri-gung-pa sub-sec influence in Ladakh. In order to facilitate trade and commerce activities, he built two roads. One was the road to Baltistan near Dha-Hanu, in the west of Leh, and the other one was the road to Zanskar, at Hanupata.[18]

Tse-dbang-rNamgyal had no heirs and he was succeeded by his younger brother Jam-dbyans-rNamgyal (1560-1590 A. D.). When Jam-dbyans-rNamgyal came to the throne, he faced a difficult situation as after the death of his brother, all the vassal princes rose in revolt. The new king tried to re-establish his prestige by intervening in a conflict between Tse-rin Malik of Cig-tan and the chief of Purig.[19] The king Jam-dbyans-rNamgyal decided to go to the assistance of Tse-rin Malik of Cig-tan.

The popular tradition has the following account about the beginning of his campaign. "It was late in the year when the Ladakhi soldiers were on the point of starting their campaign, and it was not considered lucky to start before having celebrated the New Year's festival. However, to wait for the Tibetan New Year would mean a delay of two moths. Therefore, the king decided that the New Year's festival was to be celebrated two months before it actually fell. Ever since the New Year (rgyalpo Losar) has been celebrated about two months earlier in Ladakh than in Tibet".[20]

The outcome of the conflict was a disaster. The forces of Baltisan under the ruler of Skardo, Ali Mir, outmaneuvered the Ladakhi army and overran the whole of Ladakh, plundering its riches and destroying its religious and arts treasures.[21] The king was taken prisoner to Skardo. The king of Skardo placed the king of Ladakh in honorable confinement. The daughter of the king of Skardo, named Gyal Khatun, was placed in attendance to Jam-dbyans-rNamgyal, whereby they were married. The ruler of Skardo gave his daughter in marriage on the condition that Jam-dbyans-rNamgyal convert to Islam and a child born from this second marriage of the king would be sole heir to the throne.[22] Along with the Balti princess, a group of servants and musicians were accompanied and these musicians became the "palace musician" (mkhar-mon) of Ladakh.[23] The kingdom of Ladakh was restored to Jam-dbyans-rNamgyal and for the time being ensured peace for Ladakh's western frontier. Gyal Khatun was recognized as an incarnation of the White Tara. Abdul Gani Sheikh 'Muslim introduced some of the musical instruments like Surna (oboe) and Daman (kettledrum) in Ladakh in the 17th century'.[24] 'Ghazal and qawali songs are also contributions of Balti migrants and government officials'.[25]

After the coming back to Ladakh, the king turned towards the internal affairs of the kingdom and towards religion. To provide relief to the people, who had suffered during the war, the king granted remission from the land revenue and extended monetary help to many. He renovated various monasteries and Caves, which had been damaged by the Balti invasion.[26] The king sent presents to various monasteries and sects in central Tibet.[27] The recipients of his generosity were the Jo-bo-K'an of Lhasa, the Ge-lug-pa monastery of Bras-spuns, and the Brug-pa monastery of Ra-lung.[28] He also sent an invitation to sTag-ts'an-ras-pa, a learned Brug-pa lama, who was in Zanskar on a journey to Uddiana enjoined upon him by his master.[29] He turned down the invitation for the moment, as he had not yet accomplished his journey to Uddiana.

Jam-dbyans-rNamgyal's Muslim wife bore him two sons, Sen-ge-rNamgyal and Norbu-rNamgyal.[30] Before he married Gyal Khatun, he had another wife named Ts'e-rin rgyal-mo. His first wife also bore him two sons, Nag-dban-rNamgyal and bsTan-dzin-rNamgyal, who were excluded from succession. Later the elder brother Nag-dban-rNamgyal became the head lama of Lahul.[31] According to the Chronicles, his religious name was Dzam-gling-grags-pa and in 1630, he left for central Tibet as the head of a religious mission.[32] He stayed at bKra-sis-Lhun-po and Bras-spuns under his former name Nag-dban-rNamgyal.[33] And his younger brother, bsTan-dzin-rNamgyal, was appointed as Gyalpo (King) of Spiti by Sen-ge-rNamgyal[34], when Sen-ge-rNamgyal succeeded to the throne of Ladakh.

During Jam-dbyans-rNamgyal's reign the first recorded visit of a European to Ladakh took place, a merchant from Portugal named Dioga d'Almedia, who stayed two years in Ladakh.[35] Ladakh impressed him as a rich country. Its capital was Basgo.[36] The presence of this western merchant is explained by the fact that trade through Ladakh to Tibet and Central Asia was very active.

The next king who came to the throne was Sen-ge-rNamgyal, elder son of the king Jam-dbyans-rNamgyal. The death of Jam-dbyans-rNamgyal was followed by an interregnum, during which Gyal Khatun carried on the government on behalf of her elder son Sen-ge-rNamgyal.[37] According to Luciano Petech, there was a quarrel between the king and his younger brother Norbu-rNamgyal. An agreement arranged by Lama sTag-ts'an-ras-pa[38] resulted in the younger brother Norbu-rNamgyal being placed on the throne.[39] But the younger brother reigned only for a short time, after which Sen-ge-rNamgyal ascended the throne.[40]

Sen-ge-rNamgyal was very strong, brave and an expert in archery and horsemanship from his childhood. His was one of the most glorious and eventful reigns in the history of Ladakh. The main problem of his first years of reign, and one whose solution won him his greatest success was the conflict with Guge. It started immediately after the death of his father. For a long time there had been a violent quarrel between Guge and Ladakh. Some more information on this subject is from the letter written by Andrade[41] in 1633 which tells us:

> "That eighteen years before the king of Guge had a son, the heir to the throne, born to him, but at his birth the queen had lost her reason, 'so that she is still ailing'. When after two years all effort to cure her proved useless, the king resolved to contract a fresh marriage, although the Tibetan religion permits no bigamy. The new bride was a sister of the king of Ladakh. The marriage-contract was made by proxy, but when the new queen, on her way to her husband, was at two days distance from Tsaparang, he suddenly forbade her to proceed and ordered her to go back to Ladakh."[42]

The Ladakhi king immediately declared war against the king of Guge, which with occasional intervals continued for eighteen years impoverishing the country by rendering impossible the working of fields or mines.

The bride may have been Nor-dzin dban-mo, elder sister of Sen-ge-rNamgyal.[43] The long period of tension between Guge and Ladakh led to the military conflict between Guge and Ladakh. Sen-ge-rNamgyal and his troops marched into Tsaparang.[44] The information on this subject from Coresma[45], who described about the people and the area, and tells us that the king of Ladakh had appointed a governor for Tsaparang.[46]

The conquest of Guge in the east brought Ladakh into direct contact with central Tibet.[47] During this period, the relations between Ladakh and Tibet were cordial as envoys and missions were exchanged. In 1632, the Ladakhi king Sen-ge-rNamgyal sent envoys to Brug-c'en and to the abbots of bDe-c'en-c'os-kor and rgyal-byed-ts'al: along with them he dispatched a complimentary mission to the sTan sde-srid.[48] In 1634, the sTan ruler sent reply of his to Ladakh.[49]

In the southwest, king Sen-ge-rNamgyal conquered Zanskar.[50] Zanskar at that time was ruled by Sen-ge-ide, also called Dzo-ki who had married Sen-ge-rNamgyal's sister rgyal-dzom.[51] This matrimonial relation contributed to maintain cordial relations between the two courts. But in 1638, the husband and wife quarreled and it gave Sen-ge-rNamgyal a reason to conquer Zanskar. Sen-ge-rNamgyal also conquered Lahul and got hold of upper Lahul.[52] Against the Muslims in the west, he invaded Cig-tan, spelt as Pyi-btan, and other places in that area.[53] Cig-tan, like most of Purig had become by then a Muslim area, as shown by its local genealogical tradition.[54] There are contradictory reports about the outcome of this military campaign of Sen-ge-rnamgyal in the west against the combined Balti-Mughal army. The Chronicles of Ladakh record a victory of Sen-ge-rNamgyal over the combined Balti-Mughal army at Bodh Kharbu (mk'ar-bu).[55] The Muhgal sources recorded the defeat of Ladakhi forces who settled for peace and promised tribute to the Mughal Empire in Delhi, a promise which Sen-ge-rNamgyal never kept.[56]

Whatever the military outcome, this conflict had a serious consequence on the trade relations in the area. According to Luciano Petech:

> "As an economic reprisal against the Mughals, the king prohibited the passage of caravans through Ladakh and even forbade any person from Kashmir to enter his dominions. As a result, traffic from India to central Tibet shifted to Patna-Nepal-Lhasa, while the trade of Kashmir with central Asia had to take via Skardo and Shigar to Kashgar."[57]

It was not a good decision keeping in view the economic realities at that time, because the economy of Ladakh then, as always, depended above all on the transit trade.

Apart from his military successes, Sen-ge-rNamgyal is remembered for his contribution to the promotion of religion and cultural development in Ladakh. The religious life of Ladakh flourished under him. He is remembered for his association with the great Lama sTag-tsan-ras-pa from Tibet who came to Ladakh during his reign. The great Lama achieved the gradual conversion of the royal house to the Brug-pa sub-sect.[58] The king was assisted by the great Lama in founding many monasteries of the Brug-pa sub-sect of bKa-dgyud-pa, including Hemis, the most famous and the richest monastery in Ladakh even today. Besides Hemis, which became and remained the royal monastery of Ladakh[59], the other major monastery which was built by this king was De-c'en-rNamgyal monastery at Wam-le.[60] At Hemis monastery, Sen-ge-rNamgyal installed the images that he brought from an ancient monastery at village Meru. According to A. H. Francke, the Meru monastery used to be one of the important monasteries in Ladakh, but its founder was not known. It lost much of its glory when king Sen-ge-rNamgyal made it the "mother" of Hemis monastery. On that occasion, not only the "spirit" of the Meru monastery was carried off in a bundle of twigs, but also most of the images were transferred to Hemis.[61] Another remarkable building was the Maitreya temple at Basgo. In memory of his father, Sen-ge-rNamgyal built the two-storey Maitreya statue as big "as he (Maitreya) would be in his eight years" out of clay and cooper guilt.[62]

The king along with his teacher, sTag-tsan-ras-pa, built several Mani walls to gain religious merit, and one at Basgo with rNamgyal (symbolizing victory) and bYang-chub (symbolizing enlightenment) Chortens at either end.[63] This Mani wall is said to be the longest in Ladakh.[64] Another one is at Lingshed that bears the inscription 'built by Sen-ge-rNamgyal'. During his reign, many talented monks and lay people were taught to write letters with gold and silver.[65] The king appointed dPon-Gnan-mkha-dPal-mgon as the chief calligrapher and under his supervision the king had the bKa-gyur text written with gold and silver letters. Some of it is still preserved at the temple in Basgo.[66]

The most important and magnificent secular structure built by the king Sen-ge-rNamgyal was Slel-c'en dPal-mkar, the nine-storeyed royal Palace towering over Leh.[67] The Palace contains many auspicious rooms, chapels and Buddhist symbols, and it was completed in three years and all the workers were rewarded.[68] Although far less imposing now, it resembles the Potala[69], the palatial fort in Lhasa, which was built by the fifth Dalai Lama. Besides, the king also built a wooden bridge across the Indus River at Alchi.[70] The construction of monasteries and other buildings were encouraged with guidance from Buddhist Tibet through Lama Missionaries. Apart from the building activity, Sen-ge-rNamgyal also sent frequent missions with presents to the various religious establishments in central Tibet.[71]

During the reign of Sen-ge-rNamgyal, the Portuguese Jesuit Francisco de Azevedo visited Ladakh. The purpose of his visit was to obtain permission from the king to preach the Gospel in Tsaparang.[72] He passed through Hanle and rGya[73], and reached Leh on 25 October 1631. The king received him, and Azevedo gives descriptions of the physical appearance of the king and the queen bsKal-bzan.[74] After some negotiations, he obtained a document ensuring the freedom of preaching the Gospel.[75]

Sen-ge-rNamgyal died at Wam-le on 27 November 1642.[76] He was less than fifty years old. His reign is remembered as a glorious period in the history of Ladakh. After his death, there was an interregnum during which, his widow, bsKal-szang, acted as regent for her sons who must still have been minors. bsKal-szang and Sen-ge-rNamgyal had three sons between them. bDe-Idan-rNamgyal was the eldest followed by Indrabodhi, also called Indrabodhi-rNamgyal, and bDe-mc'og-rNamgyal.[77] The second son Indrabodhi-rNamgyal, initially joined the monkhood and become a disciple of sTag-tshang-ras-pa.[78] However, on 15 February 1647, all the three brothers were consecrated as kings, but the eldest as paramount ruler.[79] The kingdom was divided between the three brothers. Indrabodhi-rNamgyal, who became a monk, received Guge; bDe-mc'og-rNamgyal, the youngest, obtained Zanskar and Spiti and rest of the 'mNa-ris-skor-gsum' in upper and lower Ladakh was assigned to the eldest son, bDe-Idan-rNamgyal.[80] Nevertheless, the two younger brothers acknowledged the supremacy of their elder brother, bDe-Idan-rNamgyal, who in turn responded to that gesture by patronizing his younger brothers.

Ladakh suffered a raid by Turki (Hor) forces from Kashgaria in the year 1647, led by Babak Beg and Sara Beg (Bha-bag-bhi, Sa-ra-bhi), who reached C'u-sod-gzun. The fight that took place resulted in many casualties and damages.[81] It was the Lama sTag-tstan-ras-pa who mediated on the request of the Ladakhi prince[82], and avoided further casualties and damage. The Turks called the Lama by the Muslim title Pir.

bDe-Idan-rNamgyal showed great interest in the governance of the kingdom even during his youth. He had thus acquired competent knowledge in the statecraft under the guidance of his father. Fifteen years after his accession, bDe-Idan-rNamgyal faced a major problem in relations with Kashmir and through Kashmir with Mughal India.[83] As mentioned earlier, after the battle of mK'ar-bu, king Sen-ge-rNamgyal had promised tribute to the Mughals but this tribute was never paid. But when in 1663, the new emperor Aurangzeb made his first and only visit to Kashmir[84], "the Ladakhi king, perhaps feeling uneasiness about the presence on the border of a ruler who nursed a rightful grievance against Ladakh and had the means to enforce redress of the same, sent him an embassy."[85] The envoys were received by the emperor and repeated to him the king's pledge tribute, promised that a mosque would be built, have the 'khutba', the prayer for the secular authority recited, and coins struck in the name of the emperor.[86] These promises were also ignored, until few years later, when a mosque was built in Leh, the first in central Ladakh.[87] According to Janet Rizvi, 'the added pledge to encourage Islam in Ladakh was certainly not taken seriously, nor the tribute paid regularly or at all'.[88] The trade between Kashmir and Ladakh, which was blocked earlier by Sen-ge-rNamgyal, was lifted.

Whatever the relations between bDe-Idan-rNamgyal and the Mughals, he adopted a forward policy to the west. The Ladakhi soldiers under the command of Sakya-rgya-mtso invaded the chiefships of lower Ladakh and Purig in 1673.[89] A year later, Ladakhi activities extended to Baltistan, where K'a-pu-lu and C'or-bad were seized[90], the first chiefship being conferred upon Hatim Khan and the second upon Sultan Khan.[91]

Ladakh's religion and cultural relations with Tibet were cordial. This was reflected in the continuance of the mission to central Tibet. Lama sTag-ts'an-ras-pa, in spite of advancing age, was very active in the construction of temples and sending missions. In 1643, he sent a mission to bDe-c'en-cos-k'or.[92] Two years later, in 1645, a mission was dispatched to Lhasa, headed by 'Brug-pa-rdo-rje on behalf of Hemis monastery and Tub-bstan-Lha-dban and A-ku dkon-mcog on behalf of the Ladakhi court. This mission arranged for the funeral rites for Senge-rNamgyal at Lhasa during the Smon-lam festival of 1646.[93]

Like his father, bDe-Idan-rNamgyal took keen interest in religious activities. With the advice and guidance from Lama sTag-ts'an-ras-pa, the king built several temples, Mani walls, Chortens and palaces. For the spiritual welfare of his father, king bDe-Idan-rNamgyal built a temple and the three-storey statue of Lord Buddha, made up of clay, copper and guilt[94], at Shey.[95] We can see this magnificent image of Buddha and beautiful mural paintings inside the temple at Shey even today. He also built a Chang-chub Chorten (a stupa symbolizing the enlightenment of Buddha), decorating the wheel, the Sun and the Moon on the upper portion of the stupa with copper.[96] The present Avalokitesvara temple in Leh was built during his reign.[97] Besides, the king constructed the eight hundred and fifty metres long Mani wall, below Leh, known as Taire-rong Mani wall.[98] Following the tradition of his father, the king annually invited hundred monks from Zanskar, Nubra and Timosgang to recite a million mantras.[99] Apart from the temples, he also built a few palaces, including one at Shey and another at Rudok in a similar style to the palace of Leh.[100]

The great Lama, sTag-tsan-ras-pa, who played a major role in the religious and cultural development in Ladakh, passed away on the 29 of January 1651 at Hemis.[101] The death of sTag-tsan-ras-pa left a gap, which was difficult to fill. Although his incarnation was soon found in Ladakh, he never exerted any substantial influence.[102] Under the influence of sTag-tsan-ras-pa, the Brug-pa sub-sect had become predominant in Ladakh and enjoyed the special patronage of the royal family. The relations with the Yellow Church in Tibet, which had been fairly cordial in the lifetime of sTag-ts'an-ras-pa, tended to deteriorate, ushering in a serious political problem. It concerned the treatment of Ge-lug-pa in Ladakh and Guge and of Brug-pa; under the dominance of the Dalai Lama, both sects felt themselves discriminated against by the ruling power.[103] This resentment was sorted out for the time being. But the mutual suspicions remained and in fact, this was the background to the quarrel that broke out between the two countries in the late 1680s, under the next king of Ladakh.[104]

bDe-Idan-rNamgyal had three wives[105]; his first wife Ku-dzon bore him a son, bDe-legs-rNamgyal; the second wife was dPal-mdzes and the third was Bu-k'rid rgyal-mo. Joseph Gergan mentions that the king married Bu-k'rid rgyal-mo as his third queen[106], who bore the king three sons: Nag-dban-p'unogs-rNamgyal, Jig-bral-rnamgyal and T 'ub-bsatn rNamgyal[107].

The next king, who came to the throne, was the eldest son, bDe-legs-rNamgyal.[108] According to Alexander Cunningham, bDe-legs-rNamgyal succeeded his father.[109] Some other sources, including Luciano Petech, had serious doubts whether bDe-legs-rNamgyal was a full king.[110] Whoever was the king during the time, the decisive event in the history of Ladakh at the time was the three-corner conflict between Ladakh, Tibet, and the Mughals, which brought to an end the short-lived paramount of Ladakh in the western Himalayas and reduced it to the present boundaries.[111]

From the Tibetan point of view the causes of the war were the increasing hostility of the Ladakhi kings towards the Ge-lug-pa sect and the raids carried out by the people of Glo-bo and Rudok against the Tibetan districts of Sa-dga and Gro-sod.[112] According to another source, the cause was the king of Ladakh's support to Bhutan during the war between Lhasa and Bhutan in 1676. The Ladakhi king, as a supporter of the Brug-pa sub-sect, sent a letter to Tibet saying that he would help the Brug-pa ruler of Bhutan.[113] Eventually the conflict between the two countries started in 1681.[114] According to Luciano Petech:

> The decision for war was taken by the Dalai Lama himself, without the concurrence of the Qosot Khan, his patron and protector, although the latter was responsible for the defense of the realm.[115]

In 1679, a small Tibetan force consisting of 250 men, marched west[116], and met the Ladakhi advanced guard in some inconclusive skirmishes in different places in Guge[117]. These initial meetings of the two forces were by no means decisive. Both the forces were small, hardly more than vanguard. But the main Tibetan army of about 5000 men in all[118] arrived in the summer of 1680. According to Janet Rizvi, the Ladakhi forces were decisively defeated in the battle on the approaches to the Chang-la; the king and his generals fled the field.[119] The Tibetan army continued their westward march without much resistance until they came upon the remnants of the Ladakhi army, blocking their advance to Basgo for three years, which was one of the best defensive positions. The king and government resided at gTin-mo-sgan[120], about thirty miles further west. The king of Ladakh asked the

Mughals to help him and with the help of the Mughal army the Ladakhis forced the Tibetan forces to retreat to Tashigon, beyond the present border.

After the retreat of the Tibetan army, the Mughals presented their condition for the help and it was rather heavy. The condition was that the king had to accept Islam, which he did under the name of Aqibat Mahmud Khan.[121] Other conditions were that every encouragement was to be given to Mohammedanism in Ladakh, to build a mosque at Leh[122], and to send the king's younger son Jigs-bral-rnamgyal as a hostage to Kashmir[123]. Another important clause of the treaty according to Luciano Petech, was the concessions to Kashmir of the monopoly of the wool export and transit trade, which was important for the shawl industry, the main produce of Kashmir along with saffron.[124] Besides, the kingdom also had to send a small tribute to Kashmir, which consisted of 18 piebald horses, 18 pods of musk and 18 white yak tails[125]. In exchange, the king was to receive yearly 500 bags of rice from Kashmir.[126]

After hearing that the king of Ladakh had embraced Islam, the Tibetan regent Sans-rgya-mtso, who ruled the country after the death of the 5th Dalai lama, was seriously concerned for the Buddhist religion in Ladakh and he requested the 6th Brug-cen-Mi-pam-dban-po (1641-1717 A. D.),[127] who wielded great influence on the Ladakhi royal house to travel to Ladakh. The Brug-cen accepted the proposal. According to Luciano Petech, Brug-cen started his journey in the winter of 1683-84 A. D., traveled to gTin-mo-sgan and pleaded with the king for the case of Buddhism in general and the Brug-pa sub-sect and the Ge-lug-pa sect in particular.[128]

The mission of the 6th Brug-cen was successful; the king and the ministers of Ladakh declared their return to Buddhism. A treaty was signed at gTin-mo-sgan in 1684 called the gTin-mo-sgan Treaty.[129] According to the treaty, it was declared that the quarrel between Ladakh and Tibet should be considered things of the past and to maintain friendly relations. The boundary between the two countries was fixed bisecting the Pangong Lake, as it exists presently.[130] As for the trade relation is concern, the goat-wool (pashmina), produced in mNgaris-skor-gsum would be sold to the merchants of Ladakh only.[131] According to Luciano Petech, the price of pashmina fixed was two dnul-dmar-zog (red silver goods) or one rin-dnul (price-silver; a rupee) for eighty nags (15 nags= one kilogram).[132] Only Ladakhi merchants sent by the king would have the right to do business in Rudok.[133] The pashmina traders from Kashmir would not be proceeding beyond dPe-t'up. For the purposes of pashmina trade, four Kashmiri merchants would reside at dPe-t'up and after having made their purchases they would have to return to Kashmir.[134] The Ladakhi merchants, who went to Changthang, the far southeastern uplands of Ladakh, to purchase pashmina, would be allowed to sell it to Kashmiri dealers within the territorial jurisdiction of Ladakh only.[135] Besides, the exchange of trade missions between Ladakh and Lhasa, the annual trade caravan from Lhasa to Ladakh popularly called C'a-pa or 'tea man' would consist of 200 animal-loads of tea and in return, Ladakh sent offerings to Tibet for the Smon-lam and for the blessing of the Dalai Lama every third year, known as Lapchak.[136] The exchange of these missions further strengthened the old institutional links between the monasteries of the two countries. Several of the larger Buddhist monasteries in Ladakh periodically sent combined religious and trading missions to Lhasa. As per the treaty, Rudok, Guge, etc., were to be annexed to Tibet for the purpose of providing the wherewithal for the sacred lamps and for the Smon-lam festival in Lhasa.[137]

Thus, as far as Ladakh's religious and spiritual ties with Tibet was concerned, it remained more or less constant and was not much affected by the three-corner conflict. This is shown by the fact that the gTin-mo-sgan treaty was the result of the effort of the 6th Brug-c'en, the head Lama of the Brug-pa sub-sect from Tibet.

The next king who came to the throne was Nyi-ma-rNamgyal who succeeded his father. He began ruling in 1691 and became the titular king around 1694/95.[138] He occupies a special place among the kings of Ladakh in the field of justice. He always consulted the state officers when delivering judgment. He appointed elders (rgan-po) on a lower level from each district to assist him. He instituted the council of state officers and elders, and laid down the rule that the primary origin of any dispute must be traced before the verdict was pronounced. On the whole, this resulted in a sharp decline of crime, such as robbery and theft.[139]

In the field of culture, the king encouraged printing and printing blocks of some devotional works were carved.[140] According to A. H. Francke, the art of painting had come to Tibet from China, where for many ages whole pages of books had been engraved on wooden tablets from which they were printed on paper.[141] The king brought one hundred and eight volumes of the bKa-gyur text from Tibet, which is now kept at the palace of sTok.[142] Besides, the king built a Mani-wall close to the village of Choglamsar.[143] Many Ladakhi folk-songs were written during his reign and are popular even today.[144]

During this period relations with Lhasa were cordial. According to the Chronicle, the king presented to all the monasteries of Tibet, from Lhasa to bSam-yas, gold water and sacrificial lamps.[145] To all the great lamas he gave presents. The contacts between various monasteries were continuing. This period witnessed a greater Ge-lug-pa influence in Ladakh. bDe-ldan-rNamgyal's second son, blo-bzan-nag-dban-p'un-ts'ogs, who was studying in Tibet, came back during this period. He became the abbot of Thiksay (K'rig-se) and the head of the seven ser-po-dgon (Ge-lug-pa) monasteries in Ladakh.[146] These seven monasteries were, according to Luciano Petech, Lha-k'an dBur-ma on the rTse-mo hill at Leh, K'rig-se, dPe-t'ub, Likir (klu-k'yil), Disket (bDe-skid) in Nubra, Karsha (dkar-sa) in Zanskar and bSam-dkar near Leh was added later.[147] During this period, not only the close institutional relations between Ladakh and Tibet but also the direct contacts between the two countries were not lacking. Luciano Petech, citing from Tibetan sources mentioned that, on 10th August 1655, envoys of Ladakhi kings arrived in Lhasa.[148]

The Ladakhi king also maintained good relations with the Mughal emperor. The traffic on the Kashmir route was regular. This was witnessed by the Jesuits Manael Freyre and Ippolito Desideri who came to Ladakh in 1715 from the Zoji-la.[149] The Italian Jesuit Ippolito Desideri and company reached Leh on 26th June 1715, and he gives a graphic account of the country, the court, the lamas, etc. The king was Nyi-ma-rNamgyal, who treated them with courtesy and honour.[150] The whole country is described as mountainous and fairly unproductive. It produced plenty of barley, little wheat, and as regards fruit, chiefly apricots. Trade with other countries was limited to very fine wool, a small quantity of gold-bearing sand, musks, etc. There were numerous monasteries and many monks, all of whom lived under a chief Lama. To attain to this dignity, however, study in one of the universities of Tibet was necessary, which indeed, was required of everyone who wanted to rise.[151] But the relations with Balti chieftains were not cordial. Dynastic ties with the chief of Ka-pu-lu[152] could not be translated into good relations. Rather, it exposed Ka-pu-lu to anemity to the other chiefs and compelled Ladakh to shoulder a heavy military responsibility in the medieval period.

Nyi-ma-rNamgyal was married twice[153]. His first wife died after the birth of a son, bDe-skyon –rNamgyal.[154] Then the king married Zi-Zi Khatun, who was from K'a-pu-lu.[155] She bore him a son, bKra-sis-rNamgyal and a daughter bKra-sis-dban-mo.[156] bDe-skyon-rNamgyal became the next king.[157] bDe-skyon-rNamgyal's mother died early, he was brought up by his stepmother, Zi-Zi khatun, whom he loved dearly. Hence, at her request, bKra-sis-rNamgyal was given Purig as a separate kingdom, with the capital Mulbhe.[158] bKra-sis-rNamgyal, son of Zi-Zi Khatun was a monk and renounced his monkhood by contracting marriage with a daughter of a noble family of the village Stok (sTog).[159] The couple, however, remained childless.

Coming back to bDe-skyon-rNamgyal, one of the most vexing problems of his reign was a family quarrel. The issue was the marriage of aKra-sis-dban-mo, daughter of Zi-Zi Khatun, to the ruler of Kashtwar. The royal house was divided. bKra-sis-rNamgyal and his mother were in favour of the proposal while bDe-skyon-rNamgyal and his ministers were against the idea.[160] The wedding, however, took place but this matrimonial alliance was short lived. bKra-sis-dban-mo could not live comfortably for long with her husband under the restriction of purdah, where she could not see even the sunlight of the day.[161] The Kashtwar family had been converted to Islam in 1687.[162] As the news reached Ladakh, Zi-Zi Khatun recalled her daughter back to Ladakh. Her husband claimed her and he also came along with her to Ladakh so that he could settle the matter amicably. At this point, Zi-Zi Khatun, being afraid of the arrival of her son-in-law, suspected he might conspire with bDe-skyon-rNamgyal at Leh to oust her son bKra-sis-rNamgyal from Purig. As Luciano Petech mentioned, "His (son-in-law) arrival might represent a menace to bKra-sis-rnamgyal's rule over Purig, caused him to be murdered, a servant of her pushing him into the river from a bridge marking the frontier between Keshtwar and Paider."[163] It was intended to pass this incident as an accident but the news leaked out and the people denounced the action of Zi-Zi Khatun. The widow bKra-sis-dban-mo was married a second time in the royal house of K'a-pu-lu.[164]

bDe-skyon-rNamgyal married thrice: his first wife was Ni-zla-dban-mo, a princess from Glo-sMon-t'an[165], what is presently called Mustang, situated in the northwest of Nepal. She gave birth to Sa-skyon-rNamgyal, but the couple soon separated on account of disagreement of temper, and the queen returned to Glo-bo[166]. The king then contracted a second marriage with Bu-k'rid-dnab-mo from Nubra, who gave birth to P'un-t'ogs-rNamgyal.[167] His third wife was bstan-dzin-dban-mo, a princess of Zanskar (Zanskar), but the king sent her back to rule Zanskar.[168]

The king bDe-skyong rNamgyal died in 1739. He reigned for about twenty years. He continued the policy of his father towards Ladakh's neighbors. Regular direct contacts with Lhasa took placed during his reign. Besides, the king was also in contact with the Chinese through Tibetan authorities. As Luciano Petech mentioned, "bDe-skyong rNamgyal had sent communication to the Chinese court through the Tibetan authorities in Lhasa regarding the movements of the Dsunger in the Yarkand region."[169] The queen Bu-krid-rgyal-mo sent to the Dalai Lama general offerings for her deceased husband bDe-skyon.

P'un-ts'og-rNamgyal (1740-1760 A.D.)[170] was the next king who came to the throne. He was bDe-skyong rNamgyal's second wife's son. Sa-skyon-rNamgyal, the eldest son of king's first wife had joined the Hemis monastery as a monk.[171] Queen Bu-k'rid-dban-mo was active in royal politics. In fact, Tashi Rabgias mentioned that she ruled for about ten years from 1740-50 A.D.[172] She played an important part in influencing the eldest son to join Hemis monastery so that her son may become the king. During this period, Purig was still ruled by his uncle bKra-sis-rNamgyal. Not much had been mentioned about these kings except a crisis, which was mediated by a Lama, sent by the Dalai Lama.[173]

According to the Chronicle of Ladakh, the upper Ladakhi view of the matter was that bKra-sis-rNamgyal, the king of Purig, tried to seize exclusive control of the lucrative Kashmir trade and to encroach with fair or foul means on Ladakh proper.[174] Whatever the case, the conflict between uncle and nephew became more and more embittered and a potential threat to the commercial interests of central Tibet. Both parties addressed themselves to the government of Lhasa and the government of Kashmir. The seventh Dalai Lama, Skal-bzang-rgya-mtsho (1708-1758 A. D.)[175], was ruling that time. He deputed Ka'-t'og Rig-dzin Ts'e-dban-nor-bu (1698-1755 A.

D.)[176], who was the rNin-ma-pa incarnate from Kham, to Ladakh to resolve the conflict. Ka'-t'og Rig-dzin was in Nepal at the time when he was asked for the job, and he left Nepal on 11th May 1752.[177] Both the king of Leh and the king of Purig along with their ministers were at Wam-le where negotiations were taking place. When the Ka't-'og arrived there, the real negotiations began and they concluded in December 1752.[178]

After listening to the different parties grievances, the Lama resolved the dispute of succession and related matters by laying down the following guidelines for resorting to peace and deciding for the future the question of succession. These guidelines were, first of all, that whatever the number of sons, only the eldest son of the ruler shall succeed to the throne of Ladakh. Secondly, all the younger brothers shall become Lamas. Third, in no case shall there be two kings in Ladakh, nor shall the kingdom be divided.[179] However, bKra-sis-rNamgyal was allowed to retain his kingdom of Purig so long as he lived. Since he had no child, it was decided that the territory he ruled should be merged into Ladakh after his death. The other exceptions were the king of Zanskar bsTan-srin-rNamgyal, having his dominion at the Indian frontier, shall remain king as before;[180] the Chief of Hi-nas-sku was also allowed to retain his principality on the plea of his royal descent and smallness of that Chiefdom.[181] Lastly, commercial traffic between Ladakh and Kashmir would continue without disturbance and the custom duties were inscribed on copper plates in five copies, of which four were deposited at Leh, Mulbhe, Zanskar and Hemis, and the fifth probably sent to Kashmir.[182] Thus, this meant the introduction of 'primogeniture' and it saved further partitions of Ladakh. In 1758, the king of Purig died and the kingdom was reunited with Ladakh.[183] This agreement is popularly known as the "Wam-le agreement". The successive kings had to follow the rule that the eldest son became the king and the younger sons became monks.

Whatever the domestic problems, cultural relations with Tibet were continuing and consistent. The government missions were also continuing. Luciano Petech, citing from Tibetan sources mentioned that, in 1740 envoys of the La-dvags rgyal-po (Ladakhi king) bKra-sis-rNamgyal were in Lhasa.[184] Besides the continuation of the Ge-lug-pa influence, this period saw a revival of Brug-pa influence in Ladakh. This is indicated by the visits of the 7th Brug-c'en dKar-brgyud P-rin-las-sun-rta to Ladakh.[185] Also, rGyal-sras Rin-po-c'e came on to the scene around this period. He was the son of king bDe-skyon-rNamgyal and queen Ni-zla-dban-mo[186], who became a monk at Hemis.[187] He is also known as the Hemis sprul-sku, the head of the monastery. Luciano Petech, citing from Tibetan sources states that Hemis sprul-sku in January 1740 came to Lhasa and shortly after he arrived at bKra-sis-lhun-po, he was recognized as a younger brother of the Pan-c'en.[188] In Ladakh, under the abbotship of rGyal-ras Rin-po-c'e, Brug-pa in general and Hemis in particular continued to develop. The number of monks increased and monastic rule was enforced more strictly.[189] Many of the silver stupas, which can still be seen in the monastery, were constructed during this period.[190]

Three kings were to come to the throne after Pun-tsog-rNamgyal, till the first Dogra invasion of Ladakh. They were Ts'e-dban-rNamgyal (1760-1780 A.D.) Ts'e-brtan-rNamgyal (1780-1790 A.D.) and Ts'e-dpal-mi-gyur-don-grup-rNamgyal (1790-1841 A.D.).[191] About these kings not much has been written about. Ts'e-dban-rNamgyal II (1760-1780 A.D.), reigned for about twenty years. The Chronicle names Kun-dzom as his mother.[192]

During the first year of Ts'e-dban-rNamgyal's rule government affairs were entrusted to the minister Kun-skyun-dpal-p'el, usually known as Kun-skyob.[193] During this period, the relations with Lhasa were maintained. Diplomatic missions were also taking place. As Luciano Petech mentioned, envoys of the La-dvags Sa-skyon were received at bKra-sis-lhun-po on 2nd February 1760.[194] Religious and spiritual ties with Tibet were consistent. Normally novices who went to different monasteries in Tibet for their higher studies were not mentioned and recorded, unless they were sent by the royal court. But in 1767, the abbot of Hemis came to bKra-sis-lhun-po, bringing with him thirty novices from Hemis, who were given their vows in solemn congregation.[195] It is remarkable that a Brug-pa abbot should seek ordination for his disciples in that great Ge-lug-pa center. It shows the closeness of religious ties between the two countries.

Ts'e-dban-rNamgyal contracted several marriages. One wife was from Zanskar[196], who however, deserted him when the king felt in love with a low-caste Bheda woman and married her.[197] Then the king married a princess, Begum-dban-mo, of Sod village in Purig.[198] She bore him two sons, Ts'e-brtan-rNamgyal and Ts'e-dpal-mi-gyur-don-grub-rNamgyal[199]; she also bore him three daughters. The king contracted a fourth marriage, with Kha-tun-Ts'e-rin, who bore him a son, Jigs-med-rNamgyal.[200]

Nothing much is known about the construction enterprise of Ts'e-dban-rNamgyal. According to an inscription, he restored the Likir monastery after a fire; and the restoration of the Mangyu monastery was apparently carried out during his reign.[201] The next king who came to the throne was his eldest son, Ts'e-brtan-rNamgyal (1780-1790 A.D.).[202] As per the "Wam-le agreement", his younger brother Ts'e-dpal entered the Hemis monastery[203] and their half-brother Jigs-med-rNamgyal took holy orders at Thiksay.[204] According to the Chronicles, of his three sisters, one was married in the royal house in the royal house of Pa-skyum, another was married off to No-no Ts'e-dban-don-grub and the last one probably lived unmarried.[205]

Ts'e-brtan-rNamgyal grew to be strong, and handsome, and had proficient knowledge in the material arts as well literature and above all in calligraphy.[206] The king was proficient in Tibetan grammar and arithmetic and could speak many languages including Kashmiri, Yarkandi, Turkomoni and Persian.[207] The king was devoted and treated the people with respect. In the funeral memory of his father, the king built the Kiudrag mani-wall, with the rNamgyal and the Jangchub mChorten at each end.[208] He also erected a two-storey tall silver mChorten (stupa) in his Palace at Leh.[209]

The official relations with Lhasa continued. In 1784 A.D., a mission of twenty-five Ladakhi persons was received in the Tibetan capital. The most important was the invitation tendered to the 8th Brug-c'en Kun-gzigs-c'os-kyi-sna-ba (1768-1822 A.D.).[210] The Brug-c'en set out on his journey in the 5th month of 1801, visiting the Kailash en route and reached at Hemis in October the same year.[211] The king and nobles honored him by offering many valuable things, including gold, silver, horses, goats and sheep.[212] So, the Brug-pa sub-sect influence in Ladakh still continued during this period.

Ts'e-brtan-rNamgyal died very young, leaving a posthumous daughter. He was barely twenty-four years old.[213] After the death of the young king, his even younger brother Ts'e-dpal-mi-gyur-don-grub-rNamgyal, was called from the Hemis monastery, where he was living as a monk.[214] He was made to abandon monkhood and shoulder the responsibility of the kingdom. That happened in about A.D. 1790.[215] He reigned until about 1841 A.D.[216] According to another source, he reigned until about 1830 A.D.[217] Unlike his elder brother, Ts'e-dpal-mi-gyur-don-grub-rNamgyal lived an easy life, and was lazy in every respect. He was an ineffective ruler, who left affairs in the hands of his ministers.[218]

The relation with Baltis in the west was not good. During his reign there were a few clashes with the Baltis. Besides, plenty of trouble also arose in the south. In 1822 A.D. armed parties from Kulu, as a result of a long-standing commercial dispute, invaded Spiti and ravaged it; the local people clamored for retaliation but the king was unable.[219] Then again, forces from Kulu, Kunawar and Lahul raided and sacked Zans-dkar.[220]

The relations with Tibet were cordial. The bDe-c'en-c'os-kor Yons-dzin-ye-ses-grub-pa accepted the invitation of the Ladakhi king and undertook the voyage to Ladakh in 1814 A.D.[221]. The missions were going on, on a regular basis. It was during Ts'e-dpal-mi-gyur-don-grub-rNamgyal reign that William Moorcroft and George Trebeck traveled to Leh. They reached Leh in September 1820 and remained there for a period two years, until September 1822.[222] They described about the general character, trade and commerce, population etc. in their travelogue travels in the Himalayan provinces on Hindustan and Punjab; in Ladakh and Kashmir; in Pashawar, Kabul, Kunduz and Bokhara, from 1819-1825. The king was Ts'e-dpal-mi-gyur-don-grub-rNamgyal. As Moorcroft and Trebeck mentioned: "the present Raja of Ladakh was a lama, but on the demise of his elder brother was called from his convent to rulership."[223]

Another important person to visit Ladakh was Alexander de Koros[224], called the founder of modern Tibetology.[225] He arrived at Leh on 9th June 1822, and stayed there for 25 days.[226] Then he started back for Kashmir and on the way he met Moorcroft at Dras[227], and agreed to return to Leh.[228] Moorcroft mentioned this meeting as:

> "On my journey to Dras I was met by Alexander Csoma De Koros, European in the garb of an Armenian, who traveled over land from Hungary to Tibet. He remained with me for some time, and after I had quitted Ladakh I obtained permission from the Khalon for him to reside in the monastery of Yangla in Zanskar, for the purpose of acquiring a knowledge of the Tibetan language, and from his erudition and acquirement accurate information on these points may be expected."[229]

Alexander de Koros returned to Leh, where the prime minister received him well and recommended him to the Lama of bZan-la in Zanskar, upon which he left at once for that place.[230]

Coming back to Ts'e-dpal-rNamgyal and his contribution towards religious and secular building activities, he built the present sTog palace.[231] Besides the palace, the king erected a number of statues mostly made of gold and silver.[232] Ts'e-dpal-rNamgyal married the widow of his brother Ts'e-brtan-rNamgyal.[233] She bore him a daughter and a son, called Ts'e-dban-rab-brtan-rNamgyal, who according to some sources, got the royal title around1830, but the Chronicle is silent on the subject.

From 1834-1842, Ladakh witnessed several invasions from the Dogra army of Raja Gulab Singh of Jammu, under the commands of Zorawar Singh and Dewan Hari Singh Chand. Finally, by the signing of an agreement between Buddhist Tibet and Dogra on 17th September 1842, Ladakh lost her independence.[234] The agreement confirmed the existing border, allowed the continuation of the Lapchak and C'a-pa missions on a commercial basis without political implications, and provided for the supply of transportation service (u-lag) for Tibetan traders in Ladakh and for Ladakhi traders in western Tibet.[235] The monarchy was abolished and the royal family was given as Jagir the sTog estate with the Palace and the Ma-spro estate.[236]

Government and Administration

The government of the kings of Ladakh was quite different from that of the Dalai Lamas of Lhasa. The supreme ruler was a lay king, popularly known as 'Gyalpo'. His office was hereditary. The king was assisted by a Council of offices. According to the Chronicles of Ladakh this Council was made of three grades of officials. The first were Chief Ministers (bka-blons) four or five in number and hereditary. The second were Ministers (blon-po), and the third the elders (dganpo). According to Cunningham and Moorcroft, the conduct of affairs was generally entrusted to the Prime Minister.

The territory of proper Ladakh was divided into a certain number of small districts called Yul, under an official.[237] The territory of outlying regions was under the feudatory chief.

At the end of the kingdom there were eight feudatory chiefs including four Muslim chiefs of Pa-skyum (Purig), bStod (Purig), Suru and Dras, and usually they were called rzong. Others were the king of Zanskar, the only one for whom the royal title was normally employed, the No-No of Spiti, the chief of Nubra, and the chief of rGya who was the only one situated within Ladakh proper.[238] Nono means junior, and the younger son of the king of Ladakh ruled Spiti that time.

Justice was ministered on the old patriarchal pattern. There was no distinction between administration and judicial officers. As per procedure, punishment (C'ad-pa) included fines, imprisonment (btson-c'ad) and in extreme cases, banishment with branding and even death. However, the death penalty was seldom awarded and still rarely executed.[239]

The Important Monasteries Built in Ladakh during the Period

There are many monasteries that have been founded in Ladakh. The foundations of these monasteries were associated with the effort of active lama missionaries and with the encouragement, guidance and support from Buddhist Tibet. The earliest foundations of monasteries in Ladakh mentioned in the second chapter are mostly associated with the activities of Rin-chen-bzang-po, the Indian yogin Naro-pa, etc., and several of them belong to the bKa-dams-pa sub-sect. With the arrival of the Ge-lug-pa monks in Ladakh in the 15th century many monasteries of the Ge-lug-pa sect were founded in Ladakh.[240] By the second half of the 16th century this sect was firmly established in Ladakh. The establishment of the Brug-pa branch of the bKa-gyud-pa sect in Ladakh was due to sTag-t'san-ras-pa and the other Brug-pa Lamas. Also in the case of the Bri-gun-pa sub-sect, rNi-ma-pa and Sa-skya-pa sects, the establishment was due to the active Lama missionaries and royal patronage. All the four major sects and several sub-sect of Mahayana Buddhism were established in Ladakh in due course of time.

Spituk (dPe-t'up)

This monastery is on the hilltop near the Indus, about seven kilometers from Leh. This monastery was founded in the 11th century by Od-ide, the king of Guge.[241] Initially it belonged to the dKa-dams-pa sect. Then during the time of King Grags-pa-ide, it was transfered to the Ge-lug-pa sect.[242] It is regarded as the first Ge-lug-pa establishment in Ladakh.[243] The name dPe-t'up is of Tibetan origin, introduced by the first Ge-lug-pa monks[244], who visited Ladakh during the reign of Grags-pa-bum-ide. dPe-t'up means 'Effective as Examples' and thus was a suitable base for their first monastery in Ladakh.

Inside the monastery there are several temples of various sizes. The first one is the Jokhang (Jo-bo-k'an), which takes its name from the central statue of Buddha Shakyamuni in a tantric form, called the Jowo Rinpoche. This statue was brought from Tibet and assembled and gilded with gold by the Ladakhi artists. The other main statues in this room are that of a Padmasambhava and of White Tara, besides, a rNamgyal chorten (stupa). The next temple is called Drolma Lha-khang, dedicated to the twenty-one manifestations of the goddess Green Tara. Tsering Stobgais, 88 years monk from Spituk monastery who had studied in Dre-pung in Tibet for 11 years said that these statues were brought from Tibet. Besides, there is a seat for the Rinpoches[245], near the window. Above this seat is a photograph of the former Ling Rinpochey, tutor to the present Dalai Lama.[246]

The Tsogchen is the main assembly hall for the large ceremonies attended by monks of all the branch monasteries of dPe-t'up.[247] Inside the Tsogchen, several long rows of seats lead up to two high thrones. The left one is reserved for the Dalai Lama who visited this monastery on several occasions. The other one is for the head Lama. The walls on either side of the room are lined with old texts. A door leads to the inner room, where several statues can be seen including the large one of Buddha Shakyamuni. The Chikhang is another assembly hall for the monks living at the dPe-t'up monastery.

On either side of the main entrance are paintings of the four guardian kings. Inside, there are several rows of seats for the monks, a throne reserved for the Dalai Lama and various statues. A door leads through to the near room, where the main statue dedicated is to the protector of the Chikhang. The Gon-khang (mGon-k'an) another room, dedicated to the protector divinities, which is a little apart from the main monastery buildings, at the very summit of the hill. It is the oldest part of the monastery.

The dPe-t'up branch of monasteries has more than one hundred monks. These branches are dSang-mkhar, Stok and Sabu (Sa-phu), each with about thirty monks[248], who all assemble during the major festival. Of these smaller branches, dSang-mkhar serves as the head Lama's private residence. It is smaller and well maintained. The Du-khang is well decorated and contains various statues including those of Buddha Shakyamuni, Tsong-kha-pa and the Eleven-Headed Avalokitesvara.

Thiksay (Krig-rtse)

This is the most impressively positioned of monasteries in Ladakh. This is also a big Ge-lug-pa monastery, which was built probably about the middle of the sixteenth century, the original period of Ge-lug-pa influence in Ladakh.[249] According to Thupstan Paldan, "Shes-rab bzang-po of sTod (upper Ladakh) first built the temple of Stagmo Lkhang at the top of the Thiksay and then his nephew called Paldan Sherab founded the Thiksay Monastery".[250] There are many well-decorated temples in this huge complex.

A few steps above from the courtyard is the Du-khang, the assembly hall. Every morning about 6.30, all the monks of this monastery assemble in the Du-khang for prayer, which normally lasts for about an hour but on special occasions gets extended. Many statues and religious objects can be seen in this room. It also contains racks of books on both sides of the wall. A door leads to the inner room, where the main images are that of the Buddha, Padmasambhava and Avalokistesvara.

The Gon-khang is a smaller and dark chamber. It contains the protector divinities. The faces of the protector divinities are kept veiled and are unveiled once in a year during festival time. The festival (Krig-rste dGu-gtor) takes place on the 17th and 18th of the 12th Tibetan month.[251] The other temples are Chamba-Lhakhang and Drolma-Lhakang, added to the building complex recently. The monastery has also a small old library that contains old religious books and objects.

Hemis

This monastery lies at a distance of about 45 kilometers south of Leh. It is one of the largest and richest monasteries in Ladakh. It belongs to Brug-pa, a sub-sect of the bKa-gyud-pa sect, of Tibetan Buddhism. It was found in 1630 by sTag-ts'an-ras-pa[252], under the royal patronage of King Sen-ge-rNamgyal. The annual festival commemorating the birth anniversary of Guru Padmasambhava held in summer, which is why it is well known to outside visitors. Lama Mipam Tsewang introduced this festival.[253] It has also now probably the biggest courtyard for the monastic dances.

The main temple of the monastery is the Du-khang, and it contains seats for the monks and the head Lama. Apart from these, there are many images including that of sTag-ts'an-ras-pa and of Vajradhara, the bKa-gyud-pa hierarchy and of various Brug-pa sub-sect Lamas. The biggest Thangka is also in this temple. The Tshogs-khang is another important and interesting temple of the monastery. This contains in the central position a huge and impressive image of Buddha Shakyamuni, and many chortens (stupas) adorned with silver and gild. Guru-Lhakhang is another temple where a huge image of Padmasambhava can be seen. It was built around the 1980s. Besides, there are several smaller temples in the monastery.

Chemde

This is another monastery that was built by sTag-san-ras-pa[254] and it also belongs to the same sect as that of Hemis, the

Brug-pa sub-sect. It is situated to one side of a tributary valley of the Indus, just off the road leading to the Chang-la, about 45 kilometers from Leh. The Du-khang contains images of sTag-san-ras-pa and other Brug-pa Lamas. Behind the images are murals of Shakyamuni flanked by his chief disciples. A smaller temple upstairs, known as the Lama temple (bLa-ma-lha-khang)[255], contains images of various Brug-pa Lamas and of the Buddha, as well as a copy of the Tibetan Canon. There is also another small temple dedicated to the twenty-one manifestations of the goddess Tara. The last temple, almost at the very top of the monastery contains many images, including that of Guru Padmasambhava. This temple and Drolma Lhakhang have been constructed recently.

Thak-Thok (Brag-tok)

This monastery is situated a few kilometers from Chemday, above the village of Sakti. It was founded in the reign of Ts'e-dban-rNamgyal in the second half of the sixteenth century.[256] The monastery is constructed around Padmasambhava's Cave, in which he is believed to have meditated.[257] This is the only monastery of Nin-ma-pa, the oldest sect of Tibetan Buddhism in Ladakh. The Cave contains images of Padmasambhava and Avalokitesvara. The Du-khang contains a big image of Padmasambhava and several other statues. The Kanjur-Lhakhang contains a copy of the Tibetan tripitaka (Canon) and image of Buddha Shakyamuni. A new and bigger courtyard has been constructed near the road. According to Thupstan Paldan, "Monks of this monastery become skilled in the 'white' astrology (of India) and the 'black' astrology (of China)."[258]

Stakna (stag-sna)

It lies at a distance of about 40 kilometers south of Leh on a hill shaped like a stag-sna (Tiger-nose). A great scholar saint Chosje Jamyang Palkar founded it during the reign of King Jam-dbyans-rNamgyal. This monastery has several well-maintained temples, including the Du-khang, which contains a silver gilt chorten (stupa), images of three Brug-pa Lamas, Padma-dkar-po, Ngag-dban-rnamgyal, the strong man of Bhutan in the 18th century, and Ngag-dban-rGyal-mtshan.[259] Most of the murals in the monastery look new, presumably of fairly recent date except in a few smaller chapels where some murals and images probably date from the monastery's foundation. This monastery had close ties with monasteries of Bhutan.

Matho (Ma-spro)

This monastery lies across the Indus and directly opposite of Thiksay. It is also known as the 'Thuptan dPal-bzang Chokhor'. It is also the only monastery that belongs to the Sa-skya-pa sect of Tibetan Buddhism in Ladakh.[260] The Sa-skya scholar rDorje dPal-bzang who arrived there after having extensively traveled throughout Tibet founded this monastery.[261] The most famous event of the monastery is its annual festival of oracles which takes place on the 25th and 26th of the 2nd Tibetan month.[262] It is known as Ma-spro Nag-hrang.[263] The oracles are two Lamas, chosen by lot every five years. The two chosen Lamas have to meditate for a few months before the festival and become the receptacles for the particular deity. These local deities are said to have come to Ladakh from Tibet. Once possessed of the god the oracles do the most extra ordinary things. According to Jamyang Gyaltsan:

> "The oracle tradition has existed here since the establishment of the monastery. Originally, the protectors were brothers who lived at a place called Khawa Karpo in Kham (in eastern Tibet). Having become attached to the Sa-skya Scholar, rDorje dPal-bzang, he propitiated them with sacrificial cakes, and when he came to Ladakh, they followed him."[264]

The monastery contains an old and a new temple; a special shrine housing the Buddhist Canon, and a shrine in honour of the Sa-skya Lamas which contains the images of Sa-skyapandita and of other important Lamas of the same sect. Another shrine houses the protectors of the Dharma. Women are not permitted to enter the old shrine of the protectors. The cave near the monastery is where rDorje dPal-bzang, a scholar of the Sa-skya sect, is believed to have resided when he first arrived in this area.

Phayang (P'yi-dban)

This monastery occupies a hilltop of a valley north from the Indus, about 20 kilometers west of Leh. It is also known as the sGan-snon-bkra-sis-c'os-rdzon monastery.[265] It was founded by Chos-rje Idan-ma, who was invited by the king of Ladakh in the late fifties of the 16th century.[266] This monastery along with Lamayuru[267] is represented by the Bri-gung-pa, a sub-sect of the bKa-gyud-pa sect of Tibetan Buddhism.

Many temples can be seen in this monastery. The Du-khang contains images of Vairocana, Shakyamuni and the important bKa-gyud-pa Lamas.[268] Another temple, known as Du-khang gsar-pa contains several interesting images. It also contains Kashmiri bronzes. Snellgrove describes it as, "a small group of Kashmiri bronzes, which by the very nature of the case cannot be later than the 14th century or so."[269] The Gon-khang as always contains the protector divinities. Besides, the monastery contains several smaller old and new temples and a private room for the head Lama.

Rigzong (Ri-dzong)

This monastery lies at a distance of about 80 kilometers west of Leh. It is known as 'Vuma Changchubling' and was founded by Lama Tsultim Nime about 140 years ago.[270] The monastery belongs to the Ge-lug-pa sect of Mahayana Buddhism. It has maintained its strict discipline, more than in most of the monasteries in Ladakh. According to Thupstan Paldan, "since the monastic community places particular importance to the observance of the 'Vinaya' precepts, the traditions of the coercive rites which include sacred dances and hurling votive offering are not especially observed."[271] A few kilometers down the gorge is the Chomoling (Nunnery). The Nuns come up to the monastery when there is special prayer. Besides, the nuns perform the works of spinning wool, milking, and extracting oil for the temple lamps.

Karcha (dkar-cha)

This monastery is the largest in Zanskar. It was founded by Shes-rab bzang-po of sTod, a native of Mar-yul (Ladakh), who introduced the Ge-lug-pa sect in this monastery.[272] Many temples can be seen in the monastery. The Du-khang was redecorated after being destroyed by fire. Next is the Gon-khang, which contains the protector divinities. The oldest part of the monastery is the 'Maitreya's place' (Byams-pa-gling).[273] In fact, the Chronicles of Zanskar translated by A. H. Francke suggest that the foundation of Byams-pa-gling along with Kanika Chorten and Pipiting are the earliest religious establishments in Zanskar.[274] Besides, there are several smaller other temples containing images, the Buddhist Canon etc.

Stongde (sTon-sde)

sTon-sde is situated at the extreme end of the Padum valley. The monastery is renowned as having been founded by Lama Marpa and its name is Marpaling, belonging to the bKa-gyud sect.[275] Later, Gyaltsan Ludub Palzang introduced there the Ge-lug-pa sect,[276] the Ge-lug-pa. Like most of the monasteries, this also occupies a hilltop. Many temples in the monastery like the Du-khang, the Gon-khang, the Kanjur Lha-khang, and the Nyung-gnas-Lha-khang, contain images, murals, and the Buddhist Canon.

Rangdum (Rang-ldum)

Driving from Kargil to Zanskar, the first monastery one comes across is the Rangdum. It was founded by Blo-bzang dge-legs Ye-shes grags-pa of mNga-ris-tshang during the reign of King Ts'e-dban rNamgyal (1753-1782 A.D.).[277] It belongs to the Ge-lug-pa sect of Mahayana Buddhism. There are several smaller temples containing a number of statues, and the Tibetan Canon. In addition, there is a private quarter (gzin-chung) of the head Lama. The successive reincarnations of mNga-ris Tulku act as the incumbents.[278]

Bardan (Bar-gdan)

This monastery lies at a distance about of 15 kilometers from Padum, the capital of Zanskar. The monastery was founded by bDe-ba-rgya-mtsho in the 17th century.[279] It belongs to the Brug-pa sub-sect of Mahayana Buddhism. Bardan along with dZong-khul and Tagrimo, all in Zanskar, are associated with the monastery of sTag-sna in central Ladakh.[280]

Zongkul (dZong-khul)

This spectacular cave monastery of Zanskar falls on the Padum-Kishtwar trekking trails. The monastery is associated with the famous Indian yogin Naropa. The two caves present in the monastery are said to have been used by the famous yogi for solitary meditation.[281] There are few smaller temples in the monastery, which contain old thangkas of Mi-la-ras-pa, Marpa and Vajradhara. Besides, there are several images and holy objects. As mentioned above, this monastery belongs to the Brug-pa, sub-sect of the bKa-gyud-pa sect and it comes under the jurisdiction of the head Lama the of sTag-sna monastery in central Ladakh.

Sani

This monastery is situated a few kilometers before Padum on the main road leading from Kargil. Unlike most other monastic foundations, it is built on flat land. Sani is also believed to have been visited and blessed by Guru Padmasambhava.[282] The famous Kanika chorten (stupa) is at the back of the monastery. This monastery is associated with the Brug-pa sub-sect and comes under the jurisdiction of sTag-sna.

Lingshed

This monastery lies at a distance of about three days journey from the south of Yuru village, on the Yuru-Padum trek routes. According to Thupstan Paldan, "originally this monastery was established by the translator, Rinchen Zangpo, later Changsem Shesrab Zangpo, having expanded it, established the Ge-lug-pa order there."[283]

Disket

This monastery is situated in the Nubra Valley, about 120 kilometers north of Leh. This monastery is one of the largest in the area. It was founded in about 1420 A.D. by Shes-rab bzang-po of sTod and it is reckoned as one of the branches of Thiksay monastery.[284] Several treasured thangkas, murals and other holy religious objects are found in this monastery.

Samstanling

This monastery is also in the Nubra valley. Lama Tsultim Nima founded it about 130 years ago.[285] The monastery maintains the same discipline as that of Rigzong (Ri-dzong).[286]

Monastic Role in Ladakh: Religious/Spiritual and Social

As mentioned above, many monasteries have been established in Ladakh due to its close religious and spiritual contacts with Tibet. In fact, many writers called Ladakh as 'the land of monasteries and lamas'. The population of the central and Zanskar regions of Ladakh is predominantly Buddhist and the central religious institution is the monastery (Gonpa). The monastery essentially functions as the religious and social centre of the people. A Buddhist life is based on the achievement of religious merit. And the importance of this religious merit is transmitted through the Lamas and Nuns. Besides, they also function as teacher, astrologer, prescribe and supply traditional medicine, participate and direct drama and dance at the time of monastic festivals and conduct the birth, marriage and death rites for the people.

The monasteries also run educational institutions, which teach religion, art, culture, the traditional system of medicine and the philosophy of the Buddha.

Some Important Royal Castles

Many important royal castles have been built in Ladakh. The largest one is the Palace at Leh known as Slel-c'en dpal-mk'ar. It was built in 1600 A.D. by King Se-ge-rNamgyal.[287] This Palace still looks magnificent.

Shey (Shel)

This is another important castle situated at a distance of about 16 kilometers from Leh. It was the castle of the first king of Ladakh, Lha-chen aPal-gyi-mgon.[288] The ruins of this fortress may be seen at several higher levels above the present Palace. The temple contains a sacred copper-gilt statue of Lord Buddha, which was built by King bDe-idan-rNamgyal in the memory of his father.[289]

Basgo

Basgo lies at a distance of about 40 kilometers west of Leh. It is the most impressive of Ladakhi Citadels. It was built by King Jam-dbyans-rNamgyal and Se-ge-rNamgyal, father and son.[290] According to Luciano Petech, Basgo was the capital of King Jam-dbyans-rNamgyal around 1603 A.D.[291] The present Matreiya temple there was built by Se-ge-rNamgyal.[292] Besides two magnificent Maitreya statues, there are many scriptures and commentaries written out in gold and silver, which can still be seen.

gTin-mo-sgan

It was also an important royal citadel, which lies at a distance of about 90 kilometers west of Leh. This castle was built by Grags-pa bum, the younger brother of Grags-bum-ide.[293] Presently there are two temples, of which one is dedicated to Avalokitesvara and the other to Padmasambhava.

sTok

This palace is at a distance of about 15 kilometers south of Leh. It was built by King Ts'e-dPal-rNamgyal.[294] Not long after it was built, Ladakh came under Dogra rule. The monarchy was abolished and the family was given as 'Jagir' the sTok estate and the Palace.[295] Since then the royal family has resided there. Besides the residence, it houses a museum in which many religious objects, and a collection of war-like quivers, arrows, guns, and swords. Coins and seals and the queen's ornaments can be found. There is also a temple. All the temples of royal citadels belong to the Bru-pa, sub- sect of bKa-gyud-pa sect.

Important Lama Visitors to Ladakh during the Period

There are many lamas who visited Ladakh during the period. They played a major role in spreading Mahayana Buddhism in Ladakh.

sTag-ts'an-ras-pa

sTag-ts'an-ras-pa Nag-dban-rgya-mtso (1574-1651 A.D.), was a Brug-pa lama who visited Ladakh during the time of Sen-ge-rNamgyal. Stag-ts'an-ras-pa was the scion of the K'on family, i.e., of the house of the Sa-skya prince-abbot, and an outstanding member of the Brug-pa sub-sect.[296] The King Jam-dbyans-rNamgyal invited him when the Lama was in Zanskar enroute to Uddiyana when he was enjoined by his master.[297] The Lama turned down the invitation for the moment, as he had not yet accomplished his journey. He came to Ladakh at the time of Sen-ge-rNamgyal and stayed mostly at rGya and Hemis.[298] sTag-ts'an-ras-pa became the religious teacher of the king of Ladakh. With the help from King Sen-ge-rNamgayl, sTag-ts'an-ras-pa built many monasteries in Ladakh, as mentioned above.

After sTag-ts'an-ras-pa, many other important lamas visited Ladakh from Buddhist Tibet. One of them was a Brug-pa scholar Nag-dban-rgyal-mts'an (1697-1732 A.D.)[299]. He became the court chaplain (dbu-bla) of Nyi-ma-rNamgyal.[300]

Another important Lama who visited Ladakh was bDe-c'en-c'os-k'or Yons-dzin ye-ses-grub-pa (1781-1845 A. D.).[301] But most important was the 7th Brug-c'en dKar-brgyud-P'rin-las-sin-tra (1718-1766 A. D.), who visited Ladakh.[302] They all played a major role in the establishment of the Brug-pa sub-sect of Mahayana Buddhism in Ladakh.

C'os-rje dam-ma

C'os-rje dam-ma Kun-dga-grags-pa was invited by the kings of Ladakh, bKra-sis-rNamgyal and Ts'e-dban-rNamgyal.[303] The Lama accepted the invitation and came to Ladakh. C'os-rje dam-ma requested the king to donate some land so that he could build a monastery.[304] The king gave him the permission to take land wherever he wished for his purpose. The Lama chose a place about 20 kilometers west of Leh. Then he built the present monastery of Phyang (P'yin-dban).[305] As mentioned above, this monastery along with Lamayuru belong to the Bri-gung-pa sub- sect of Mahayana Buddhism in Ladakh.

rDorje dPal-bzang

rDorje dPal-bzang, a sa-skya scholar, visited Ladakh from Tibet. He was responsible for the founding of Matho (Ma-spro), a Sa-skya monastery.

Shes-rab-bzang-po

He was from sTod (upper) Ladakh and was a very well known Lama. He along with his nephew Paldan Shes-rab was responsible for building many Ge-lug -pa monasteries in Ladakh. These monasteries are mentioned above.

Conclusion

Thus, lama missionaries played an important role in spreading all the four major sects and several sub-sects of Tibetan Buddhism in Ladakh.

This chapter has surveyed the medieval period of Ladakhi history, characterized by the emergence of the rNamgyal dynasty and its patronage of the Mahayana Buddhism sustained by Ladakh's spiritual ties with Buddhist Tibet. The emphasis shifted to primarily Buddhist preoccupation such as the patronage and support of construction of monasteries and stupas in Ladakh, and moved away from violence as a policy and way of life of the entire population. In terms of long historical development and evolution Ladakh earned the present day reputation as a peaceful Buddhist Community. During this period, the cultural influences in Ladakh not only come from east but also from the south and west as well.

REFERENCES

1. A. H. Francke, *Ladakh: The Mysterious Land;* A *History of western Tibet (*London, 1907 and reprinted, New Delhi: Cosmo Publication, 1978), p. 82.
2. Tashi Rabgias, *Maryul La dvags Kyi Snon Rabs Kun gsal melong Zhes bya ba zugso: History of Ladakh Called the Mirror which Illuminates All* (Delhi: n/d, 1984), p. 145.
3. Luciano Petech, *The Kingdom of Ladakh, C. 950-1842 A.D.* (Roma: *Istituto Italiano Per IL Medio Ed Estremo Orient 1977)*, p. 24.
4. Janet Rizvi, Ladakh: *Crossroad of High Asia* (New Delhi: Oxford University Press, 1983), p. 45.
5. A. H. Francke, *Antiquities of Indian Tibet, The Chronicles of Ladakh and Minor Chrinocles, Part II* (New Delhi: S Chand and Co., 1926), p. 37.
6. *Ibid.* p. 37.
7. Luciano Petech, op. cit. 3, p. 28.
8. A. H. Francke, op. cit. 5, p. 38.
9. *Ibid.* p. 37.
10. Luciano Petech, op. cit. 3, p. 28.
11. A. H. Francke, op. cit. 1, p. 85.
12. Luciano Petech, op. cit. 3, p. 26.
13. Tashi Rabgias, op. cit. 2, p. 150
14. Luciano Petech, op. cit. 3, p. 28.
15. *Ibid.* p. 27.
16. *Ibid.* p. 32.

17. A. H Francke, op. cit. 5, p. 38.
18. Tashi Rabgias, op. cit. 2, p. 158.
19. A. H. Francke, op. cit. 5, p. 38.
20. A. H. Francke, op. cit. 1, p. 91.
21. Luciano Petech, op. cit. 3, p. 33.
22. Pascale Dollfus, The History of Muslims in Central Ladakh, *Tibet Journal (Autumn, 1995)*, pp. 36-37.
23. *Ibid*, p. 37
24. Abdul Gani Sheikh, Ladakhi Culture Over the centuries, *New Hope*, Volume 3, No. 1, January-February, 2002, p. 111
25. *Ibid*, p. 111
26. Nawang Tsering Shakspo, An Insight into Ladakh, Francesca Merritt *(eds.)* (Sabu-Leh: n/d, 1993), op. cit, p. 26.
27. Luciano Petech, op. cit. 3, p. 34.
28. A. H. Francke, op. cit. 5, p. 39.
29. Luciano Petech, op. cit. 3, p. 35.
30. *Ibid*, p. 36.
31. O. C. Handa, *Buddhist Western Himalaya- part-I* (New Delhi: Indus Publishing company, 2001), p. 141.
32. A. H. Francke, op. cit. 1, p. 39.
33. Luciano Petech, op. cit. 3, p. 55.
34. O. C. Handa, op. cit. 31, p. 141.
35. Luciano Petech, op. cit. 3, p. 36.
36. *Ibid*. p. 37.
37. *Ibid*. p. 38.
38. A learned Brug-pa lama from Tibet visited Ladakh.
39. Luciano Petech, op. cit. 3, p. 40-41.
40. *Ibid*. p. 41.
41. He was a Jesuit missionary and was traveling in the area.
42. S.L. Wessels, Early *Jesuit Travelers in Central Asia, 1603-1721* (First published in 1924 and reprinted at New Delhi: Asian Educational Services, 1992), pp. 75-76.
43. Luciano Petech, op. cit. 3, p. 42.
44. *Ibid*. p. 45.

45. Another Jesuit missionary in the area.
46. S. L. Wessels, op. cit. 42, p. 84.
47. Luciano Petech, op. cit. 3, p. 46.
48. *Ibid*. p. 46.
49. *Ibid*. p. 46.
50. David Snellgrove and Skorupski, *the Cultural Heritage of Ladakh, volume two* (New Delhi: Vikas Publication House, 1980), p. 13.
51. Luciano Petech, op. cit. 3, p. 48.
52. *Ibid*. p. 49.
53. Tashi Rabgias, op. cit. 2, pp. 179-80.
54. A. H. Francke, op. cit. 5, pp. 172-75.
55. *Ibid*. p. 40.
56. Janet Rizvi, op. cit. 4, p. 50.
57. Luciano Petech, op. cit. 3, p. 51.
58. *Ibid*. p. 52.
59. *Ibid*. p. 52.
60. Now known by Hanle, a place in the Southeast of Leh.
61. A. H. Francke, *Antiquities of Indian Tibet, part one* (Calcutta: n/d, 1915), p. 65.
62. Tashi Rabgias, op. cit. 2, p. 181.
63. Nawang Tsering Shakspo, op. cit. 26, p. 26.
64. Tashi Rabgias, op. cit. 2, p. 181.
65. Nawang Tsering Shakspo, op. cit. 26, p. 27.
66. *Ibid*. p. 27.
67. A. H. Francke, op. cit. 5, p. 40.
68. Tashi Rabgias, op. cit. 2, pp. 183-84.
69. *Ibid*, p. 184.
70. A. H. Francke, op. cit. 5, p. 100.
71. Luciano Petech, op. cit. 3, p. 52.
72. S. L. Wessels, op. cit. 42, p. 101.
73. Two places in the Southeast of Leh.
74. S. L. Wessels, op. cit. 42, pp. 103-109.
75. Luciano Petech, op. cit. 3, p. 54.

76. *Ibid.* p. 56.
77. A. H Francke, op. cit. 5, p. 41.
78. Nawang Tsering Shakspo, op. cit. 26, p. 29.
79. Luciano Petech, op. cit. 3, p. 93.
80. A. H. Francke, op. cit. 5, p. 41.
81. Luciano Petech, op. cit. 3, p. 58.
82. The name of the prince is not available but it should be one of the sons of Sen-ge-rNamgyal.
83. Janet Rizvi, op. cit. 4, p. 52.
84. *Ibid.* p. 52.
85. Luciano Petech, op. cit. 3, p. 63.
86. *Ibid.* p. 63.
87. Janet Rizvi, op. cit. 4, pp 52-3.
88. Janet Rizvi, op. cit. 4, p. 53.
89. Luciano Petech, op. cit. 3, p. 67.
90. A. H. Francke, op. cit. 5, p. 41.
91. Luciano Petech, op. cit. 3, p. 67.
92. A. H. Francke, op. cit. 5, p. 40.
93. G. Tucci *Tibetan printed Scrolls,* 2 Vols. (Rome: n/d, 1949), p.256.
94. A. H. Francke, op. cit. 1, p. 102.
95. About fifteen kilometers southeast of Leh.
96. Nawang Tsering Shakspo, op. cit. 26, pp. 29-30.
97. *Ibid.* p. 30.
98. Tashi Rabgias, op. cit. 2, p. 225.
99. *Ibid.* p. 227.
100. *Ibid.* p. 223.
101. Luciano Petech op. cit. 3., p.59.
102. *Ibid.* p. 60.
103. *Ibid.* p. 60.
104. We shall see more on this subject later.
105. Luciano Petech, op. cit. 3, p. 69.
106. Joseph Gergan, *Bla-dvags rgyal-rabs c'-med gter* (New Delhi: n/d, 1976), p. 405.

107. *Ibid*, p. 405.
108. Tashi Rabgias, op. cit. 2, p. 233.
109. A. Cunningham, Ladakh: *Physical, Statistical and Historical* (London: W. H. Allen, 1854, Reprinted, New Delhi: Sagar Publication, 1970), p. 330.
110. Luciano Petech, op. cit. 3, p. 70.
111. Ibid. p. 70.
112. Life of P 'o-lha-nas bSod-nams-stobs-rgyas (1689-1747), this Tibetan sources is cited in Luciano Petech, op. cit. 3, p. 70.
113. A. H. Francke, op. cit. 5, p. 42.
114. C. L. Datta, *Ladakh and Western Himalayan Politics, 1819-1948* (New Delhi: Munshiram Manoharlal Publishers Pvt. Ltd. 1973), p. 62.
115. Luciano Petech, op. cit. 3, p. 71.
116. Janet Rizvi, op. cit. 4, p. 54.
117. *Ibid*. p. 54.
118. Luciano Petech, op. cit. 3, p. 72.
119. Jenet Rizvi, op. cit. 4, p. 54.
120. Luciano Petech, op. cit. 3, p. 73.
121. Tashi Rabgias, op. cit. 2, p. 245.
122. A. H.Francke, op. cit. 1, p. 111.
123. Luciano Petech, op. cit. 3, p. 75.
124. *Ibid*. p. 75.
125. Tashi Rabgias, op. cit. 2, p. 246.
126. A. H. Francke, op. cit. 1, p. 112.
127. Luciano Petech *op. cit*. 3, p. 76.
128. *Ibid*. p. 76.
129. Jenet Rizvi, op. cit. 4, p. 55.
130. A. H. Francke, op. cit. 5, p. 112.
131. Tashi Rabgias, op. cit. 2, p. 251.
132. Luciano Petech, op. cit. 3, p. 77
133. Tashi Rabgias, op. cit.2, p. 251.
134. Luciano Petech, op. cit. 3, p. 77.
135. O. C. Handa, op. cit. 31, pp. 159-60.
136. Luciano Petech, op. cit. 3, p. 78.

137. A. H. Francke, *op. cit. 5, p.* 42.
138. Luciano Petech, op. cit. 3. p. 81.
139. G.·Tucci and E. Ghersi, *Secrets of Tibet* (London: n/d, 1985), pp. 43-44.
140. A. H. Francke, op. cit. 5, p. 44.
141. A. H. Francke, op cit. 1, p. 118.
142. Tashi Rabgias, op. cit. 2, p. 288.
143. *Ibid*. p. 289.
144. Nawang Tsering Shakspo, op cit. 26, p. 34.
145. A. H. Francke, op. cit. 5, p. 44.
146. Luciano Petech, op. cit. 3, p. 85.
147. *Ibid*. p. 85.
148. *Ibid*. p. 86.
149. C. L. Wessels, op. cit. 42, pp. 211-15.
150. *Ibid*. pp. 214-15.
151. *Ibid*. p. 213.
152. A. Cunningham, op, cit. 109, p. 30.
153. A. H. Francke, op. cit. 1, p. 119.
154. Tashi Rabgias, op. cit. 2, p. 301.
155. Luciano Petech, op. cit. 3, p. 95.
156. A. H. Francke, op. cit. 5, p. 44.
157. Luciano Petech, op. cit. 3, p. 96.
158. A. H. Francke, op. cit. 5, p. 44.
159. *Ibid*. p. 44.
160. Luciano Petech, op. cit. 3, p. 98.
161. O. C. Handa, op. cit. 31, p. 167.
162. Luciano Petech, op. cit. 3, p. 98.
163. *Ibid*. p. 98.
164. Tashi Rabgias, op. cit. 2, p. 302.
165. *Ibid*. p. 301.
166. Luciano Petech, op. cit. 3, p. 99.
167. *Ibid*. p. 99.
168. *Ibid*. p. 99.

169. *Ibid*. p. 97.
170. A. H. Francke, op. cit. 1, p. 120.
171. *Ibid*. p. 120.
172. Tashi Rabgias, op. cit. 2, p. 317.
173. Luciano Petech op. cit. 3, p. 103.
174. A. H. Francke, op. cit. 5, p. 45.
175. Nawang Tsering Shakspo, op. cit. 26, p. 36.
176. Ka'-t'og is a rN in-ma-pa monastery some forty miles South-East of sDe-dge.
177. A. H. Francke, op. cit. 5, p. 45.
178. Luciano Petech, op. cit. 3, p. 105.
179. A. H. Francke, op. cit. 1, p. 121.
180. Luciano Petech, op. cit. 3, p. 105.
181. O.C. Handa, op. cit. 31, p. 170.
182. A.H. Francke, op. cit. 5, p. 46.
183. Luciano Petech, op. cit. 3, p.110.
184. *Ibid*. p. 100.
185. Tashi Rabgias, op. cit. 2, p. 332.
186. *Ibid*. p. 334.
187. A.H. Francke, op. cit. 5, p. 45.
188. Luciano Petech, op. cit. 3, p. 107.
189. Nawang Tsering Shakspo, op. cit. 26, p. 37.
190. Tashi Rabgias, op. cit. 2, p. 335.
191. A.H. Francke, op. cit. 1, pp. 122-28.
192. A.H. Francke, op. cit. 5, p. 44.
193. Luciano Petech, op. cit. 3, p. 112.
194. *Ibid*. p. 114.
195. *Ibid*. p. 119.
196. Tashi Rabgias, op. cit. 2, p. 340.
197. O. C. Handa, op. cit. 31, p. 172.
198. Tashi Rabgias, op. cit. 2, p. 344.
199. *Ibid*. p. 344.
200. O.C. Handa, op. cit. 31, pp. 172-73.

201. A.H. Francke, op. cit. 5, p. 123.
202. Tashi Rabgias, op cit. 2, p. 349.
203. A.H. Francke, op. cit. 1, p. 126.
204. A.H. Francke, op. cit. 5, p. 46.
205. *Ibid.* p. 46.
206. A.H. Francke, op. cit. 5, p. 46.
207. Tashi Rabgias, op. cit. 2, pp. 349-50.
208. *Ibid.* pp. 351-52.
209. *Ibid.* p. 352.
210. Luciano Petech, op. cit. 3, p. 124.
211. *Ibid.* p. 124.
212. Tashi Rabgias, op. cit. 2, p. 350.
213. A.H. Francke, op. cit. 5, p. 47.
214. Tashi Rabgias, op. cit. 2, p. 365.
215. A.H. Francke, op cit. 1, p. 128.
216. O.C. Handa, op. cit. 31, p. 175.
217. Tashi Rabgias, op. cit. 2, p. 365.
218. Janet Rizvi, op. cit. 4, p. 58.
219. A.H. Francke, op. cit. 1, pp. 130-31.
220. A.H. Francke, op. cit. 5, p. 47.
221. Luciano Petech, op. cit. 3, p. 132.
222. W. Moorcroft and George Trebeck, *Travels in the Himalayan provinces on Hindustan and Punjab; in Ladakh and Kashmir; in Pashawar, Kabul, Kunduz and Bokhara, from 1819-1825, two volumes. Vol. 1* (New Delhi: Sagar publication, 1971), p. xxxvi.
223. *Ibid.* p. 334.
224. Tashi Rabgias, op. cit. 2, p. 376.
225. Luciano Petech, op. cit. 3, p. 131.
226. *Ibid.* p. 131.
227. W. Moorcroft and George Trebeck, op. cit. 222, p. 338.
228. Luciano Petech, op. cit. 3, p. 131.
229. W. Moorcroft and George and Trebeck, op. cit. 222, p. 338.
230. Luciano Petech, op. cit. 3, p. 131.

231. A.H. Francke, op. cit. 1, p. 132.
232. A.H. Francke, op. cit. 3, p. 48.
233. A.H. Francke, op. cit. 1, p. 128.
234. Luciano Petech, op. cit. 3, p. 151.
235. C.L. Datta, op. cit. 114, pp. 149-50.
236. Luciano Petech, op. cit. 3, p. 151.
237. *Ibid.*, p. 156.
238. A. Cunningham. op. cit. 109, p. 258.
239. *Ibid.*, pp. 262-3.
240. David Snellgrove and Tadeusz Skorupski, op. cit. 50, p. 42.
241. A. H. Francke, op. cit. 5, p. 37.
242. Tashi Rabgias, op. cit.2, pp. 86-87.
243. David Snellgrove and Tadeuszki Skorupski, The *Cultural Heritage of Ladakh, Volume one* (England: Aris & Phillips Ltd., 1977), p. 107.
244. *Ibid*. p. 107.
245. The incarnate lamas.
246. Michael Harris Good man, *The Last Dalai Lama* (first published in Great Britain, 1986, New Delhi: Rupa & Co, 1998), p. 107.
247. dSang-mkhar, Sa-bu etc. are the branches.
248. David Snellgrove and Tadeusz Skorupski, op. cit. 243, p. 109.
249. Janet Rizvi, op. cit. 4, p. 175.
250. Thupstan Paldan, *The guide to the monasteries and royal Castle of Ladakh* (Delhi: n/d, 1997), p. 18.
251. David Snellgrove and Tadeusz Skorupski, op. cit. 243, p. 115.
252. Luciano Petech, op. cit. 3, p. 52.
253. Thupstan Paldan, op. cit. 250, p. 21.
254. Ibid. p. 57.
255. David Snellgrove, and Skorupski, op. cit. 243, p. 132.
256. Janet Rizvi, op. cit. 4, p. 179.
257. Tashi Rabgias, op. cit. 2, pp. 50-51.
258. Thupstan Paldan, op. cit. 250, p. 23.
259. David Snellgrove, and Tadeusz Skorupski, op. cit. 243, p.131.
260. Janet Rizvi, op. cit. 4, p. 181.

261. Thupstan Paldan, op. cit. 250, p. 19.
262. David Snellgrove, and Tadeusz Skorupski, op. cit. 243, p. 133.
263. *Ibid.* p. 133.
264. Jamyang Gyaltsan, "Monks of Mangtro Gonpa" in Osmasten, Henry and Philip Denwood, (eds.) *Recent Research of Ladakh 4 & 5. Proceedings of the fourth and fifth International Colloquium on Ladakh* (Bristol, 1989 and London: SOAS Studies, 1992), p. 56.
265. Luciano Petech, op. cit. 3, p. 29.
266. Tashi Rabgias, op. cit.2, pp. 169-72.
267. Situated about 130 kilometers west of Leh.
268. David Snellgrove, and Taduez Skorupski, op. cit. 243, p.123.
269. *Ibid.* p. 123.
270. Thupstan Paldan, op. cit. 250, p. 13.
271. *Ibid,* p. 13.
272. David Snellgrove, and Tadeusz Skorupski, op. cit. 50, p. 42.
273. *Ibid.* p. 48.
274. A. H. Francke, op. cit. 5, p. 160.
275. Thupstan Paldan, op. cit. 250, p. 27.
276. *Ibid.* p. 27.
277. David Snellgrove, and Tadeusz Skorupski, op. cit. 50, p. 55.
278. Thupstan Paldan, op. cit. 250, p. 29.
279. David Snellgrove, and Tadeusz Skorupski, op. cit. 50, p. 55.
280. John Crook, and Tsering Shakya, "Monastic Communities In Zanskar: Location, Function and Organization" in John Crook and A. Henry Osmaston (eds.), *Himalayan Buddhist Village: Enviroment, Resources, Society and Religious Life in Zanskar- Ladakh* (Bristol and New Delhi: Motilal Banarasidass), 1994), op. cit, p. 562.
281. David Snellgrove, and Tadeusz Skorupski, op. cit. 50, p. 55.
282. Thupstan Paldan, op. cit. 250, p. 27.
283. *Ibid.* p. 29.
284. *Ibid.* p. 24.
285. *Ibid.* p. 24.
286. Thupstan Paldan, op. cit. 250, p. 13.
287. A.H. Francke, op. cit. 5, p. 40.

288. Thupstan Paldan, op. cit. 250, p. 17.
289. A. H. Francke, op. cit. 1, p. 102.
290. Thupstan Paldan, op. cit. 250, p. 12.
291. Luciano Petech, op. cit. 3, pp. 36-37.
292. Tashi Rabgias, op. cit. 2, p. 181.
293. Luciano Petech, op. cit. 3, p. 25.
294. A. H. Francke, op. cit. 1, p. 132.
295. Luciano Petech, op. cit. 3, p. 151.
296. Luciano Petech, op. cit. 3, p. 35.
297. Tashi Rabgias, op. cit. 2, pp. 175-76.
298. Luciano Petech, op. cit. 3, p. 38.
299. *Ibid*. p. 87.
300. Luciano Petech, op. cit. 3, p. 87.
301. *Ibid*. p. 132.
302. Tashi Rabgias, op. cit. 2, p. 332.
303. Luciano Petech, op. cit. 3, p. 29. According to Tashi Rabgias, the king was Jam-dban-rNamgyal.
304. Tashi Rabgias, op. cit. 2, p. 171.
305. Luciano Petech, op. cit. 3, p. 29.

5
Pilgrimage and Trade

Trade appears to be one of the most fundamental activities of human societies, going hand in hand with the development of complex form of social organization. 'Perhaps in its earliest form it involved no more than the barter of subsistence commodities between people living off the land in adjacent ecological zones; such simple barter has persisted alongside more developed trading patterns almost down to the present times.'[1] In the western Himalayas, inspite of the huge mountain ranges like Karakoram and Hindu Kush, traders could not deter the overland trade that existed among various countries, exchanging their produce with others, across high and difficult passes. With the passage of time, this trade developed further.

In the olden days, Leh, the capital of Ladakh due to its strategic location in the Western Himalayas had developed into an active and important centre for commercial intercourse with Tibet, Persia, Yarkand, China and even Russia on one hand, and Kashmir, the Punjab, and the plains of Hindustan on the other.[2] In 1872, R.B. Shaw, the British Joint Commissioner on special duty, Ladakh, mentioned that the town of Leh had become an important point, where the great majority of traders from both sides were always coming but not going beyond Ladakh, and they were present there at Leh, bartering their goods with other merchants and returning to their homes.[3] The origins of these trades are undocumented. But it seems to have started long ago. The trade relation between Ladakh and Tibet is an old one. It is quite possible that the inhabitants of Ladakh felt the Tibetan influence as early as the mid-seventh century, for the nomadic Tibetans of Changthang would have good reason to have contacts with the Mons and Dards, exchanging grains for animal's products. The Tibetan nomads occupied the higher pasture ground for their animals and the Aryan tribes (Mons and Dards) irrigated in the lower plains. According to A.H. Francke, the products of the fields were as welcome to the Tibetans as were the produce of the flocks to the Dards and the peasants.[4] During this period the Tibetan nomads of Changthang probably inter-married with the Mon and Dard population and allowed a trading or bartering system to develop between the two groups of people. This trade continued to develop for many years. Luciano Petech mentioned that "about 900 A.D., Ladakh, still inhabited by a Dardi-speaking population, was no longer connected politically with Tibet, at the most it maintained trade relations with it."[5]

By the 16th and the 17th centuries, the trade in the Western Himalayas through Ladakh was well established as several references supported this fact. It may be assumed that by then it was already an institution of many centuries, standing. The people of Nubra petitioned King Ts'e-dban-rNamgyal (1530-1560 A.D.), to refrain from undertaking a campaign in the North of Leh, against the Khan of Yarkand, as it would have seriously damaged the trade through the passes, which was of vital importance to Nubra; the king saw the point and decided in favour of the petition.[6] The Chronicle of Ladakh also mentions this petition.[7] After ascending the throne, King Ts'e-dban-rNamgyal waged war in the West, the East, and the South, and when he planned to go to war against Yarkand in the North of Leh, the people of Nubra petitioned to the king against the war:

> "Chnag Hor la dmag gyab gsun wa la Nobra pa nrams kyis ju wa phyul nas ma mdzad."[8]

It means that when the king would have waged a war against the Hor (the Turks) in the North, the people of Nubra petitioned him and he desisted.

Many travelers in the 17th and 18th centuries have documented the trade through Ladakh. The first most comprehensive analysis of this trade is by W. Moorcroft who was on his way to Yarkand. He reached Leh in September 1820 and remained there for a period of two years, until September 1822.[9] He reported that a considerable number of people from Kashmir and some Turani merchants were engaged in commerce at Leh.[10] He also mentioned that Leh, because it was centrally situated, became the great thoroughfare for an active commercial intercourse between Tibet, Turkistan, China, and even Russia on one hand, and Kashmir, the Punjab and the plains of Hindustan on the other.[11] In fact, this trade became an important source of income not only for Ladakh but also for other countries including Kashmir. This point is substantiated by the fact that King Sen-ge-rNamgyal of Ladakh in the middle years of the 17th century closed the main trade route between Ladakh and Kashmir as an economic reprisal against the Moghul.[12] This economic blockade, which lasted for about twenty years, was lifted by King bDe-Idan-rNamgyal.[13] This decision of King Sen-ge-rNamgyal to close the commercial caravan was not good economic sense and it also affected the economy of his own country. As Luciano Petech writes that this blockade of the Kashmir trade must have dealt a serious blow to the commercial interest of the country (Ladakh).[14]

There was trade not only with different countries but also among different regions of Ladakh, exchanging the produce of one region with that of others. The internal trade consisted in articles both imported and produced in the country and the trade was between the inhabitants of one region and those of others. This trade was carried by barter.[15] For example, people of Rupshu brought salt to Zanskar and took barley in exchange; the Zanskaris further exchanged this salt with inhabitants of Suru for Pattu (woolen cloth), some cash and barley.[16] In 1846, the quantity of wool used in making blankets and sacks was 20,000 small mounds of wool.[17] Maund was a measure of weight of two sizes; bigger one 'the pukka maund' being approximately 37 kilograms and the small maund was about 15 kilograms. According to Frederic Drew, the chief profit was in the trade of salt; by acting both as carriers and merchants of this they increased its value enough to provide themselves with the luxuries that must come from outside.[18] The lower region of Ladakh, locally called Sham, produced various kinds of fruits including apricots and the peasant-traders from the region used to take dried apricots, and other necessary articles of trade to Changthang, exchanging it for goat wool (pashm) and salt. According to Janet Rizvi, every year the traders from Sham traveled with their donkeys via Chang-la to Rudok, some reaching as far as Gertse, over 500 kilometers from the border, while others worked the intervening valleys and plateau of Gerge and Rundor.[19] Earlier, many monks from Ladakh used to go to Tibet for monastic education, with the traders. There are still many monks who have been to Tibet through this route. Lobsang Tomba,[20] about eighty years old, is one of them. When he was about thirteen years old, he went through this route with the traders to Tibet. He studied for twenty-two years in Dre-pung and Tashi-Lhunpo monasteries in Tibet. After keeping enough for their domestic consumption, the peasant-traders of Sham loaded their donkeys once more with the salt and wool they had brought from Changthang, and took it further down as far as Skardu in Baltistan. The traders followed two routes to Skardu. On the first route, the traders made a detour over the Fatu-la and Namika-la, to Kargil, the two passes between Leh and Kargil. From Kargil, the route followed the Dras-Suru River down to it confluence with the Indus at Marol, and then took a trail, which goes along the steep mountainside above the river down to Skardu.[21] The other route goes down along the Indus for about 45 kilometers, then takes a right turn up the Hanu River, over the Chorbat-la and down into the Shayok Valley to Skardu.[22] There are still many traders especially in Sham region of Ladakh, who had been involved in the trade and Tashi Angchok, about 90 years old from the village Skurbuchan, is one such trader. He started involved in the great trade of Ladakh at the age of 20 years. Initially he works as assistant with his elder brother for few years and then with another trader named Namgyal Titapa of the same village again as assistant for two years. And then, he started his own business with just three donkeys. After four years, he could buy another 6 donkeys. With 10 donkeys, he had been to different regions of Ladakh like Nubra, Changthan and Kargil and also to neighboring areas like Shigar, Skardo, Kashmir, Gartok, Rudok etc. exchanging different articles of trade. He preferred travel to Shigar and Skardo and he traveled to these two places many times. He took different routes from Skurbuchan to Skardo. He mentioned that there are three routes to Shigar/ Skardo from Skurbuchan. One route is via Hanu crossing Chorbat-la to Kapula and then to Shigagar/ Skardo, second routes go along the Indus River via Batalic and third routes via Kargil. But mostly he travelled to Shigar/Skardo via Batalic routes. 'From Skurbuchan to Beema to Hordas to Danbudoo to Dantharthang to Marol (here one has to cross the Indus River on boats made up of local juniper trees. Four donkeys with their loads can cross on a board at one time. They used to charge 2 Anna for one donkey, a rupee has 16 annas. Then to Changmar to Tarkachik to Bayulchan to Kharmag Rog to Tolti to Ggyasing to Parkuta to Zillung to Dhaphays (there is no village, there is the Legendry Kessar arrow). Next is to Gol to Narthang-(plains areas, there is no village) to Thorgu Thapchung to Skardo'. At Skardo they have to cross a river to go Shigar, here also there were local boats and one can carry about 10/15 donkeys with their loads at a time. It costs 4 Anna for one donkey, 8 Anna for bigger animals like Dzo or Yak to cross it. It costs more because the river is bigger as it consisted of three rivers that come from Ladakh i.e., the Shayok, the Indus and the Suru rivers. It takes about 18 days to reach Shigar/Skardo via Batalic routes. It takes 4/5 days more via Kargil routes. He makes profit by exchanging of different trade articles. For example, he bought apricots from Ladakh and Baltistan and takes it to Changthang; eastern part of Ladakh and Tibetan areas, where it exchanged for wools, butter and pashmina called in Ladakh as 'lena'. In Changthang, he used to exchange a 'Bati' equal to two kilograms of apricots to equal weight of pashmina and butter. Wool gets double and khulu (Yak wool) gets three times. Loaded these wools on his 10 donkeys, he traveled back to Leh and takes some of the wools and other articles to Baltistan, where he exchanged for one 'Bati' of wool to seventeen times of apricots. So, in this process he makes profits. He said that 'I have not much agriculture land but the profits that I earned from the trade were enough to feed my 18 children'.

Though the majority of the Ladakhis lived by subsistence agriculture, yet trade played a vital role in development of its economy and culture.

Trade Routes

In the Tibetan and Ladakhi language every road is called Lam; but the high roads are distinguished by the name of Lam-chen, or "Great Roads," and Gya Lam or "Passable Roads."[23] Ladakh is connected with many trade routes; the Central Asian trade routes, the Southern route, the Northwestern route and Southwestern route. The principal route is that between Kashmir and Yarkand; the next in importance is the route to Lhasa, and the third is that which leads to Rukchu, Lahul, and Kulu and the fourth route goes to Baltistan. It was through these routes that social, cultural and trade exchanges between Ladakh with neighboring areas were taken placed. The following are some of the important roads that connected Ladakh with different countries.

The Western Roads

The Western Road connects Ladakh with the Kashmir valley. The whole distance from Leh to Kashmir is 228 miles.[24] La means pass, and there are three main passes on this route; the Namyki-la, (about 3,000 feet), the Fatu-la (13,240 feet)[25] and the Zoji-la (11,300).[26] The Zoji-la is passable from March till November; it is closed in winter by the vast masses of snow. This route became important for the trade between Ladakh and Kashmir. In fact, in 1873, J. E. T Aitchison while reporting upon Ladakh routes to the Secretary to the government of Punjab suggested for "the formation of a covered way across the Zoji-La in order to secure a permanent passage throughout the whole year between Kashmir and Ladakh."[27] Normally it took travelers on horseback some 14 to 16 days to reach Leh from Kashmir.[28] Ladakh trade reports from years 1869 to 1874 show the average improvement of imports into Ladakh and export from Ladakh to Kashmir on this route:

Table 5.1. Imports and Exports of Ladakh with Kashmir

Year	*Imports value in (Rs.)*	*Exports value in (Rs.)*	*Total value in (Rs.)*
1869	40,002	71,919	1,11,921
1870	1,18,185	81,393	1,99,578
1871	69,555	1,58,232	2,27,787
1872	42,054	1,01,380	1,43,434
1873	76,386	1,84,014	2,60,400
1874	95,614	1,42,932	2,38,546

Source: Ladakh Trade reports of the respective years, National Archives, Delhi.

The above total value of imports and exports figures for six years from years 1869 to 1874, show slight improvement; it was about one lakh and twelve thousand in the year 1869 and increased to two lakhs thirty eight thousand five hundred in the year 1874.

This route is now familiar to visitors driving in from Kashmir since Ladakh was opened to tourists in 1974.

The Southwestern Road

This road linked Leh to Zanskar, and Kishtwar with Jammu.[29] The distance between Leh to Jammu is almost the same as the distance from Leh to Kashmir, mentioned above.[30]

From Jammu it took an easterly direction, through Chandra Bhaga valley near Chatargarh and after crossing Umasi-la (pass), entered Padum, the capital of Zanskar.[31] From Padum there are two roads to Leh; the direct route through Zanskar and the winter route through Rupshu.[32] Zorawar Singh, a commander of the Dogra army, took the latter in the winter of 1835, when all the passes on the more direct road had been closed.[33]

The Southern Road

This road connected Leh to Lahul, Kulu, Kangra valley, Bashahr, Nurpur and other trade marts of Punjab.[34] The establishment of mule traffic on this route was due to the creation in 1870 of the Kulu mule train by Captain Harcourt, under the orders of Colonel Coxe, Commissioner of the Jalander division.[35] According to Cunningham, by this route the shawl wool was brought to the large cities of Nurpur, Amritsar, and Ludhiana, all of which made a return in manufactured shawls and coarse brocades.[36]

The Northwestern Road

This road led from Baltistan and other neighboring districts up the bed of the Indus to Leh[37]. During the summer season, when the water level of Indus increased due to the melting of snow, the travelers preferred ascending the Shayok river as far as Chhorbad, and thence crossing the mountains by the Hanu pass (16,890 feet) and descended into Ladakh at the fort of Hanu[38]. This road was frequently traversed by Baltis and Ladakhi, who carried dried apricots, which were in great favour and demand in the cold countries of Ladakh and Tibet[39]. Zorawar Singh who conquered Baltistan in 1839-40 also followed this route.[40]

The Northern Road

This road leads from Yarkand and Kotan, over the Karakoram mountains (18660 feet) to Leh.[41] The Karakoram route from Yarkand to Leh is about 500 miles in length.[42]

There are several possible routes from Leh to Yarkand, all converging at the Karakoram pass[43], the travelers' choices of which depended on the season. As for the distance, whatever the season, it was a march of about 500 miles and took about a month.[44] The Karakoram route was a very difficult one; there were several formidable obstacles. From Leh, the first is the Kardong-la pass (about 18380 feet), where no road can be constructed over a steep glacier, and then the Shayok River, which was difficult to cross in summer, as there was no bridge.[45] The British Joint Commissioner of Ladakh reported in March 1872 that the Shayok River has a boat plying across it opposite Tirit (a village in Nubra) at a certain season.[46] He further added that any bridge over the river near the village "would have to be of such a span as practically to forbid its construction in a region devoid of large trees like in Leh and Nubra."[47] The next difficult obstacle on this route is the Sasser Pass- a large glacier, and it is difficult to climb over it. B.R. Shaw, the British Joint Commissioner of Ladakh, who crossed this pass mentioned that:

> "It is difficult and toilsome for even a foot passenger to climb over these slippery masses of ice, while the hollows between them are filled with small lakes or pools which force the travelers to make way over sloping moraine at the side, consisting of rocky masses of all sizes and shapes poised unsteadily as they have been deposited by melting ice. Traveling on foot, as I was when I crossed this pass, I could scarcely have believed that a horse could advance a yard on such ground, had not the skeletons on the track born witness to the fact."[48]

Traders traveled through these routes in the summer as well as in the winters. The autumn and winter traveling between Yarkand and Ladakh possessed the advantage of greater ease in crossing the streams which in the spring and early summer were much swollen by the melting snows, yet this advantage was more than counterbalanced by the intense cold that prevailed late in the year in those elevated regions, and the drying up of the grass.[49] Snow was another disadvantage that was faced by the travelers in winter, especially as it increased the difficulty of the baggage animals to cross the passes. But whatever the reason, the Yarkand traders much preferred to start southward at an earlier season so that they would have reached Ladakh not later than the beginning of September at least.[50] They were thus enabled to meet at Leh the Punjab traders, who could not wait for them beyond the beginning of October on the account of closing of the passes between Ladakh and India.[51] Despite such difficulties, the trade on this route had been improving year by year as the following figures from the Ladakh Trade Reports from 1868 to 1874 show:

Table 5.2. Imports and Exports of Ladakh with Central Asia

Year	*Imports value in (Rs.)*	*Exports value in (Rs.)*	*Total Value in (Rs.)*
1868	1,58,054	1,23,999	2,82,053
1869	2,78,799	1,96,323	4,75,122
1870	2,64,000	3,46,543	6,10,543
1871	2,61,242	1,92,579	4,63,821
1872	3,21,763	1,61,165	4,82,928
1873	3,30,690	2,55,660	5,86,3501
1874	3,81,802	8,02,563	1,84,365

Source: Foreign Department, Political. A. Branch, Nos. 214-216, Consultation July 1874, National Archives Delhi.

The above figures show increased of both imports and exports of Ladakh with central Asia. The imports value was about one lakh and fifty eight thousand rupees in the year 1868 and it increased to three lakh eight one thousand eight hundred in the year 1874. The exports value was also increased from one lakh twenty four thousand in the year 1868 to eight lakhs two thousands five hundred in the year 1874. The increased was due to the improvement of the trade route between them.

The Southeastern Road

This road connected Ladakh with Tibet. From Leh it followed the course of the Indus upstream; then through Gartok and Lake Mansarowar it entered the valley of Tsang-po and reached Lhasa.[52] Gartok was situated on the Indus, about 15 days journey from Leh.[53] It was the main trading and administrative centre of Western Tibet, where only three possible routes could reach it. The first and direct one was the road that goes straight up the Indus through Upshi and Chumathang.[54] But this was possible only in winter, so one alternative in other seasons was to make a detour south over the Taglang-la to Debring, crossing Polo-kongka-la, and following down to the Puga river down to the Indus at Mahe.[55] The other one was to detour north over the Chang-la to Tangtse, Chushul, and to cut over to the Indus Valley via the Tsaka-la. Sven Hedin followed the last one, when he was traveled from Leh to Tibet in 1906.[56] The three routes converged at Thangra on the Indus; from there it was about nine days march through Demchok to Gartok.[57] The route from Leh to Lhasa was extended over 90 stages, and along the road there were nomads, who grazed large herds of sheep, yaks and goats.[58] Imports into Ladakh and exports from Ladakh to the Tibetan area from 1867 to 1874 showed a steady improvement. The following figures are taken from Ladakh Trade Reports from 1867-1874:

Table 5.3. Imports and Exports of Ladakh with Tibet

Year	*Imports value in (Rs.)*	*Exports value in (Rs.)*	*Total Value in (Rs.)*
1867	68,888	62,832	1,31,720
1868	1,39,057	1,45,239	2,84,296
1869	1,33,788	57,889	1,91,677
1870	1,58,413	67,751	2,26,164
1871	1,49,537	52,084	2,01,621
1872	2,61,242	55,153	3,16,395
1873	78,511	56,133	1,34,644
1874	1,20,529	1,11,521	2,32,050

Source: Foreign Department, Political. A. Branch, Nos. 214-216, Consultation July 1874, National Archives Delhi.

The total value of imports to and exports from Leh to Tibetan territories was also rising; it was about one lakh thirty one thousand seven hundred in the year 1867 and rose to a total value of about two lakhs thirty two thousand in the year 1874. The large proportion of tea imported in the year 1872 turned out to be of bad quality, and remained in the hands of Lhasa tea merchants.[59] This may be the reason behind the sudden decrease in the imports value shown in the year 1873.[60]

Some of the Important Articles of Ladakh Trade

Due to its central location and being connected with the famous Silk Route, Ladakh became a transit centre in the Western Himalayas. Traders from different countries in the region used to travel through respective roads to Ladakh and exchange their goods with others. Following are some of the important articles of trade that were exchanged through Ladakh

Goat Wool (Pashm)

The goat wool (Pashm) was the most important article of the trade between Ladakh, Tibet, Kashmir and Yarkand. It was the trade of Pashm which formed the most substantial link, a link which for centuries was political as well as commercial.[61] It was the Pashm business that induced Maharaja Gulab Singh, the Raja of Jammu to undertake the conquest of Ladakh in 1834. As Alastair Lamb pointed out:

> "There can be little doubt that it was the attraction of the Ladakh carrying trade, particularly, in shawl wool, which brought the Sikhs into this barren and mountainous region and there can be equally little doubt that the Sikh conquest and the consequent exaction imposed upon this trade upset the long-established commercial framework of this region."[62]

Wool, in both Tibetan and Ladakhi is called 'Bal' and there are two kinds: first, goat wool or 'Le-na', which is used for shawls, and secondly sheep-wool or 'Bal' which is used for blankets and coarse clothing, and for stuffing pillows and bedding.[63] The goat wool (Pashm) is the soft warm undercoat of a particular breed of domestic goat found in the bitter cold of the trans-Himalayan winter.[64] This wool is produced in many areas in Ladakh and Tibet. Some of the important areas where wool is produced are Rupshu, Rodokh and Changthang.[65] Besides the above areas, some fine Pashm known as 'Turfan' was also imported into Ladakh from Yarkand.[66] Strictly speaking, pashm should be described as the wool of the domesticated goat in contradiction to "tush," which is the wool of the wild goat, or ibex. Tush was so exceedingly rare that it cannot be said to come under the head of marketable commodities. In 1874, Captain E. Molloy, Officiating British Joint-Commissioner, Ladakh, mentioned that very small quantities of it were sent every year from Changthang to Kashmir for the use of the Maharaja.[67] It is obtained by being picked off rocks and thorny bushes where ibex have rubbed themselves; of course these animals might be shot for it. There are two kinds of tush-shahtush and tush. Shahtush is fine white down that grows only on certain parts of the body of the ibex, whereas tush is the wool of the rest of the body, and it varies in being different shades of brown.[68] I had myself seen pashm on bushes on a high pass near the Tsomoriri Lake[69] in Ladakh, in the month of August 2003, when I along with my friends was on a day trek. In fact, my friend noticed it first, as he is interested in pashmina shawl. There were lots of pashmina goats in the area. Captain E. Molloy, Officiating British Joint-Commissioner, Ladakh, mentioned in 1874 that "in Changthang the pashm was taken once a year out of the goat, this was not the case in Turfan (Yarkand), where the wool was not touched while the goat was alive."[70] In Changthang it is usual to extract the pashm in two ways, it being done always around June, either by combing it out before shearing the animal, when it is called 'Kaljack' or by shearing it with the coarser hairs of the goat, when it is called 'Chang'.[71] The former process, however, produces much finer and softer pashm than the latter. In

Turkistan, after the skin of the animal has been taken off, it is steeped for some days in a preparation of lime-water, when the upper growth of the coarse hairs were picked out of it, and the fine under-growth of wool being then collected and made up into bales for foreign export.[72] However, before the weaver used it, it was subjected to a further process of cleaning and picking.[73]

The goat wool was (and is) the most important raw material for Kashmir's shawl industry. The final product of this material is called Pashmina shawl and it is well known all over the world. The raw materials were procured from the western provinces of Tibet and Ladakh. Kashmiri merchants from Leh mostly carried it. Moorcroft mentioned that:

> "the fleece is cut once a year; and the wool, coarsely picked either in the place from whence it comes, or at Leh, is sold by the importers to the merchants at that city, by whom it is sent on to Kashmir."[74]

The important of the article is substantiate by the fact the it is mentioned in the treaty of Tingmosgang (1684), which brought an end to the three-cornered conflict between Ladakh, Tibet and the Mughal Empire at Kashmir.[75] One clause of the treaty deals with the Pashm trade between Ladakh, Tibet and Kashmir. According to this treaty, the goat wool of mNa-ris-skor-gsum must not be sold to any other country but Kashmir and the price being fixed as two dnul-dmar-zog (red silver good) for eighty nags.[76] For the purpose of pashm trade, four Kashmiri merchants were to be settled at Spituk (dPe-t'up)[77], to supply the Pashm to Kashmir.[78] Kashmiri residents of Ladakh were to travel to Byan-t'an (Changthang) to procure goat wool and bring it to Leh, where they would sell it to Kashmiri traders; Kashmiri residents of Ladakh were not allowed to bring themselves their wool to Kashmir.[79] Further, no merchants from Kashmir were allowed to enter Changthang.[80] This treaty on the Pashm gives more advantages to the Moghuls in Kashmir. In fact, C.L. Datta writes that "the entire wool export and transit trade of Ladakh was a firm monopoly of Kashmir."[81]

The Tibetan text of the treaty reported in the Chronicles of Ladakh, contain many important points on the Pashm trade between Ladakh, Tibet and Kashmir; it mentioned:

> "Kha-chul dgos chyet/ mNgaris-khor-gsum gi le-na sogs/yul gzyan la tsong mi chok pa tang/ ley rin yang chey ralnyag bGyad bChu la dngyul dmar azog gnyis rey btang gryu dang/ Ley rin chey ral nyag 40 la rin dnyul gchig ry gtang gryu/ rong pai nag la chang-pas chang mi chog/Chang-pai le-na (la) sa do'w chu sogs dyg zer lo myt Pa dang/ Ru-thok rang la mkhar tsong pa ma thogs/ gro Mi chog pa chas/ le-na nrams/ kha-chey (tshaso) tshong pa mi bzhai dPe-t'up (Spituk) tu bsdad nas/ k(sha) mir kha chey dang nyam tsong chas/ Kha-chul dro gya chas wa ma gtogs/ Kha-chul kha chey Chang-thang la gro mi chog/ Chang-thang gro wai Ladgs kha chey yis Kha-chul la rang Le-na khyor tai/ gro mi chog."[82]

Translation: the fine goat wool of mNgaris-khor-gsum should be sold only to Kashmir, the price of the fine wool and mix wool being fixed. It was two red silver good (two rupees) for eighty nags of the fine wool and forty nags of mixed wool cost one rupee. The nag used by rong-pa[83] was not allowed to be used by the people of Changthang. There should be no complaint that the wool of Changthang contains soil, stones and moisture. Only the court merchants of Ladakh were allowed to go to Rudok. Four Kashmiri merchants were to reside at Spituk to trade and supply wool to Kashmir. Besides the four merchants who settled at Spituk, no merchants from Kashmir were to be allowed to enter Changthang. And those Kashmiri residents of Ladakh who traveled to Changthang were not allowed to go to Kashmir themselves with the load of the goat wools.

Thus, the shawl wool trade became an area of mutual dependence between Ladakh, Western Tibet and Kashmir, and outsiders were excluded. Several travelers in the 17th and 18th centuries have reported about this shawl wool trade activity between Ladakh and Kashmir. Ippolito Desideri the

Jesuit priest, who visited Ladakh in 1715, has reported about the trade of fine wool between Ladakh, Western Tibet and Kashmir.[84] About a century after Desideri, William Moorcroft, who traveled to many provinces in the Himalayas from 1819 to 1825, witnessed the trade in fine wool between Ladakh, Tibet and Kashmir. He stayed in Leh from September 1820 to September 1822 and his observation during the period has confirmed that the fine wool was still the most important article of trade between Ladakh and Kashmir. As William Moorcroft writes:

> "One of the most important articles of the trade of Ladakh is shawl wool, of which it forms, in some degree, the source, but in a still greater, the entrepot between the countries whence the wool is chiefly supplied, Rudokh and Changthang, and that in which it consumed, Kashmir."[85]

The Treaty of Tingmosgang which was signed more than a century ago (1684), was still effectively in place when Moorcroft was in Leh. As he pointed out that:

> "About eighty hundred loads (wool) are annually exportedto Kashmir, to which country, by ancient custom and engagements, the export is exclusively confined, and all attempts to convey it to other countries are punished by confiscation. In like manner it is considered in Rudokh and Changthang as illegal to allow a trade in shawl wool except through Ladakh."[86]

Despite the Dogra's several expeditions to Ladakh from years 1834 to 1842, the shawl wool trade between Ladakh, Tibet and Kashmir continued as before. The Dogra expeditions in Ladakh was to divert the wool trade to Jammu via Zanskar and Kishtwar,[87] but it could not succeed. Alaistair Lamb stated that "the trade between Ladakh and Tibet was largely based on a system of traditional relationships which could hardly fail to be disturbed by the conquest of a power alien in culture and religion."[88]

The Treaty of Leh (1842) between the Dogras and the Tibetans and four years later, the Treaty of Amritsar (1846), which put Gulab Singh in possession of Kashmir in addition to his existing territories of Jammu and Ladakh, ensured the continuation of the trade of shawl wool through Ladakh to Kashmir. The treaty of Leh (1842) ensured that "the conformity with ancient usage, tea and shawl wool shall be transmitted by the Ladakh road."[89] Alexander Cunningham witnessed the continuation of this trade when he visited Ladakh in the year 1846-47. He observed that during the period export of shawl-wool, produced in the country, amounted to 2,400 small mounds or 76,800 lbs a year.[90] The goat wool was exported to Kashmir, Amritsar and Rampur.[91] During the same period, the export of goat wool was approximately about 5,000 maunds.[92]

Table 5.4. Cunningham Reported the following Data of the Goat Wool that was Produced in Ladakh and Imported from Western Tibet in the year 1847

Goat wool	*Maunds*	*=Lb*	*Value (Rs)*	*Rate of import duty per Maunds (Rs)*	*Value of duty (Rs)*
Produced in Ladakh	2400	76800	76800	—	—
Imported from western Tibet	4000	128000	128000	8as	2,000
Total	6400	204,800	204,800	—	2,000

Source: A. Cunningham, op. cit. 17, pp. 239, 249.

Table 5.5. Goat Wool Exported to Different Countries from Ladakh in the Year 1847

Goat wool	*Maunds*	*=Lb*	*Value (Rs)*	*Rate of import duty per Maunds (Rs)*	*Value of duty (Rs)*
Kashmir	3200	102,400	102,400	8as	1600
Punjab	3200	102,400	102,400	12as	2400
Total	6,400	204,800	204,800	-	4000

Source: A. Cunningham Op. cit. 17, p. 250

Table 5.4 shows that out of the total 6400 maunds of goat wool of Ladakh in year 1847, total 2400 maunds were produced in Ladakh and 4000 maunds were imported from western Tibet. And the table 5.5 shows the exports of the same wool from Ladakh. Out of total 6400 maunds, only half of it went to Kashmir; the other half was being brought by traders to Rampur and Amritsar in Punjab. It seems clear that the Ladakh and Kashmir monopoly of the goat wool trade established by the Treaty of Tingmosgang had been breached.

In the 18th and 19th centuries British India was the other player who started taking an interest in the trade that went through Ladakh, especially the trade that went to Yarkand and other places in Central Asia. It was not the profit of the trade that British India was interested in, but to gather intelligence from the traders about Russian activities in Central Asia. In the context of Anglo-Russian rivalry, and the increase of Russian activities in Central Asia,[93] British India stationed for the first time a British official at Leh in 1867.[94] Dr. Cayley was the officer on special duty, to monitor the trade.[95] That was ostensibly his brief but actually he was posted there to "monitor the developments across the border."[96] Later in the year 1870 a commercial treaty between the British government and Maharaja Ranbir Singh of Jammu and Kashmir freed the trans-Karakoram trade of all duties, and also appointed two joint commissioners, one each representing the Kashmir Durbar and the British government.[97] Their responsibilities included the maintenance of the road and the settlement of disputes between traders or travelers.[98] Thus originated the post of British Joint Commissioner at Leh who supervised the trade that went to trans-Karakoram. In 1875, Captain E. Molloy, Officiating British Joint-Commissioner, Ladakh, while submitting the trade report for year 1874 to the Government Secretary, Punjab, has reports that:

> "It is worth mentioning that 12 merchants who have been up to last year in the habit of confining their commercial trips to Yarkand to one or other of these

routes, in 1874 for the first time piloted their return consignments of goods over the Karakuram. Several of these men complained to me in strong terms of the duties exacted along these routes, and expressed themselves as much pleased with the free system that prevails on Ladakh trade route."[99]

The British Joint-Commissioner of Ladakh mostly carried out repair work of the trade routes that fell under Ladakh and settled disputes of the traders. In the year 1873, the Joint-Commissioner, Ladakh, carried out repair works to the portions of the trade routes running through the Ladakh district.[100] In the year 1895, Captain S.H. Godfrey, then the British Joint-Commissioner, Ladakh reported that "the treaty of year 1870 with Kashmir securing a free highway to Central Asian traffic has been more satisfactorily observed than in the past year."[101] Thirty years after the treaty, Captain Kenien was the Joint Commissioner of Ladakh and he had visited Rudokh to settle some disputes between the Ladakhi traders and the local Tibetan official.[102] Besides, at the important and difficult places Chowkiders were appointed to take care of the traders and goods.[103]

The exports from Leh in the years 1867 to 1872 show that the trade in goat wool was still being monopolized by Kashmir.

Table 5.6. Export of the Shawl Wool from Leh to Kashmir and Punjab in the Years 1867 to 1872

		Maunds & Seers	*Value (Rs.)*
1.	The total amount of goat wool imported into Leh from Turkestan and Changthang amounted	5,781.34	3,12,842
2.	The total amount of shawl wool exported from Leh to Punjab was	433.30	24,028
3.	The total amount of shawl wool purchased by Kashmir traders at Leh amounted	5,348.03	2,88,814

Source: Janet Rizvi, op. cit. 1, p. 284.

The total figures of the six years from 1867 to 1872 showed that Ladakh's import of wool from Yarkand and Changthang (Western Tibet) amounted to 5782 maunds with the total value rupees three lakhs twelve thusands eight hundred and out of these a total of 5348 maunds of goat wool with the total value of rupees two lakhs eighty eight thusands eight hundred was purchased by Kashmiri traders and only 434 maunds with the total value rupees about twenty four thousands went to Punjab. These figures confirmed the Ladakhi and Kashmiri monopoly of the goat wool trade during the period.

The profit for the respective governments from the goat wool business was not only via the duties the government levied on it, but the kings were also personally involved in the trade. The Kashmir Maharaja profited not only from his government leying duties on the shawl business and on the shawl industry in Srinagar, but was also personally involved in the trade.[104] For many years Ladakhi kings had their own merchants who were involved in the trade.[105]

After a long process, the industries in Srinagar produced fine shawls called 'Pashmina' which was (and still is) famous in many countries. The Pasmina shawls were in great demand in many countries including Britain, Russia and many countries in Europe.[106] By the year 1870, the demand for the Pahmina shawls from Europe declined. One of its causes was attributed to the Franco-Prussian war, which saw a sharp and immediate reduction in the demand for the shawls in France, previously the best European market.[107] On the other hand, the change in women's fashion, and "the development of the jacquard loom, making it possible to produce imitation 'cashmere' shawls for a fraction price of the real thing" resulted in the decline of the shawls' demand in Europe.[108] The export figures of shawls in the year 1886 to 1894 confirmed its decline:

Table 5.7. Exports of Shawl-goods from Kashmir during the Years 1886-7 to 1893-4

Years	*Value in Rupees*
1886-87	12,10,012
1887-88	12,68,500
1888-89	6,07,510
1889-90	7,08,300
1890-91	1,96,250
1891-92	85,250
1892-93	2,19,275
1893-94	22,850

Source: Janet Rizvi, op. cit.1, p. 286.

Table 5.8. Exports of shawls to Central Asia in the years 1867 to 1879

Years	*Value in Rupees*
1867	3414
1868	800
1869	180
1870	24100
1871	44354
1872	5200
1873	2400
1874	6140
1875	4900
1876	10700
1877	650
1878	—
1879	680

Source: Ladakh Trade report cited in K. Warikoo, op. cit.96, p. 66.

The export figures of shawls in Table 5. 8 show the decline of exports from Kashmir. In the year 1886-7 the shawl exports value was around twelve lakhs ten thousands rupees, and the export value declined to twenty-two thousands eight hundred rupees in the year of 1893-4.

The shawls export from Kashmir declined not only to Europe but also to Central Asia. The Ladakh trade reports for the periods from years 1867 to 1879 shows in table 5.8, that in the year 1867 the shawl exports to Central Asia amounted to 3416 rupees, and the highest export was in the year 1871, amounting to about 45000 rupees; then the decline in exports began and in the year 1879, the export amount came down to 680 rupees.

The shawls of Kashmir were used as turbans by Andijanis and Kokandis and were in demand in Kashgar during the rule of Yakub Beg but this demand declined after the year 1877 when the Chinese re-occupied Eastern Turkestan.[109] In the later 19th century, despite the decline of the shawls, demand from Europe and other countries, the trade in shawl wools was kept alive by a continuing demand of shawls from Bengal and some other areas[110]. However, the trade of shawl wools ceased to be an important issue.

Tea

The next article of importance in the trade of Ladakh was tea, which is more or less drunk by everybody in Ladakh. Therefore, a considerable quantity of tea was imported both for home consumption and for export to other areas.[111] The teas of China were chiefly brought from Lhasa, but some of the finer kinds were also imported from Yarkand.[112] Most of the teas that were imported to Ladakh in the 16th century were from Lhasa. The treaty of Tingmosgang in the year 1684 between Ladakh and Tibet has also mentioned the quantity of tea that was to be brought by the 'Chapba' mission from Tibet. According to the treaty, the Tibetan government sent, in return for the 'Lapchak mission',[113] an annual mission with two hundred loads of the Chinese brick tea to Leh, known as 'Chapba' or 'Zungtsong'.[114]

The tea that came from Lhasa was made into 'compressed cubes', known as brick-tea. In Ladakh this brick-tea is known as 'cha-pak' and it is still possible to find cha-pak in the few old local shops at Leh. According to Moorcroft, "the consolidation of the tea in square blocks or bricks renders it easier for transport by reducing its bulk, and obviating the necessity of wooden boxes; whether anything is used to give firmness to these masses, or for any other object, as to improve their flavour or colour is questionable."[115]

Some of those teas were exported to other areas including Kashmir and the Punjab.[116] The green tea was sold "usually at the wholesale price of three rupees per seer, a measure of weight, approximately 0.935 kilograms, and back at less then two rupees, and the retail price nearly double."[117] By the 18th century, the tea from India was available in the market at Leh. Moorcroft saw the Indian tea selling in Leh market when he was there in 1820-22. He mentioned that the green and black teas that were produced in the British dependency of Bashahr and Kulu were selling at Leh.[118] Later the Indian tea became an important article of export to Central Asia, especially to Yarkand. In the year 1889-90, Indian teas worth 37, 500 rupees was imported into Russian Central Asia from Leh.[119] Janet Rizvi writes that:

> "Whereas formerly the only import of tea into Ladakh was from China via Lhasa, in the form of bricks, and latterly also from Yarkand, now tea was being grown in India and for the rest of the duration of the trans-Karakoram trade would form an important article of export to Yarkand."[120]

Besides, the Chinese teas were also imported via Bombay or Calcutta.[121]

Thus, teas were imported from different areas for the local consumption as well as to export. Ladakh trade reports of the last ten years show the following figures of tea imported into Ladakh from different areas:

Table 5.9. The Total Value of Imported Teas into Ladakh from Different Areas

Year	*Indian tea value in (Rs)*	*Chinese tea from Bombay and Calcutta value in (Rs.)*	*Lhasa brick tea value in (Rs.)*
1885-86	67,240	15,280	57,412
1886-87	97,820	31,120	1,24,480
1887-88	1,04,600	nil	89,280
1888-89	9,160	609	1,02,600
1889-90	51,762	900	62,580
1890-91	32,947	1,840	24,460
1891-92	37,220	1,540	46,980
1892-93	39,060	4,865	39,285
1893-94	45,700	8,890	18,447
1894-95	57,280	7,070	45,448

Source: Foreign, Secret. F, Nos. 374-383, September 1895, National Archives, Delhi.

The above figures in table show the steady rise of the Indian tea demand in Ladakh compared to the Chinese and the Lhasa brick tea. In the year 1885-86, the total import value of Indian tea was 67,240 rupees; in the same year the total value of the Chinese tea via Bombay and Culcatta and the Lhasa brick tea were rupees 15280 and 57412 respectively. In the year 1894-95, the total import value of Indian tea was 57280 rupees as compared to the Chinese rupees 7070 in the same year. This is because the Andijani merchants (Russian subjects) were able to trade in Indian tea without hindrance through Chinese territory.[122] There were difficulties in selling Indian tea in Kashgar. This fact was mentioned by Captain S. H. Godfrey, Assistant to the Resident in Kashmir for Leh, while he was reporting on the trade for the year ending 31st March 1894 to Colonel D.W.K. Barr, Resident in Kashmir. He writes that "the special assistant for Chinese Affairs at Kashgar, adverted to the difficulties experienced by British

India traders in dealing in this commodity."[123] Other reasons for the increased demand for Indian tea were because it was cheaper than the Lhasa brick tea.[124] Tea being too expensive for the poor Ladakhi, even they started to prefer to drink the cheaper tea from India.[125] Thus, tea was one of the important commodities of the trade of Ladakh, and it was imported from several places.

Borax and Sulphur

The other articles of trade were borax and sulphur, which were found at Puga[126] where there were numerous hot springs. The borax was ejected in the bed of the stream by the numerous hot springs, and the annual export production of borax from Ladakh was 500 maunds, or 16,000 lb.[127] In addition to the production in Ladakh, sulphur and borax were imported from Changthang. The annual borax imported from Changthang was about 2,500 maunds, or 80,000 lb.[128] The total export of borax from Ladakh was the total local production plus the imports from Changthang, which was 3000 maunds or 96,000 lb and exported at the rate of sixteen seers per rupee,[129] being 6000 rupees. These articles were mainly exported to the Punjab and the Himalayan states.[130] The traders of Lahul, Kulu and Rampur with their flocks and herds and families used to come to Puga and other areas to take borax.[131] They would bring many hundreds of animals laden with rice, tobacco, cotton goods, and many other articles with which they paid for the borax at the rate of about one rupee per maund (80lbs).[132] It was estimated that an average 80 'tol' or set of traders used to come each season to Puga, with about 10,000 animals, and they collected and carried away some 3,500 maunds of impure borax, for which they paid in goods to the value of 3,000 rupees, half of which went to the government, and each 'tol' also paid a tax of one rupee to the government.[133] The goods in exchange for the borax were chiefly taken by the people of Rupshu to Gartok, and these were exchanged for wool and other articles, and thus considerable trade was kept up, and upon it the people in great measure depended for their livelihood.[134] Dr. Cayley, Special Duty at Ladakh in 1871, while commenting about this trade mentioned that "formerly half of the price went to the Kardar of Rupshu, and half to the Zaminders; but since the last two years half of the price has been claimed by the Maharaja."[135] And the sole right of collecting borax in Puga had been sold by the Kashmir government to Wazir Goshaon, of Mahndi, on a lease of three years.[136] Dr. Cayley, Special Duty at Ladakh mentioned in his Ladakh trade report for the year 1870, submitted to the Secretary, government of Punjab writes that:

> "The effect of this change will, I fear, prove ruinous to the Rupshu people, and to the numerous families of our hill districts engaged in the trade whose occupation is suddenly, put a stop to. This year they suffered loss, on account of not being allowed to carry the borax they had collected, no arrangement had been made by Wazir Goshan; but many of the traders had then left empty handed, and the rest lost hundreds of animals from being kept in Ladakh for several months beyond the usual time."[137]

Though these commodities did not constitute an important article of trade in terms of profit making, yet many local people depended on it and it became their livelihood.

Salt

Another article of the trade was salt, which came from the lakes and springs of Changthang. Some of it was consumed in Ladakh and some re-exported to the hill states.[138] Salt was an important article of trade not only for the local consumption but also the local traders; those traders especially from Sham, Rupshu and Zanskar regions used to take salt to different villages of Ladakh, exchange it with barley, apricots etc., and they earned reasonable profits. As Fredric Drew mentioned that:

> "Their profit seems to be in the trade for salt; by acting both as carrier and merchants of this they increase its

> value enough to provide themselves with the luxuries that must come from outside."[139]

A salt of soda, locally known as 'phuli', found in the Nubra and Rubshu areas of Ladakh was (and still is) consumed in Ladakh and was exported to Kashmir and Kulu.[140] It is used for mixing with tea so as to bring out the tea's strength. Even today most of the local people use it for the same purpose. In the year 1874, Captain E. Molloy, British Joint-Commissioner, Ladakh, had mentioned that the import of phuli had never exceed more than 500 rupees, in the year 1873, the figured was 3,400 rupees.[141] If the trade picked up, it was due to the energy of Mr. Johnson, Wazir of Ladakh, who in the summer of 1873 made elaborate arrangements for the collection of phuli.[142] Earlier locals also used it as soap to wash clothes.

Apricots

Dry fruits consisted of apricots and small seedless raisins commonly called currants. These were partly produced in lower Ladakh and partly imported into Ladakh from Baltistan.[143] Tashi Angchok, mentioned that the apricots of Baltistan are bigger in size and superior in quality, and one cannot eat more than seven fresh apricots. Dry apricot was another important article of trade that the local traders especially from the Sham region of Ladakh exchanged with various goods like barley. Dry apricot was also one of the export products of Ladakh. It was exported to many countries including Tibet and India.[144] Moorcroft himself witnessed this trade when he was in Ladakh, and he mentioned:

> "The greater part of the fruit is dried in the sun, in which state it remains good for many years, and is stored for some consumption, or exported to Lhasa and Tartary. About six hundred maunds annually exported, and ten or twelve pounds are sold for about a rupee."[145]

In year 1870 a total of 490 maunds of dried apricots and 50 maunds of currants were exported to Lhasa and Shimla.[146] Besides fruits, oil was also extracted from apricot kernels.

Locals used the oil for cooking, as hair and body oil and for oil lamps.

Carpets and Namdas

Carpets were imported into Ladakh from Central Asia, and exported from Leh to different countries including Tibet.[147] Namdas were also imported from Central Asia into Kashmir, where they were dyed, worked and sold to natives and visitors.[148] Ladakh trade report for the last nine years show the following value of Carpets and Namdas.

Table 5.10. Total Imports Value of Carpets and Namdas for the Years 1886-87-1894-95

Year	*Value of Carpets in Rupees*	*Value of Namdas in Rupees*
1886-87	28,960	19,736
1887-88	15,525	39,798
1888-89	9,800	34,320
1889-90	17,950	55,310
1890-91	8,600	434,276
1891-92	1,395	15,616
1892-93	4,815	24,688
1893-94	3,075	20,505
1894-95	5,070	29,748

Source: Foreign Department, Secret. F. Branch, Nos. 49-53, Consultation Dec. 1891, also see Foreign, Secret. F, Nos. 374-383, Sept. 1895, National Archives, Delhi.

The above table shows the total value of carpets in the year 1886-87 was rupees 28960, and in the same year the total value of namdas was 19736 rupees. And in the year 1894-95 the total value of carpets was 5070 where as the total value of namdas was 29748 rupees. The increase in the value of namdas was due to the higher prices realized in Leh bazaar, with the value of the ordinary white namdas having risen appreciably.[149] The silk Khutan carpets were also imported from Central Asia.[150]

Precious Metals

Precious metals like gold and silver were imported from Central Asia into Leh and then exported to different areas.[151] The gold came in the form of gold dust, nodules, bars and coins.[152] Ladakh trade reports from the year 1886 to 1894 showed the increase of the total import value of gold and silver.

Table. 5.11. Total Value of Gold and Silver from the Years 1886-1894

Year	*Value of Gold in Rupees*	*Value of silver in Rupees*
1886-87	66,719	2,35,787
1887-88	2,00,286	1,61,278
1888-89	82,466	68,745
1889-90	76,116	1,73,250
1890-91	1,51,300	1,86,250
1891-92	90,796	2,78,648
1892-93	2,49,114	2,96,420
1893-94	2,66,686	2,92,158

Sources: Foreign Department, Secret. F Branch, Nos. 49-53, Consultation Dec. 1891, also see Foreign, Secret. F, Nos. 425-430, September 1893, National Archives, Delhi.

The total import value of gold at Leh in the year 1886-87 was about sixty-six thousand seven hundred rupees and increased to two lakhs and sixty-six thousand six hundred and eight six rupees in the year 1893-94. The total value of silver increased from two lakhs thirty-five thousand seven hundred eight seven rupees in the year 1886-87 to two lakhs ninety-two thousand one hundred fifty eight rupees in the year 1893-94. "The increase might have been due to the gold washing at Khotan that seems to have been corroborated from Kashgar."[153] The decline noticeable in the year 1891-92 was said to have had its origin in the rise of the profit from silver at that time, and in that year gold was brought to Leh and taken back again untouched.[154]

Silk

This was one of the chief articles manufactured in Yarkand and imported into Leh, and from there exported to India.[155] Captain E. Molloy, Officiating British Joint-Commissioner, Ladakh, mentioned in his trade report in the year 1874 that traders who had brought large quantities of silk in year 1873 from Yarkand had found it difficult to turn their business into a profitable outcome.[156]

Spices

Spices were imported from India into Ladakh and then exported to Central Asia. This article was regarded as one of the most important imports to Central Asia, as that area depended on India entirely for the supply of spices.[157] The Ladakh trade report from 1886-87 to 1894-95 shows a slight decrease in the total value at Leh.

Table. 5.12. Ladakh trade report of spices from years 1886-87 to 1894-95

Year	*Value in Rupees*
1886-87	30,924
1887-88	25,887
1888-89	45,680
1889-90	61,630
1890-91	29,280
1891-92	40,810
1892-93	28,787
1893-94	26,005
1894-95	35,805

Source: Foreign Department, Secret. F Branch, Nos. 49-53, Consultation Dec. 1891.

Also see Foreign, Secret. F, Nos. 374-383, Sept. 1895, National Archives, Delhi.

The above table shows the total value of trade in spices during the years 1886-87 to 1894-95. The total value in the year 1886-87 was 30924 rupees, declined to rupees 26005 rupees in the year 1893-94 and the total value was increased to 35805 rupees in the year 1894-95. The reason for decline in its trade in the year 1892-93 to 1893-94 were that the spices were over-imported early in the year 1892, and good prices were not then realized in the Yarkand market.[158]

Precious Stones

Precious stones like Turquoise and Coral were imported into Ladakh; the former was mostly imported from Lhasa and the latter from India, and then both were exported to other areas including Central Asia.[159] Turquoises also reached Yarkand from Nisharpūr via Bokhara.[160] These stones were exported to Lhasa also because it was superior than the Lhasa gem and earned a better profit.[161] In his Ladakh trade report for 1874, Captain E. Molloy, British-Joint Commissioner, Ladakh reports that:

> "A pilgrim from Yarkand turned a rupee to very good account a few years ago at the holy shrine by an investment in turquoises. He purchased Rs. 700 worth at Macca, which on his return here he sold for Rs. 2000 to a merchant from Lhasa, realizing a profit thereby which must have enabled him to perform his pilgrimage at an exceedingly small cost for himself."[162]

Ladakh itself used a good deal of both Turquoises and Corals. All the Ladakhi women wear a headdress called 'pairak' made up of turquoises and corals. H. S. Branes, British Resident in Kashmir mentioned that "the Ladakhi women investing their earnings in ornaments of turquoises and corals in the same way that natives of India invest their savings in bracelets and anklets of precious metals, with the difference that among the Buddhists spare money was almost invariably spent upon the headdress (pairak), which all the women of Ladakh wear, and nothing on bangles or anklets."[163] Ladakh trade report from 1884-85 to 1893-94 shows the following value of Turquoise and Coral:

Table 5.13. Total Value of Turquoise and Coral in the Year 1884-85-1893-94

Year	*Value in Rupees*
1884-85	30,769
1885-86	23,140
1886-87	3,681
1887-88	6,802
1888-89	11,232
1889-90	53,167
1890-91	48,532
1891-92	56,286
1892-93	56,288
1893-94	1,47,030

Sources: Foreign Department, Secret. F Branch, Nos. 613-619, Consultation July 1894, National Archives, Delhi.

The total imported value of these two articles in the year 1884-85 was 30769 rupees, declined to 3681 rupees in the year 1886-87 and in the year 1893-94 increased to 147030 rupees. The reason was due to the rise in price in the Yarkand market.[164] There was also rise in the demand for turquoises and coral for ornamental purposes in Yarkand and Tibet.[165] A considerable quantity was also said to be in demand in Russian Central Asian territory in the year 1894, where the fashion of wearing coral appeared to have spread.[166]

Yak Tail (Chowris), Kidakh and Incenses

Yak's tails were imported from the Tibetan area and Yarkand into Ladakh, and from there exported to Kashmir.[167] During the year 1869, a total of 803 maunds of yak tails were imported from Yarkand at the rate of 1-8 rupees at Leh and the total value at Leh was 905 rupees.[168] Some of the other articles that were imported into Ladakh from Tibet were Kidakh[169] and incenses, which are mostly consumed in Ladakh. In the year 1869, a total of 2000 maunds of Kidakh were imported into Ladakh from Tibet at the rate of 8 annas per 'than'(a roll), and the total value at Leh was 1,000 rupees.[170] In the same year, 4 boxes of incenses were imported from Tibet into Leh, and the total value at Leh was 200 rupees.[171]

Drugs and Medicines

Charas was imported from Central Asia into Ladakh and then exported to Indian markets.[172] In the Ladakh trade report in the year 1872, J. E. T. Aitchison, British Joint-Commissioner, Ladakh, mentioned that the Punjab markets had become gradually glutted with a bad quality of Charas, and the prices on the whole had fallen, and the traders were not ready to invest.[173] It had fallen to 53,425 rupees in the year 1872 from 74,320 rupees in the year 1871. In the year 1870, its value was 1,29,312 rupees.[174] Ladakh trade report from the years 1888-89 to 1892-93 shows the following figures:

Table 5.14. Total Value of Charas in the Years 1888-89-1892-93

Year	*Total value in Rupees*
1888-89	1,76,250
1889-90	2,16,400
1890-91	2,19,000
1891-92	2,30,385
1892-93	1,91,565

Source: Foreign, Secret. F, Nos. 425-430, September 1893, National Archives, Delhi.

The above figures show the total value of charas in the year 1888-89 was 1,76,250 rupees. During the year the total 3,525 maunds were imported at the rate of 50 rupees per maund.[175] In the year 1889-90 about 2,164 maunds were imported but it was of better quality than the previous year and sold at Leh at the rate of 100 rupees per maund, and valued at 2,16,400 rupees.[176] In the year 1893, Captain S. H. Godfrey, British Joint-Commissioner mentioned that the charas trade between Leh and India was in the hands of Punjabis, who were making good profits.[177] In the year 1889-90, charas were sold in Punjab for about 325 rupees per 'pai,' i.e. about 220 rupees per maund.[178]

Horses

Horses were imported from Central Asia to India.[179] In the year 1871, 111 horses were imported for the total value of 16,650 rupees, which comes at the rate of 150 rupees per horses.[180] In the year 1872 the import value of horses increased to 20,400 rupees. And in the year 1873 this valued further increased to 27, 500 rupees and were imported 204 horses. Almost all of them were taken to Punjub and were used for the carriage of good.[181]

Clothing stuffs, brocade and satins

The above articles were imported from India to Ladakh and exported to Central Asia.[182] In the year 1873, the total value of import was 55,060 rupees, showing an increase of 21,160 rupees over the preceding year.[183]

Silk stuffs and brocade were also imported from India and the total import value in the year 1873 was 55,060 rupees, and in the year 1874 it increased to 75, 265 rupees.[184]

Sugar

This article was imported from India through Ladakh to Central Asia.[185] A good deal of sugar was also imported into Central Asia from Russia, but Indian sugar was, however, said to be preferred to that from Russia.[186] Ladakh Trade Report from the year 1870-71 to 1874-75 shows the following figures of import value:

Table 5.15. Import Value of Sugar for the Last Five Years

Year	*Total value in rupees*
1870-71	16,164
1871-72	13,024
1872-73	14,464
1873-74	14,911
1874-75	18,542

Source: Foreign, Political. A, 21-24, September 1875, National Archives Delhi

The total value for the first four years was more or less the same, and in the year 1874-75 it increased by more than three thousand rupees.

Dyed Goat Skins (Laki)

The article under this head was imported from India into Ladakh and then exported to other areas including Central Asia. These were extensively used for foot leather, and it was said to be a safe and paying article of commerce.[187] It was manufactured at Nurpur, in the Punjab, but a good many of them were also prepared in Kashmir.[188]

Saffron

This article was imported from Kashmir into Ladakh and then exported to Lhasa. In the year 1873 the total import value was 3,543 rupees and next year, it increased to 7,408 rupees.[189] The chief market of saffron was in Lhasa, where the lamas in their religious ceremonies extensively utilized it as a kind of incense.[190] It was also used as a condiment with food by the upper classes.[191]

Dyeing Materials

Indigo was imported from India and sent to Central Asia through Ladakh. The total imported value of indigo in the year 1891-92 was 33,885 rupees, and in the year 1892-93 the value decreased to 8,865 rupees.[192] A decrease in its production at Multan was said to be the only cause of the decline in its imports.[193]

Coarse Clothes (Garha and Chakman)

Garha and Chakman were coarse clothes brought moderately in Ladakh and a small quantity of it went to Baltistan.[194] But the chief market was in Lhasa, where it was extensively used as a material for tents.[195]

Cotton Goods from India

Cotton piece goods were imported from India into Leh and then exported to Central Asia.[196] These piece goods in

1870s formed the largest items in the trade between India and Central Asia.[197] Ladakh trade reports for the ten years from the years 1884 to 1893-94 show the following figures:

Table 5.16. Total Value of Cotton Piece Goods for the Last Ten Years

Years	*Total value in rupees*
1884	2,27,173
1885	1,09,722
1886-87	1,75,897
1887-88	3,93,120
1888-89	4,39,760
1889-90	3,19,480
1890-91	3,01,280
1891-92	3,80,820
1892-93	3,88.620
1893-94	5,29,920

Source: Foreign, Secret. F, 613-619, July 1894, National Archives Delhi.

Bazazi (cotton piece good) were also imported from India to Ladakh and taken to different areas including Central Asia.[198] The total value import in the year 1873 was about two lakh and ninety thousand rupees.[199] Figures in the above table show a steady increased of the total value of cotton piece goods. In the year 1884 the total was rupees 2,27,173, increased to rupees 3,19,480 in the year 1889-90 and in the year 1893-94 was 5,29,920 rupees. Besides all the above articles and goods, there were many more articles exchanged among different countries and regions through Ladakh. For example, from Central Asia a small quantity Yambo silver, boots, Russian leather, velvets, Jade Stone, Chinese Silver, Chinese Knives, Soap, from Kashmir embroidered cloth, Combs, Oil, Swords/guns, Shoes, Tawer (silk), chintzes, copper tinned vessels, tea-pots, spoons, turmeric, ginger, black pepper and honey, from Skardo Iron and Butter, from Punjab rice, Iron, Combs and vessels from Kulu and from Changthang paper and coarse cloths.[200]

All the commodities were carried on the backs of a variety of animals including horses, mules, yaks, dzos, donkeys, sheep and occasionally goats and camels. The Central Asian traders used camels. The present double hump camels found in the Nubra valley in Ladakh is believed to be the remains of the two-humped Bactrian breed used for carrying goods during the old caravan trade between Ladakh and Central Asia. In the year 1871, Dr. Calley, Special Duty at Leh mentioned that many camels had arrived from Yarkand heavily laden, and no loss occurred on the road.[201] Camels were of "the two-humped Bactrian breed, such as found in the Pamir steppes and mountain districts of Central Asia."[202] They were very powerful, and able to bear the most extreme cold.[203] Dr. Calley in his trade report submitted to the Secretary to the Government of Punjab in the same year had writes that "if camels should come into general use, the expense and difficulties of the journey to Yarkand would be greatly lessened."[204] Frederic Drew saw the use of sheep and goats to carry loads when he reached the Rupshu valley of Ladakh, and he mentioned that:

> "the sheep is of a large kind; it is here made use for carrying loads; the salt from the Lake is carried out of and grain is brought into the country on the back of sheep. The larger of the two kinds of goat kept here is made use of in just the same way."[205]

The average weight carried by a sheep was 24 lbs; the stronger animals could carry loads up to 32 lbs.[206] Thus, the trade through Ladakh not only involved merchants but also a variety of animals. The following figures show the number of merchants and animals involved with the trade through Ladakh in 1873:

The most number of animals used in the trade of Ladakh in the year 1873 were horses. Out of 4,520 horses, 159 were ridden horses, 288 were for sale and the rest laden with goods.[207] Yaks were the animals least used during the year and the number of attendants was three times more than the merchants. In the year 1873, out of the total (239) merchants engaged in trade, 34 percent (82) was on the central Asian routes followed by 31 percent (76) on the Kashmir routes.

Table 5.17. Number of Men and Cattle Composing the Caravan in the Year 1873 at Ladakh

Route	*Merchants*	*Attendants*	*Horses, Laden, sale and Ridden*	*Laden Yaks and Bullocks*	*Laden Donkeys*	*Laden sheep and Goats*
Kulu	46	226	645	—	36	948
Rampur	9	16	28	—	66	—
Kashmir	76	245	1,732	36	66	—
Tibet	26	136	1,209	146	182	—
Turkistan	82	302	906	—	2	—
Total	239	925	4,520	182	352	948

Source: Trade Report For 1873, Foreign, Political. A, 214-216, July 1874, National Archives Delhi.

Thus, traders came to Ladakh from different areas with their goods and exchanged them with goods from other areas. Several merchants were also taking their goods as far south as Calcutta and Bombay and as far north as Central Asia.[208] The following two tables no. 5.18 and 5.19 show the increase of the total imports and exports value at Leh in the years 1863 to 1872-73 and in the years 1885-86 to 1894-95.

Table 5.18. Total value of trade in Ladakh for the years 1863-64 to 1872-73

Years	*Value in Rupees*
1863	2,36,040
1864-66	1,00,000 (about)
1866-67	5,54,945
1867-68	10,38,401
1868-69	12,91,537
1869-70	15,48,000
1870-71	12,41,177
1871-72	15,84,800
1872-73	17,76,729

Source: Foreign, Pol. A, 214-216, July 1874, National Archives, Delhi.

Table 5.19. Total Value of Trade in Ladakh for the Years 1885-86 to 1894-95

Year	*Imports (Rs.)*	*Exports (Rs.)*	*Total value (Rs.)*
1885-86	18,31,501	15,69,321	34,00,822
1886-87	16,52,413	12,32,229	28,84,642
1887-88	17,16,245	17,12,328	34,28,573
1888-89	13,53,845	12,12,030	25,65,875
1889-90	16,00,580	15,13,626	31,14,206
1890-91	15,25,483	14,40,906	29,66,389
1891-92	15,65,278	14,47,840	30,13,118
1892-93	17,95,141	15,91,544	33,86,685
1893-94	21,54,252	18,37,375	39,91,627
1894-95	31,65,218	28,50,102	60,15,321

Source: Foreign, Secret. F, 374-383, September 1895, National Archives Delhi.

The total trade value of Ladakh increased from about two lakhs thirty six thousand rupees in 1863 to about seventeen lakhs seventy-six thousands in the year 1872-73. Ten years later, in the year 1885-86, it increased to about thirty-four lakhs eight hundred and in the year 1894-95, it further increased to about sixty lakhs fifteen thousand rupees. There were several factors that contributed towards this improvement. The most important was the introduction of the 'free highway' to Central Asian traffic. The treaty of 1870 abolished the transit duty in Kashmir territory.[209] H. S. Barnes, British Resident in Kashmir in July 1895 reports that "the condition of the treaty of 1870 with Kashmir securing a 'free highway' to central Asian traffic has been more satisfactorily observed than in past years."[210] Besides, the roads and communication had been improved. Bridges had been constructed at several places.[211] Postal services were set up between Leh, Ladakh and Central Asia and there were nineteen stages from Leh to Shadulla[212], and two people were posted at each stage.[213] The following table shows the number of postal stages and two men posted on each stage and the total expenditure between Leh and Yarkand.

Table 5.20. Costs of Postal expenses from Leh, Ladakh to Shadulla

No. of Stages	*Name of stages*	*No. men*	*Rate Rs.*	*Pay of men per month*		
				Rs.	*a.*	*p.*
1.	Polu	2	5	10	–	–
2.	Khardong	2	5	10	–	–
3.	Satti	2	5	10	–	–
4.	Tagar	2	5	10	–	–
5.	Panamic	2	5	10	–	–
6.	Chaugloog	2	5	10	–	–
7.	Tootialak	2	5	10	–	–
8.	Surthang	2	5	10	–	–
9.	Sasair	2	5	10	–	–
10.	Moorgee	2	5	10	–	–
11.	Boorsa	2	5	10	–	–
12.	Kazilongar	2	5	10	–	–
13.	Daolatbeg	2	5	10	–	–
14.	Bransu	2	5	10	–	–
15.	Wahab Jigla	2	5	10	–	–
16.	Aktagh	2	5	10	–	–
17.	Chibra	2	5	10	–	–
18.	Suket	2	5	10	–	–
19.	Shadulla	2	5	10	–	–
Total Cost	Per mensem	–	–	190	0	0

Source: Foreign, Political. A, 390-392, September 1874, National Archives Delhi.

So, a total number of thirty-eight men with a pay at the rate of five rupees each per month, totaling rupees 190, maintained postal communication between Ladakh and Yarkand. Thus Leh, because of its favorable situation became an annual meeting place where goods from all quarters were bartered as at a fair.[214] Trade fairs were taken place at Shey and Leh in Ladakh. Traders got a good price at the Leh market. Trade report of Ladakh in the year 1874 shows the comparative prices at Yarkand, Leh and Amritsar markets.

Table 5.21. Price of the Different Articles at Yarkand, Leh and Amritsar

Sl.No.	*Articles*	*Yarkand Value in (Rs.)*	*Leh Value in (Rs.)*	*Amritsar Value in (Rs.)*
1.	Long–cloth	14	13	7
2.	Spices per maund	62	40	22
3.	Sugar per maund	50	30	12
4.	Otter skins each	7	6	4
5.	Indogo	144	110	75

Source: Foreign, Political. A, 21-24, September 1875, National Archives, Delhi.

To know the proportionate difference between those rates, one has to take the cost of the carriage into consideration. This for one horse-load may be approximately put down at rupees 20 to 25 from Punjab to Leh, and rupees 40 to 45 from Leh to Yarkand, from which it is manifest that it costs almost twice as much to take a load of goods from Ladakh to Yarkand as it does to convey one from the Punjab to Ladakh, so as a matter of fact Leh prices were more remunerated than those of Yarkand.

The average profit earned by traders in the year 1874-75 at Leh was around 20 to 25 percent. For instance in the year 1874, tea, indigo, spices and goat skins yielded a profit of 25 percent each, and sugar and piece-goods yielded a profit of 20 percent each.[215] The rates of profits as given above do not represent so much money actually realized but rather the amount may fairly be anticipated to be realized as current prices stood. A trader, for instance, came to Leh with a consignment of piece goods, in exchange for which, say, he made a bargain for charas and silk. But this business is only half over, and he still had to get rid of the silk and charas, which of course depended on the state of the Indian market as regard to those goods. Then again, in balancing again, consideration must be taken of the expense of carriage, risk of loss or damage on the road, mortality of horses etc., and all those contingencies were much increased in the case of a trader's travel being prolonged to Central Asia.

As far as benefits for locals were concerned, despite the fact that Ladakh consumed little and produced less to promote and develop commerce, yet locals benefited from the trade by providing various services like supply of animals and fodders, etc. For instance, the men of Nurba reaped an annual harvest by sending their yaks with provisions across the Sasser pass to meet the traders, who paid them in Yarkand goods.[216]

Religious and Trade Missions

As mentioned in the beginning of this chapter the relation between Tibet and Ladakh was an old one as early as the 7th century, the Tibetan nomads of Changthang and the Dards and the Mons could have had contacts. But with the establishment of the first Ladakhi dynasty of Tibetan origin in the 10th century, religious and commercial relationships between them were well established. Monks from Ladakh started to go to the different monasteries in Tibet for their higher monastic education. Not only monks, ordinary people also travelled to the great pilgrimage sites of Tibet. Pilgrims to sacred places in Tibet were not only Buddhists, but many Hindus also visited to the sacred Mansarowar Lake at the holy mountain of Kailash.[217] The British Joint-Commissioner at Ladakh reports that:

> "Every autumn, a large fair is held at Gartok or Gai and the hill people from all sides assemble and purchase pashm, sheep wool, tea, and ponies from all parts of Great Tibet. The Hindus, Buddhist also flock as pilgrims to the sacred Mansarowar Lake, or 'Man Talao' the traditional sources of the four great rivers of India, and the holy mountain of Kailash or Gangri, the most lofty peak of the great trans-Indus range of mountains. Every six-year is especially observed as a great festival, and thousands of devotees collected

from all quarters and ascended the sides of the mountain to do homage at the Hindu and Buddhist shrines and bathe in the holy waters of the Lake. One of these high festivals was held in 1870 and the road leading to Rupshu and Gartok were crowded with people and traders with their families and flocks and herds, Lamas, Brahmins and beggars, all progressing towards the holy Man Talao."[218]

The total distance from Leh to the base camp for Kailash Mansarovar is about 625 kilometers.[219] The road between Leh and Damchok[220] can open throughout the year. It is reported that on the other side of the border the Tibetan towns of Tashigong and Gorzong are located 35 and 150 kilometers away from Damchok.[221] This can be the shortest route of pilgrimage to Mansarovar for Indian devotees.

The most important trade mission between Ladakh and Tibet were the Lapchak and Chapa missions, which were set up in 1684 as a result of the treaty of Tingmosgang.[222] The annual trade caravan from Lhasa to Ladakh was known as Zhung-tsong (government mission) also known as Chapa (tea man) consisting of two hundred loads of tea, and it was to cross the frontier at Demchok only.[223] The Chronicle of Ladakh mentioned that if the government fails to come every year then the stipulations of the treaty should no longer be binding; as it pointed out:

> "Pod nas gzyung Tsong khal ma ney bgyai cha tang chas yong Gry tang/ cha pak du jee di Ladags ma thogs/gdzan mtha la gdong mi chog/ gzyung-tsong lo tar ma yong chey/ Ngar gi chad don la mi gnas pa chas."[224]

Translation: From Tibet the government traders shall come with two hundred loads of tea and the rectangular brick-tea will brought only to Ladakh. Should the Zhung-tsong trader fail to come annually, then the agreement[225] shall no longer be binding.

The head of the Chapa mission was the Dalai Lama's personal trader to Ladakh, and was always a Tibetan official, either lay or monastic, of some importance.[226] The Chapa mission left Lhasa each June and arrived at Leh in December.[227] It remained in Leh the whole winter months until the following April, when it left Leh for Lhasa, taking with it dry apricots, saffron and sugar, etc.[228]

In return of the Chapa mission, Ladakh sent a mission known as Lapchak.[229] The Lapchak mission went from Leh to Lhasa every three years, with offerings to Tibet for the Smon-lam and for the blessing of the Dalai Lama.[230] According to Captain H. Ramsay, the missions start from Leh in every September and arrived in Lhasa in January or February.[231] The triennial mission would bring a specific amount of presents to the Bla-bran (treasury) in Lhasa and an unspecific amount of presents to other Lamas. The Chronicle of Ladakh mentioned the following presents:

> "Ladags nas pod la rt'en tang chas lo gsum bar du tang gos/ Bla khag sogs la rgyas Sdyos nga's pa ma't kyang/ Bla-bran chag mdz'd la/ ser thur zo chu/(C MS.) thur zo dow (tola chu); dri sran chu/(gyor gyum) Hor Z'og byb yogdryg/ bab sta byb chig phyol nas."[232]

The translation means: The mission from Ladakh should send presents to Tibet every three years. The quantity of the presents to ordinary Lamas is not fixed but the Bla-bran treasury in Lhasa shall be given gold, quantity is not known; ten sran (ounces) of perfumes (saffron); six rolls of Hor (Moghul) cloth and one roll of soft cotton cloth.

A prominent Ladakhi headed the Lapchak mission and was accompanied by a leading Ladakhi Muslem (Arghun) merchant of that class which had by a long tradition been permitted to trade in Tibet.[233] The Lapchak mission while in Tibetan territories received all facilities available including free transport (ula), and the Chapa mission while in Ladakh also got the same facilities.[234]

The two missions were the most important manifestation of the close relationship between Ladakh and Tibet. It gave rise to a number of smaller missions, and the feudatories of the king of Ladakh and several of the larger monasteries both from Ladakh and Tibet used to send lesser missions. The Raja of Stok usually sent annual trading missions to Gartok.[235] Certain Muslim traders possessed special privileges to trade in Chinese brick-tea between Ladakh and Lhasa.[236] In this respect, the history of Rangdu family recounted by Abdul Wahid Rangdu in his *Caravane tibetaine* is exemplary.[237] 'The first to settle in Ladakh was a religious man, Sheikh Asad'[238]. His son, Faruq became a caravan merchant, maintained close tie with the Ladakhi kings and he received land in the village of Stok, in Leh.[239] His eldest son settled in Leh. The well respected and high ranking Rangdu family owned handsome properties and important warehouses in several places.[240] Ghulam Muhammad had a house and family both at Leh and Lhasa.[241] In recognition of their services, the Rangdu family has received several titles from both the Maharaja's court and the British resident in Srinagar[242].

The Governors of Gartok, the Kharpons, as well as the Tibetan commander of the fort at Rudok used to come to Leh annually to trade.[243] Several of the larger Buddhist monasteries in Ladakh periodically sent combined religious and trading missions to Lhasa, and at about ten-year intervals a similar mission came to Leh from the great Tashi-lhunpo monastery.[244] For instance, during the lifetime of sTag-tsan-raspa (1574-1651)[245], he sent several religious missions to many monasteries in Tibet. Following were some of them:

> "In 1626, sTag-tsan-raspa sent a mission to the Brug-c'en incarnate and to the monastery of rNam-rgyal-thun-po and Ri-bo-rtse-brgyad (on the Manasarovar).
>
> In 1628, he sent a mission to the Brug-c'en and bDe-c'en-c'os-k'or.
>
> In 1629, he sent another mission to Brug-c'en, the Zva-dmar-pa incarnate and bDe-c'en-c'os-k'or.
>
> In 1630, he sent again a mission to Brug-c'en. The mission was headed by the king's brother Dzam-gling-graps-pa."[246]

Each of these missions carried several hundreds of ounces of gold, many more of silver, besides turquoises and shawls.[247]

Dr. Cayley, British Special Duty at Ladakh mentioned in 1871 that there were a dozen families in Ladakh who had the privilege of going as traders to Changthang and Lhasa.[248] He also mentioned that the old arrangements where still in force, that a trade mission of the Lhasa government came to Ladakh and a return trade mission from Ladakh proceeded to Lhasa, and they were allowed free carriage in their respective areas.[249] There are still traders in Ladakh who have been part of the great trade of Ladakh. Besides, there are also many monks who have been to Tibet with traders for their higher monastic education.

Conclusion

Thus, Ladakh had a long trade relation with her neighbours. The effects of the trade relationships, which continued for hundreds of years between Ladakh and Buddhist Tibet, were felt in nearly every Ladakhi village. From small local traders like Tashi Angchok to the bigger merchants and the governments caravans have greatly profit from this trade. For example, the total value of trade at Leh was more than sixty lakhs of rupees in the year 1894-95. Besides, such extensive and long period of active trade and pilgrimage also helped in developing a sustain ties between Ladakh and Buddhist Tibet. The trading Caravans of Asia's highlands gradually declined in importance, disappearing altogether after the Chinese communist rise to power in China and the subsequent occupation of Tibet when the borders were closed.

Ladakhis hope for the restoration of normal border trading and cultural relations with Tibet. The revival of border trade will not only benefit business in the region but there is also a great prospect of pilgrimage and tourism.

REFERENCES

1. Janet Rizvi, Trans-Himalayan Caravans, Merchant Princes and Peasant Traders in Ladakh (New Delhi: Oxford University Press, 1999), p. 3.
2. W. Moorcroft and George Trebeck, Travels in the Himalayan Provinces on Hindustan and Punjab; in Ladakh and Kashmir; in

Pashawar, Kabul, Kunduz and Bokhara, from 1819-182, Vol. 1 (New Delhi: Sagar Publications, 1971), p. 346.

3. Foreign Department, Political. A. Branch, Nos. 126-130, Consultation May 1872.
4. A. H. Francke. Ladakh: The Mysterious Land: A History of Western Tibet (London: n/a, 1907, reprinted, New Delhi: Cosmo Publication, 1978), p. 27.
5. Luciano Petech, The Kingdom of Ladakh, C. 950-1842 A.D (Roma: Istituto Italiano Per IL Medio Ed Estremo Orient, 1977), p. 13.
6. *Ibid.*, p. 32.
7. A. H. Francke, Antiquities of Indian Tibet, The Chronicles of Ladakh and Minor Chronicles, Texts Translation, with Notes and Maps, Part II (New Delhi: Chand and Co., 1926), p. 38.
8. *Ibid.*, p. 38.
9. W. Moorcroft, W and George Trebeck, op. cit. 2, p. xxxvi.
10. *Ibid.*, pp. 319-320.
11. *Ibid.*, p. 346.
12. Luciano Petech, op. cit. 5, pp. 50-51.
13. *Ibid.*, pp. 64-65.
14. *Ibid.*, p. 65.
15. C. L, Datta, Ladakh and Western Himalayan Politics, 1819-1948 (New Delhi: Munshiram Manoharlal Publishers Pvt. Ltd. 1973), p. 19.
16. Frederic Drew The Northern Barrier of India (Jammu: Light and Life Publishers, 1971), p. 287.
17. A. Cunningham, Ladakh, Physical, Statistical and Historical (London: W.H. Allen, 1854 Reprinted, New Delhi: Sagar Publication, 1970), p. 238.
18. Frederic Drew, op, cit. 16, p. 287.
19. Janet Rizvi, op. cit. 1, p. 39.
20. A monk of Thiksay monastery in Ladakh.
21. Janet Rizvi, op. cit. 1, p. 39.
22. *Ibid.*, p. 39.
23. A. Cunningham, op. cit. 17, p. 146.
24. *Ibid.*, p 149.
25. *Ibid.*, p. 148.

26. C. L. Datta, op. cit. 15, p. 13.
27. Reports of Ladakh Routes, Foreign Department, Political. A. Branch, Nos. 215-218, Consultation August 1873.
28. Janet Rizvi, op. cit. 1, p. 28.
29. C. L, Datta, op. cit. 15, p. 10.
30. A. Cunningham, op. cit.17, p. 151.
31. C. L, Datta, op cit.15, p. 11.
32. A. Cunningham, op cit. 17, p. 152.
33. *Ibid.*, p. 152.
34. Trade report, Ladakh, Foreign Department, Political. A. Branch, Nos. 214-216, Consultation July 1874.
35. Foreign Department, Political. A. Branch, Nos. 214-216, Consultation July 1874.
36. A. Cunningham, op. cit. 17, p. 153.
37. *Ibid.*, p. 162.
38. C. L, Datta, op. cit. 15, p. 11. Also see A. Cunningham, op. cit. 17. p. 162.
39. Fredrick Drew, op. cit 16, p.239.
40. C. L, Datta, op. cit. 15, p. 12.
41. A. Cunningham, op. cit. 17, p. 160.
42. Foreign Department, Secret. F. Branch, Nos. 613-619, Consultation July 1894.
43. Janet Rizvi, op. cit. 1, p. 28.
44. Foreign Department, Secret. F. Branch, Nos. 613-619, Consultation July 1894. Also see Janet Rizvi, op. cit. 1, p. 28.
45. Reports on trade routes through Ladakh, Foreign Department, Political. A. Branch, Nos. 126-130, Consultation May 1872.
46. *Ibid.*, P. 4.
47. *Ibid.*, P. 4.
48. Foreign Department, Political. A. Branch, Nos. 126-130, Consultation May 1872.
49. Foreign Department, Political. A. Branch, Nos. 214-216, Consultation July 1874.
50. Trade report, Ladakh, Political. A. Branch, Nos. 214-216, Consultation July 1874.

51. R. B Shaw, British Joint-Commissioner, Ladakh to the Secretary to Govt., Punjab, Foreign Department, Political. A. Branch, Nos. 214-216, Consultation July 1874.
52. C. L, Datta, op. cit. 15, p. 12.
53. Ladakh Trade Report for 1874, Foreign Department, Political. A. Branch, Nos. 21-24, Consultation September 1875.
54. Janet Rizvi, op cit. 1, p. 33.
55. *Ibid.*, p. 33.
56. Sven Hedin, Trans-Himalaya, Discoveries and Adventures in Tibet, Volume I (London: Macmillan And Co; Limited, 1909), pp. 64-70.
57. Janet Rizvi, op cit. 1, p. 33.
58. Foreign Department, Political. A. Branch, Nos. 21-24, Consultation September 1875.
59. Foreign Department, Political. A. Branch, Nos. 214-216, Consultation July 1874.
60. Trade Report, Ladakh, 1873. Foreign Department, Political. A. Branch, Nos. 214-216, Consultation July 1874.
61. Janet Rizvi, op. cit. 1, p. 50.
62. Alastair Lamb, Britain and Chinese Central Asia: The Road to Lhasa 1767 to 1905 (London: Routledge & Kegan Paul, 1960), p. 65.
63. A. Cunningham, op. cit. 17, p. 239.
64. Foreign Department, Political. A. Branch, Nos. 21-24, Consultation September 1875.
65. W. Moorcroft and George Trebeck, op cit. 2, pp. 346-47.
66. Foreign Department, Political. A. Branch, Nos. 21-24, Consultation September 1875.
67. Ladakh Trade Report For 1874, Foreign Department, Political. A. Branch, Nos. 21-24, Consultation September 1875.
68. *Ibid.*, p. 4.
69. About 170 kilometers Southeast of Leh.
70. Foreign Department, Political. A. Branch, Nos. 21-24, Consultation September 1875.
71. Ladakh Trade Report For 1874, Foreign Department, Political. A. Branch, Nos. 21-24, Consultation September 1875.
72. *Ibid.*, p. 4.

73. *Ibid.*, p. 4.
74. W. Moorcroft and George Trebeck, op cit. 2, p. 347.
75. Luciano Petech, op. cit. 5, p. 74.
76. *Ibid.*, p. 77.
77. About seven kilometers down the Indus from Leh.
78. C. L, Datta, op. cit. 15, p. 65.
79. Luciano Petech, op. cit. 5, p. 77. Also see C. L, Datta, op. cit. 15, p. 65.
80. *Ibid.*, p. 77.
81. C. L, Datta, op. cit. 15, p. 65.
82. A. H. Francke, op. cit. 7, p. 42.
83. Rong means gorge, Rong-pa probably mentioned of the people of the Indus.
84. C. Wessels, Early Jesuit travelers in Central Asia 1603-1721 (New Delhi: Asian Educational Services, 1992), p. 213.
85. W. Moorcroft and George Trebeck, op cit. 2, pp. 346-47.
86. *Ibid.*, p. 347.
87. Janet Rizvi, op. cit. 1, p. 60.
88. Alastair Lamb, op. cit. 62, p. 65.
89. C. L Datta, op. cit. 15, p. 214. Also see Alastair Lamb, op. cit. 62, pp. 70-71.
90. A. Cunningham, op. cit. 17, p. 239.
91. *Ibid.*, p. 239.
92. *Ibid.*, p. 239.
93. W. Moorcroft and George Trebeck, op cit. 2, pp. 385-86.
94. Janet Rizvi, op. cit. 1, p. 65.
95. *Ibid.*, p. 196.
96. K Warikoo, Central Asia And Kashmir: A Study in the context of Anglo-Russian Rivalry (New Delhi: Gian Publishing House, 1989), p.122.
97. *Ibid.*, p. 139.
98. Janet Rizvi, op. cit. 1, p. 202.
99. Foreign Department, Political. A. Branch, Nos. 21-24, Consultation September 1875.

100. Trade Report from Captain E. Molloy, Officiating British Joint-Commissioner, Ladakh to The Secretary to Government, Punjab, Foreign Department, Political. A. Branch, Nos. 21-24, Consultation September 1875.
101. Foreign Department, Secret. F. Branch, Nos. 374-383, Consultation September 1895.
102. An official letter from the British Resident in Kashmir to the Vice-President of the Jammu and Kashmir State Council, July 14, 1900; for details, see Appendix i
103. An official letter from the British Joint commissioner to the Wazir Wazrat, Ladakh, January 2, 1909, for details, see Appendix iv.
104. Janet Rizvi, op. cit. 1, pp. 64-65.
105. A. H. Francke, op. cit. 7, p. 42.
106. K. Warikoo, op. cit. 96, p. 62.
107. Janet Rizvi, op. cit. 1, p. 67.
108. *Ibid.*, p. 67.
109. K. Warikoo, op. cit. 96, pp. 66-7.
110. Janet Rizvi, op. cit. 1, p. 67.
111. A. Cunningham, op. cit. 17, p. 248.
112. W. Moorcroft and George Trebeck, op cit. 2, p. 350.
113. A trade mission from Ladakh sent by the king to Tibet.
114. Foreign, Secret. F, 613-619, July 1894.
115. W. Moorcroft, and George Trebeck, op cit. 2, pp. 350-51.
116. *Ibid.*, p. 350.
117. *Ibid.*, p. 351.
118. *Ibid.*, p. 352.
119. K. Warikoo, op. cit. 96, p. 59.
120. Janet Rizvi, op. cit. 1, pp. 198-99.
121. Foreign Department, Secret. F. Branch, Nos. 613-619, Consultation July 1894.
122. A Trade Report from Captain S. H. Godfrey, Assistant to the Resident in Kashmir for Leh to Colonel D. W. K. Barr, Resident in Kashmir, Foreign Department, Secret. F. Branch, Nos. 613-619, Consultation July 1894.
123. Foreign Department, Secret. F. Branch, Nos. 613-619, Consultation July 1894.

124. Foreign Department, Secret. F. Branch, Nos. 425-430, Consultation September 1893.
125. Foreign Department, Political. A. Branch, Nos. 146-176, Consultation July 1873.
126. A place in the South-east of Leh.
127. A. Cunningham, op. cit. 17, pp. 239-40.
128. *Ibid.*, p. 245.
129. *Ibid.*, p. 240.
130. W. Moorcroft and George Trebeck, op cit. 2, p.356.
131. Foreign Department, Political. A. Branch, Nos. 560-597, Consultation June 1871.
132. *Ibid.*, pp. 8-9.
133. *Ibid.*, pp. 8-9.
134. *Ibid.*, pp. 8-9.
135. Ladakh Trade Report, Foreign Department, Political. A. Branch, Nos. 560-597, Consultation June 1871.
136. Foreign Department, Political. A. Branch, Nos. 560-597, Consultation June 1871
137. Ladakh Trade Report, Foreign Department, Political. A. Branch, Nos. 560-597, Consultation June 1871.
138. W. Moorcroft and George Trebeck, op cit. 2, p. 356.
139. Fredric Drew, The Jammu and Kashmir Territories (London: Edward Stanford, 1875. Repr. New Delhi: Cosmo Publication, 1975), p. 284.
140. C. L, Datta, op. cit. 15, p. 20.
141. Foreign Department, Political. A. Branch, Nos. 21-24, Consultation September 1875.
142. *Ibid.*, p. 10
143. C. L. Datta, op. cit. 15, p. 20.
144. Foreign Department, Political. A. Branch, Nos. 560-597, Consultation June 1871.
145. W. Moorcroft and George Trebeck, op cit. 2, p. 297.
146. Foreign Department, Political. A. Branch, Nos. 560-597, Consultation June 1871.
147. Foreign Department, Secret. F. Branch, Nos. 374-383, Consultation September 1895.

148. Foreign Department, Secret. F. Branch, Nos. 613-619, Consultation July 1894.
149. Foreign Department, Secret. F. Branch, Nos. 374-383, Consultation September 1895.
150. The Statistics of the trade of India with Turkestan and Changthang, 31st March 1895, Foreign Department, Secret. F. Branch, Nos.374-383, Consultation September 1895.
151. Foreign Department, Secret. F. Branch, Nos. 374-383, Consultation September 1895.
152. Foreign Department, Political. A. Branch, Nos. 146-176, Consultation July 1873.
153. H.S. Barnes, Resident in Kashmir to the secretary to the government of India, Foreign Department, Secret. F. Branch, Nos. 374-383, Consultation September 1895.
154. Foreign Department, Secret. F. Branch, Nos. 425-430, Consultation September 1893.
155. Foreign Department, Political. A. Branch, Nos. 21-24, Consultation September 1875.
156. *Ibid.*, p. 12.
157. Ladakh Trade Report for 1874. Foreign Department, Political. A. Branch, Nos. 21-24, Consultation September 1875.
158. Foreign Department, Secret. F. Branch, Nos. 613-619, Consultation July 1894.
159. Foreign Department, Secret. F. Branch, Nos. 374-383, Consultation September 1895.
160. Foreign Department, Political. A. Branch, Nos. 21-24, Consultation September 1875.
161. *Ibid.*, p. 3.
162. Trade Report for 1874, Foreign Department, Political. A. Branch, Nos. 21-24, Consultation September 1875.
163. Foreign Department, Secret. F. Branch, Nos. 374-383, Consultation September 1895.
164. Foreign Department, Secret. F. Branch, Nos. 613-619, Consultation July 1894.
165. The Trade of India with Turkistan and Changthang, Foreign Department, Secret. F. Branch, Nos. 613-619, September July 1894.
166. Foreign Department, Secret. F. Branch, Nos. 613-619, September July 1894.

167. Foreign Department, Political. A. Branch, Nos. 286-291, Consultation May 1870.
168. Ladakh Trade Report for 1869, Foreign Department, Political. A. Branch, Nos. 286-291, Consultation May 1870.
169. Scarf used by Ladakhi during ceremonies.
170. Foreign Department, Political. A. Branch, Nos. 286-291, Consultation May 1870.
171. *Ibid.*, p. 11.
172. Foreign Department, Political. A. Branch, Nos. 146-176, Consultation July 1873.
173. *Ibid.*, p. 2.
174. *Ibid.*, p. 2.
175. Foreign Department, Secret. F. Branch, Nos. 425-430, Consultation September 1893.
176. The Statistics of the Trade of India with Turkistan and Changthang, Foreign Department, Secret. F. Branch, Nos. 425-430, Consultation September 1893.
177. Foreign Department, Secret. F. Branch, Nos.425-430, Consultation September 1893.
178. *Ibid.*, p. 316.
179. Foreign Department, Political. A. Branch, Nos. 146-176, Consultation July 1873.
180. Foreign Department, Political. A. Branch, Nos. 214-216, Consultation July 1874.
181. Foreign Department, Political. A. Branch, Nos. 146-176, Consultation July 1873.
182. Foreign Department, Political. A. Branch, Nos. 214-216, Consultation July 1874.
183. *Ibid.*, p. 5.
184. Foreign Department, Political. A. Branch, Nos. 21-24, Consultation September 1875.
185. *Ibid.*, P. 8.
186. Foreign Department, Political. A. Branch, Nos. 146-176, Consultation July 1873.
187. Foreign Department, Political. A. Branch, Nos. 21-24, Consultation September 1875.
188. Ladakh Trade Report, Foreign Department, Political. A. Branch, Nos. 21-24, Consultation September 1875.

189. Foreign Department, Political. A. Branch, Nos. 21-24, Consultation September 1875.
190. *Ibid.*, p. 10.
191. *Ibid.*, p. 10.
192. Foreign Department, Secret. F. Branch, Nos. 425-430, Consultation September 1893.
193. *Ibid.*, p. 317.
194. Foreign Department, Political. A. Branch, Nos. 21-24, Consultation September 1875.
195. Ladakh Trade Report For 1874, Foreign Department, Political. A. Branch, Nos. 21-24, Consultation September 1875.
196. Foreign Department, Secret. F. Branch, Nos. 613-619, Consultation July 1894.
197. Foreign Department, Political. A. Branch, Nos. 214-216, Consultation July 1874.
198. Foreign Department, Political. A. Branch, Nos. 21-24, Consultation September 1875.
199. Ladakh Trade Report for 1874, Foreign Department, Political. A. Branch, Nos. 21-24, Consultation September 1875.
200. Foreign Department, Political. A. Branch, Nos. 286-291, Consultation May 1870.
201. Foreign Department, Political. A. Branch, Nos. 560-597, Consultation June 1871.
202. *Ibid.*, p. 9.
203. *Ibid.*, p. 9.
204. *Ibid.*, p. 9.
205. Fredric Drew, op. cit. 139, p. 288.
206. *Ibid.*, p. 288.
207. Foreign Department, Political. A. Branch, Nos. 214-216, Consultation July 1874.
208. Foreign Department, Political. A Branch, Nos. 21-24, Consultation September 1875.
209. Foreign Department, Political. A. Branch, Nos. 214-216, Consultation July 1874.
210. Foreign Department, Secret. F. Branch, Nos. 374-383, Consultation September 1895.

211. *Ibid.*, p. 376.
212. A Place in Yarkand.
213. Foreign Department, Political. A. Branch, Nos. 390-392, Consultation September 1894.
214. Foreign Department, Political. A. Branch, Nos. 214-216, Consultation July 1874.
215. F)reign Department, Political. A. Branch, Nos. 21-24, Consultation September 1875.
216. Foreign Department, Political. A. Branch, Nos. 126-130, Consultation May 1872.
217. Ladakh Trade Report For 1870, Foreign Department, Political. A. Branch, Nos. 560-597, Consultation June 1871.
218. Foreign, Political. A, 560-597, June 1871.
219. www.Ladakh.free.fr/news/html/2004/04.
220. The last Ladakhi village nears the border.
221. www.Ladakh.free.fr/news/html/2004/04.
222. A. H Francke, op. cit. 7, p. 42.
223. *Ibid.*, p. 42. Also see Luciano Petech, op. cit. 5, p. 78.
224. A. H Francke, op. cit. 7, p. 42.
225. For the detail agreement see footnote no. 82.
226. Alaistair Lamb, op. cit. 62, p. 57.
227. *Ibid.*, p. 57.
228. C. L Datta, op cit. 15, pp. 65-66.
229. Alaistair Lamb, op. cit. 62, p. 57.
230. Luciano Petech, op. cit. 5, p. 78.
231. Cited in John Bray, The Lapchak Mission From Ladakh to Lhasa in British India Foreign Policy, *Tibet Journal, 15 (4), 1990*, p. 85.
232. A. H Francke, op. cit. 7, p. 42.
233. Alaistair Lamb, op. cit. 62, p. 57.
234. A. H Francke, op. cit. 7, p. 42. Also see C. L Datta, op. cit. 15, p. 65.
235. Alaistair Lamb, op. cit. 62, p. 57.
236. Janet Rizvi, op. cit. 1, p. 160.
237. Cited in Pascale Dollfus, The History of Muslim in Central Ladakh, *Tibet Journal, 20/3 (Autumn, 1995)*, p.43

238. *Ibid.*, p. 43
239. *Ibid.*, p. 43.
240. *Ibid.*, p. 43
241. The Diary of British Joint-Commissioner, Ladakh, 18th June 1890, Foreign, Secret. F, 1-9, January 1892.
242. Pascale Dollfus, The History of Muslim in Central Ladakh, *Tibet Journal, 20/3 (Autumn, 1995)*, pp. 43-44
243. Alaistair Lamb, op. cit. 62, p. 57.
244. *Ibid.*, p. 57.
245. He founded several monasteries including Hemis, in Ladakh.
246. Luciano Petech, op. cit. 5, p. 53.
247. *Ibid.*, p. 53.
248. Foreign Department, Political. A. Branch, Nos. 560-597, Consultation June 1871.
249. *Ibid.*, p. 8.

6
Conclusion

To conclude, Ladakh's cultural ties with Buddhist Tibet were close and consistent for centuries. Even during the conflict between Ladakh and Tibet in the 1680s, the cultural relations between the two countries continued. This is illustrated by the fact that the peace treaty of the conflict was signed in 1684 by the effort of the 6th 'Brug-c'en' Mi-p'am-dban-po (1641-1717 A.D.), the head lama of the Brug-pa sub-sect in Tibet, who came to Ladakh in 1683-84. There were several factors responsible for developing a close and sustain relationships between Ladakh and Buddhist Tibet.

Though the cultural influences in Ladakh come from east, south and west, this book has placed importance mainly on the religious, spiritual, education and trade factors between Ladakh and Buddhist Tibet. I briefly summarize here the main points that have been analyzed.

It is certain that before the Tibetan influence, the cultural influence on Ladakh was from Kashmir. But very little remains as evidence except, some rock-carvings. The first important and widespread cultural influence from Tibet came with the establishment of the first Ladakhi dynasty rule in the tenth century. The origin of the first Ladakhi dynasty is connected with the decline of and fall of the Tibetan monarchy. The survey of the early and the medieval Ladakhi history characterized by the establishment of the Lhachen dynasty and then the emergence of the rNamgyal dynasty, and their patronage of Mahayana Buddhism propagated and sustained Ladakh's spiritual ties with Buddhist Tibet. The emphasis shifted to primarily Buddhist preoccupations such as the patronage and support of the construction of monasteries and stupas in Ladakh, and moved away from violence as a policy and way of life of the entire population. In terms of long historical development and evolution, Ladakh earned the present day reputation as a peaceful Buddhist community.

There were several important mediums through which the Tibetan influences came to Ladakh; they were the lama missionaries, trade and pilgrimage, the Ladakhi monk's monastic education in Tibet, and the royal patronage to Mahayana Buddhism.

Lama missionaries played an important role in the spread and development of Mahayana Buddhism in Ladakh. Many important lamas from Tibet and other areas visited Ladakh. Lotsawa Rinchen Zangpo, Chos-rje Gdan-ma, and Stag-tsan-Ras-pa, etc., were some of the important lamas who visited Ladakh and played a vital role in development of religious and spiritual ties between Ladakh and Buddhist Tibet. The more lama missionaries were active, the more diffusion of Mahayana Buddhism in the area.

Monastic education of Ladakhi monks in Tibet was another important medium through which Mahayana Buddhism from Tibet came to Ladakh. Tibet became an important center for monastic education and many Lamas from Ladakh went to the different monasteries in Tibet for studies. After coming back from Tibet, they played a vital role in spreading Mahayana Buddhism in their native places. Many royal princes also became monks and went for higher studies to Tibet. After returning to Ladakh, they became heads of important monasteries and played an important role in the spread of monastic education in Ladakh. For example, King Deldan Namgyal's second son named Lobsang Nawang Puntsog studied at the university of Brans-spun, and after nine years study he obtained the high degree of dge-bses-rab-byams-pa. After coming back from Tibet, he was appointed the abbot of Thikse monastery. The Ladakhi monks not only played an important role in their native country but also made their contributions to the mainstream religion tradition of Tibet. The contribution of Zanskar Lotswa's translation works in Tibet was one such example.

There are still today more than one hundred monks in various monasteries in Ladakh, who have been to Tibet for monastic education. They are still active in religious activities of the monasteries and teaching the younger monks. The hallmark of Ladakhi lamas was their perusing a comprehensive study in various branches of Buddhist studies in some renowned monastic institution in Tibet, and for the lamas, a visit to Lhasa, their spiritual home, was a cherished dream. There are two reasons why the lamas went to Tibet. First of all, the Mahayana Buddhism came directly from Tibet to the Himalayan areas, and secondly, Tibet in due course of time became a centre of Mahayana Buddhism and the residence of leading Lamas who taught Mahayana Buddhism.

Both lama missionaries and the monastic education of Ladakhi monks in Tibet contributed towards the construction of various monasteries, stupas and other religious structures in Ladakh. Monastic organization and monastic education was a sustaining factor in the relationship between Ladakh and Buddhist Tibet.

Trade and pilgrimage was another important medium through which the Tibetan influences impacted Ladakh. The trade relation between Ladakh and Buddhist Tibet is an old one. It is quite possible that the inhabitants of Ladakh felt the Tibetan influence as early as mid-seventh century, for the nomadic Tibetans of Changthang (Western Tibet) would have good reasons to have contact with the sedentary Mon and Dard, exchanging grains for the animal products. Then, the two trade missions called 'Lapchak' and 'Cha-pa' between Ladakh and Buddhist Tibet, which were setup as the result of the Tinmosgang Treaty. This treaty brought to an end the three-corner conflict between Ladakh, Tibet and the Moghul Empire, and established the border between Ladakh and Tibet, and some trade regulation especially about wool and pashm. The Lapchak mission went from Leh to Lhasa once in every three years. In return, the Tibetan government sent an annual trade caravan from Lhasa to Leh, popularly known as the Cha-pa mission or 'tea man', as the mission used to come with loads of tea. This mission gave rise to a number of lesser missions. The major monasteries sent half-religious and half-commercial missions to Tibet. The participants ranged from the big merchants to ordinary peasants, from bigger monasteries to a Lama entrepreneur. From a small local traders like Tashi Angchok to the bigger merchants and the governments caravans have greatly profit from this trade. The value of trade increased at Leh substantially, it was more than sixty lakhs of rupees in the year 1894-95. Thus, such extensive and long period of active trade and pilgrimage also helped in developing a sustain ties between Ladakh and Buddhist Tibet.

The Tibetan influences can be seen on Ladakhi language, literature, dress, customs, food and drinks. The influence can also be seen on the Ladakhi architecture, astrology and paintings. As regards religion, the four major sects and several sub-sects of Mahayana Buddhism were developed in Ladakh. The advent of Mahayana from Tibet Buddhism in the Himalayan states where the people were having faith in primitive religions did not create any serious conflict, as they were peaceful diffusions. Mahayana Buddhist ideas and values, which came into contact with the indigenous culture, ecology and psyche of the Himalayan people added into the Himalayan character.

Problems and Prospects

The tradition of going to Tibet for education, which continued for hundreds of years, was suddenly stopped when the Chinese occupied Tibet. Most of the monks from Ladakh had to come back. This abrupt end would have had a major impact on the standard of monastic educational levels in Ladakh. But luckily three important developments have worked in Ladakh's favour. First of all, the monks who came back to Ladakh after the Chinese occupation of Tibet played a major role in teaching the young monks in Ladakh, and soon a Buddhist institute named the Central Institute of Buddhist Studies was established in 1959 at Leh, where initially novices from different monasteries in Ladakh came for their education. Secondly, the major monasteries in Ladakh set up their own schools in their monasteries. Lastly, with the establishment of the Tibetan government-in-exile in India and the establishment of some Tibetan monastic institutions in India, many monks from Ladakh go to these institutions for higher education. Some of these institutions are in Karnataka and few other places in India, where many well-known teachers from Tibet are teaching.

At present all the major monasteries in Ladakh have their own schools. In these schools, besides the monastic education, they teach subjects like mathematics, social sciences and Hindi and English languages. Many novices are studying in these schools and after the completion of their courses they go for higher studies to the Tibetan institutions in southern India and few other places.

Relevance of the Reopening of the Border

The effect of the traditional relationships, which continued for hundreds of years between Ladakh and Buddhist Tibet were felt in nearly every village in Ladakh. The links of the relationship disappeared after the Chinese occupation of Tibet, when the borders were closed. Of late, India and China have made progress in boosting economic ties, prompting both sides to look at opening up new routes to encourage cross-border trade. In June 2003, India and China agreed to open the border trade along the eastern stretch of the rugged Himalayan border between Sikkim and Tibet. In this changed environment, the people of Ladakh are optimistic about the opening of the old trade route through Demchok on the Ladakhi side and Tashigang on the Tibetan side for pilgrimage and trade. Trade and subsistence agriculture have been the Ladakhis' only livelihood through the ages. At the moment there is no border trade, but there is smuggling and goods-selling in the streets of Leh. There is no reason why this old trade route should not be reopened. Reopening of the route will benefit both the local economy as well as the government trade. Since age-old routes and relationships already exist, they only need the government approval to start functioning again, leading to economic benefits for both India and China. As the two countries work towards greater cooperation in the economic sphere, Ladakh as an economic area of activity should be focused upon.

The hope for Ladakhis is the restoration of normal border trading and cultural relations between them and Tibet. The opening of the old trade routes will not only help trade in the region but also promote pilgrimages to the Kailash Mansarovar Lake and other holy places in Tibet and tourism. One of the important advantages of the route to Kailash Mansarovar Lake through Ladakh is that there is a motorable road on both sides of the border; one can drive all the way up to Kailash.

APPENDICES

APPENDIX-1

A Letter from the British Resident in Kashmir to the Vice-President of the Jammu and Kashmir State Council Regarding Disputes Settlement (Traders). Dated the 14th July 1900

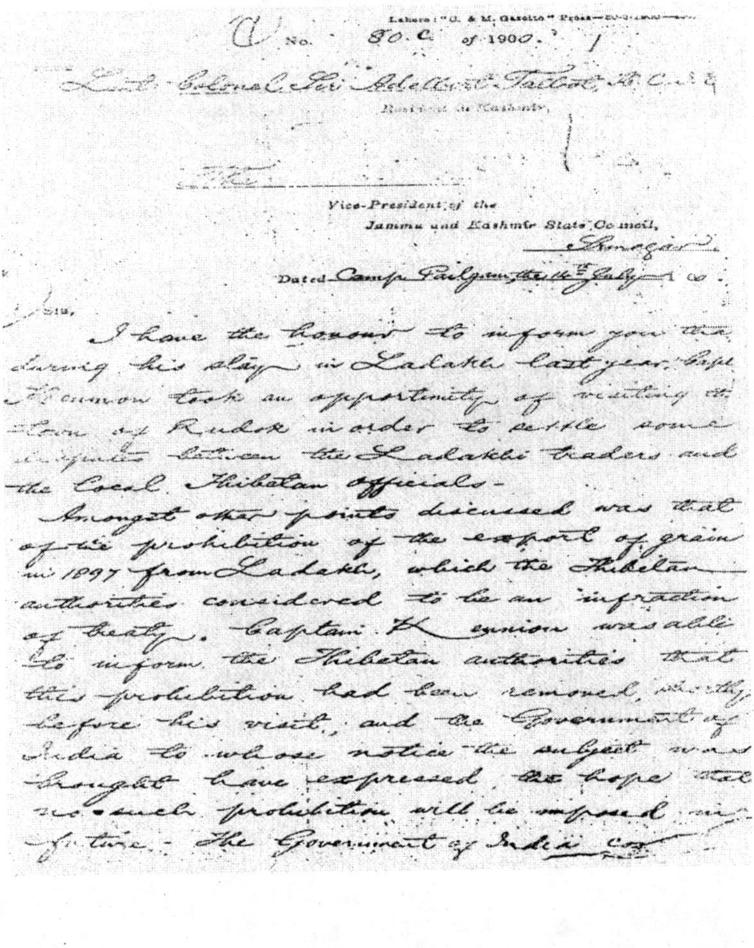

No. 80 C. of 1900.

Lieut.-Colonel Sir Adelbert Talbot, K.C.I.E.,
Resident in Kashmir,

To

The Vice-President of the
Jammu and Kashmir State Council,
Srinagar.

Dated Camp Pailgam, the 14th July 1900.

Sir,

I have the honour to inform you that during his stay in Ladakh last year, Capt. Kennion took an opportunity of visiting the town of Rudok in order to settle some disputes between the Ladakhi traders and the local Thibetan officials.

Amongst other points discussed was that of the prohibition of the export of grain in 1897 from Ladakh, which the Thibetan authorities considered to be an infraction of treaty. Captain Kennion was able to inform the Thibetan authorities that this prohibition had been removed shortly before his visit, and the Government of India to whose notice the subject was brought have expressed the hope that no such prohibition will be imposed in future. The Government of India con-

that interference with trade is in the long run hurtful to the State as well as to the Community at large. I have no doubt but that the Durbar will agree in the wisdom of these views and I should be glad if you would kindly have orders issued to the Wazir Wazarat, Frontier Districts, to prevent the imposition of any such prohibition in future.--

Yours truly

[illegible]

Resident in Kashmir

No. 2381

Submitted to H. H. the Maharajah in Council. [illegible]

[illegible]

Vice President of State Council.

Date 17/7/1903

For Council

[illegible]

17/7/1903

APPENDIX-2

A letter from Khan Bhadur Ghulam Ahemad Khan, Revenue Member of the State Council to the Vice-President of the Jammu and Kashmir State Council Regarding the Export of Grain from Ladakh to Tibetan Territory. Dated the 10th September 1900

REVENUE DEPARTMENT.

JAMMU AND KASHMIR STATE.

FROM

KHAN BAHADUR GHULAM AHMED KHAN,

Revenue Member of the State Council,

Srinagar

TO

THE Vice President of State Council Srinagar

No. 3232 Dated 10th September 1900.

SIR,

With reference to your office No: 2535 dated 21st July 1900, regarding the export of grain from Ladakh to the Thibetan territory, I have the honor to enclose herewith a copy of Resolution No: 35 dated 20th August 1900, and to request the favor of your transmitting the same to the Resident in Kashmir for his information.

2. I beg to add that the Wazir Wazarat Frontier districts has been asked to comply with the orders of the State Council.

APPENDIX-3

Report on Ladakh Trade Routes from J.E.T. Aitchison, British Joint-Commissioner, Ladakh, to the Secretary to Government of Punjab. Dated the 4th March 1873

No. 137, dated Lahore, 4th March 1873
From—J. R. T. Aitchison, Esq.,
Joint. Commissioner, Ladakh
To—The Secretary to government, Punjab

I. Hati the honor herewith to forward a report upon Ladakh trade routes, as called for by your latter No. 1527, dated 2nd December 1872.

Report on Laddkh Trade Routes

In reporting upon the several trade routes between Yarkand and India, and as in which of these is the one likely to be finally selected for the jurisdiction of the Joint. Commissioners as appointed by the two Governments, I would class them under the following heads taking the town of Leh as their starting point:

I. The routes leading from Leh to Yarkand.

II. The routes from Leh to India.

2. I. *The Routes leading from Leh to Yarkand:* During the year 1872 no traders departed from or arrived at Leh *vid* the Changehenmoo routo, the whole of the traffic having been carried on over the Korakoram routes—the former having been altogether forsaken as, with the exception of the guides sent by the Joint-Commissioners to meet the coming caravan from yarkand, which they did at Shadulla, no one went over the Changechenmoo route this year.

3. I do not believe traders will ever of themselves be induced to attempt again the Changehenmoo roules; nor will those feelings of distrust which originated with the disasters of Mr. Forsyth's upward march to Yarkand, during which some two hundred horsos were lost and whose bodies still remain as permanent monuments of misfortune, be readily obliterated unless some steps be at once taken to remove them.

4. To do so I would recommend that the British Joint-Commissioner himself should go by the new route given in Mr. Shaw's report sufficiently early this next season, so as to meet the Yarkand caravan at Shadulla and himself guide them in their journey to Leh. He would thus have the opportunity of taking such means as he might consider necessary to establish throughout his whole route landmarks at certain distances so as to render it quite impossible for any future travellers to lose the proper track. Besides it would enable him to see that efficient preparations in the way of supplies, and C, were made.

5. I spoke to several merchants and carriers, more especially to *Gul Morad,* who was the *first to bring camels vid the Changehenmoo route.* All without exception were against any route in that direction, unless supported by the presence of a European, saying that they would willingly attempt any proposed new route if preceded by the British Commissioner.

6. I strongly urged Gul Morad again bringing camels, and told him that any one displaying so much energy and enterprise would be supported and probably rewarded by the British Government.

7. The great difficulty that they held out was want of *water, rather than fodder or supplies; but even this* by their own account could always be obtained at no great depth. I feel confident that during the summer months at least this difficulty might be overcome by means of Norton's tube wells, the soveral lengths of which could easily be conveyed and distributed through a caravan.

8. I incline, therefore, to the opinion that at present it would be premature to fix upon any special route to the north of Leh for the jurisdiction of the Joint-Comissioners, and consider that Para XIII of the Treaty should be adhered to in its integrity for some years yet; that the town of Leh should under away circumstances, and for the various reasons given by Dr. Cayley, Mr. Forayth and Mr. Shaw, be kept within the jurisdiction of the Joint-Commissioners.

9. *II—The routes from Leh to India:* Mr. Shaw, in para 1 of his report on trade routes through Ladakh, says—"If a free choice is given, undoubtedly the route taken by the traders for so many generations is as far as the vallcy of the Indus the most suitable for traffic," and agrees with Dr. Cayley in thinking that the route *"from Lahoul to Ladakh is certainly the best."*

10. Had Mr. Shaw added "for five months only during the year" I would certainly agree with him in the above opinion.

11. Admitting that the progress of civilization in its effects upon the trade of India is at a stand-still, and taking only into consideration the enormous development of the Ladakh trade since 1863 from Rs. 2,00,000 to Rs. 15,00,000 this increase of itself demands the use of a route capable of being employed with safety for a longer period of time; and this demand must necessarily be one of the effective causes for removing the trade from the present Lahoul route to that through Ladakh to Kashmir.

12. From the vast increase of Central Asian trade the relative proportion of traders late for crossing by the Lahoul route also becomes greater. These must, as they have does this was all comes by the Kashmir route, along which they have seen that supplies were play difficulties law as need and the using to be process of the British Commissioner accompanying the caravan and his being in Kashmir during its progress through the country obstruction and oppression on the part of the Kashmir officials were totally absent, the natural result of which will be that such traders as came

through this year vid the Kashmir route, should they happen to be at all late in their ventures, rather than run any risk by going the Lahoul route, will most probably prefer this one for the future. I certainly do not agree with Mr. Shaw in thinking that they are willing to run any risk rather than proceed through Kashmir Territory, as in my opinion the Yarkand traders are yearly becoming bolder and they will not allow themselves to be plundered to the same extent as formerly. Owing to this the potty local authorities have begun to recognise that the traders passing through are not to be treated with impunity, and that the best way of making money from them is by establishing friendship and aiding *them with supplies and carriage.*

13. The presence of a British Resident at Srinagar, the very numerous Europeans who during the summer visit the valley of Kashmir as well as traverse the various trade routes, enable the traders to find a publicity and support for their complaints quite sufficient to create a wave of influence over Kashmir petty officials beneficial to them. This is yearly becoming greater and it is this influence that is making traders bolder, and is giving to them a spirit of self-protection and independence which enables them to act on the offensive when necessary.

14. His Highness the Maharajah of Kashmir having removed all taxation from goods passing through his territories, there is new no opportunity afforded to tax collectors for pilfering a trader's goods. The trader for his own safety does not break bulk, confirming Mr. Forsyth's views, as given in his report of 1868, that, "as the Maharajah has lowered his duties, and perhaps ere long may abolish transit dues, it may be taken for granted that in a few year's time fiscal considerations will have no weight in determining the line taken by traders". The only real difficulties which he has to overcome are supplies and carriage. The latter he has probably engaged as through carriages, or he may have brought it with him; the former are on the whole scarcely, if ever, difficult to procure.

15. Colouel T.G. Montgomerie, in Mr. Davies' Report "Trade with Central Asia," Appendix A., says:—"I consequently think that, all other things being equal, the trade conuection would favor the Kashmir route." With this opinion I agree, as also with—"every endeavour should of course be made to improve the roads where a small outlay is likely to be effectual"..."The Kashmir road offers great facilities for allowing camels to pass, and a very small expenditure would be sufficient to make the present roads passable for camels".

16. As far as this I have not taken into consideration the progress of civilization and its probable effects upon Indian trade. Mr. Forsyth, in a memorandum on "Routes from the Punjab to Eastern Turkestan," says, at page 7—"In a few years' time the railroad to Rawalpindi will be opened, and possibly this may cause some alteration in the point at which Kashmir is entered." Again he states—"It may safely be predicted that there will be a vast increase of trade along this line, and perhaps the greater advantages of the Kashmir route with its frequent villages may induce merchants to take that line in preference to auother shorter one."

The road from Kala-ki-Sorai to Garhi Habibula is a good cart road.

From Garhi to top of ascent, four miles, is an excellent camel road. From the top of the pass to Mozafferabad, four miles, scarcely fit for laden horses. From Mozafferabad to Srinagar well fit for laden horses.

Route from Kala-ki-Serai vid Mozafferabad to Kashmir

Kala-ki-Serai from Lahore, on the Grand Trunk Road, 180 miles

To Haripur	—	22 miles	British Territory	D. B.*
To Abbottabad	—	21 miles		D. B.
To Mansehra	—	155 miles		R. B.
To Garhi Habibula	—	182 miles		R. B.

To Mozafferabad	—	7 miles		R. H.
To Sirun	—	8 miles		R. H.
To Huttain Dobutta	—	16 miles		R. H.
To Kanda	—	11 miles		R. H.
To Kathai	—	10 miles	Kashmir	R. H.
To Shah Derah	—	15 miles		R. H.
To Gingla	—	10 miles		R. H.
To Baramula	—	15 miles		
To Patan	—	14 miles		
To Srinagar	—	17 miles		

*D.R. Bak Banglore
R.B. Road Bangalor
R.H. Geet House

Within the next two years at the very furthest the Lahore and Peshawar railway will be finished. This will enable goods to be conveyed twenty miles to the north of Rawalpindi, from which there is a good cart road for five marches *vid* Abbottabad to Garhi. From Garhi to Mozafferabad is eight miles; from Mozafferabad to Srinagar is nine marches upon an old and well-known road, which during winter certainly is the best, being scarcely, if ever, known to be closed by snow, and is besides the most rapid way by which one reaches British Territory from Kashmir. That portion of the road between Garrhi and Mozafferabad that belongs to Kashmir is execrable for about four miles. From Mozafferabad to Baramula it is, on the whole, at present in fair condition for laden hoses, with the exception perhaps of one march. Throughout its whole length it could be easily converted at little expense into a road capable of allowing camel traffic, chiefly by the removal of a few trees.

17. A large through traffic exists between Peshawar and Kashmir *vid* Mozafferabad; there would thus upon this route be combined the Peshawar with the Punjab and Central Asian traffic. Now it is known that nearly all Peshawar goods are carried on camels in all directions except from Mozafferabad to Baramulla, between which oxen, ponies and mules alone

are used. Were this portion of the route improved as proposed, the Peshawar traders would be the means of originating a camel traffic; and I have no doubt that traders with Yurkand would get from the Pashawaris camels to convey their goods at least as far as Kashmir.

18. Moreover, the Hazara District is well known for its capabilities in supplying grazing, and, as it is completely off the line of the Grand Trunk Road, the traffic, especially round Garhi Habibulla, near Mozafferabad, would never be high, and carriage through Kashmir is always moderate, whereas that by the Kulu and Lahoul route has always been expensive.

19. Under the above circumstances it would therefore be better not for some years to make any change in the jurisdiction of the Joint–Commissioners until substantial proofs are given by the trade itself of what route it is likely permanently to occupy.

20. I cannot well conclude this report without respectfully laying the following suggestion before you for consideration, *vis*:–the formation of a covered way across the Zoji La Pass, in order to secure a permanent passage throughout the whole year between Kashmir and Ladakh.

21. From the Punjab *vid* Mozafferabad to Srinagar, and as far as Baltal in the Sind valley, the road towards Leh is open during the whole winter, with the exception perhaps of occasional short stoppages. Again, from Dras to Central Asia the roads are open during the whole winter. With our present scientific knowledge, it is hard to think that we cannot remove the existing barrier between Kashmir and Ladakh which causes an obstruction of intercommunication for five months yearly. From what I myself have seen of the country I cannot help thinking that it would prove quite feasible, and not expensive, to construct a covered way from Baltal to Dras, or such portion of the road as it may be found necessary upon practical examination. This covered way may be spoken of as divisible into three parts *viz*:-

1. The Portion between Baltal and the gorge of the pass.
2. The portion through the gorge to the summit.
3. From the summit towards Dras.

Portions 1 had 3 would merely consist of two strong walls made of unhewn stone work, and roofed in with timber. Portion 2 would be the costly part of the project, *vis,* a gallery cut in the rock along its face through the gorge. There would be no difficulty whatever in obtaining the materials for building the walls of the covered way, and any amount of timber for the roofing is procurable round Baltal.

22. To those who have not seen the religious edifices throughout Ladakh called "mani" the above proposition may appear extravagant; but it was from reflecting upon the uselessness of those labored constructions and to what service they possibly could be applied that it occurred to me that it two of them were placed side by side and roofed in an admirable construction would thus be formed for a permanent way through any depth of snow.

23. Were such a work accomplished across the Zoji-Ja Pass, its value would be inestimable. Not only to Kashmir itself would it prove an immediate benefit in admitting of a perpetual and free communication of the inhabitants with their Ladakh neighbours and thus develope a far more 'extensive local trade, but it would also be a means of safety for Ladakh in case of an invasion from the countries to its north and west, which, were such to take place now, the Ladakhis would be quite unable to prevent, and it would be impossible for Kashmir to send assistance. Besides, supposing Kashmir to have sent assistance in summer, during the winter the armies would be completely cut off from their base. For trade with foregn countries it would prove invaluable.

Appendix-4

A Letter from the British Joint–Commissioner Ladakh to the Wazir Wazarat Ladakh Regarding the Payment of the Chowkidar Appointed on the Trade Routes Dated the 2nd January 1909

No. 0/70 of 1909.

From

Captain D.G. Oliver, I.A.,
British Joint Commissioner Ladakh.

To

The Wazir Wazarat Ladakh Leh.

Dated Srinager, the 2nd January 1909.

Sir,

With reference to my endorsement No. 204, dated the 1st April 1908 I have the honour to enclose a Hundi for Rs. 100 on account of the pay of the ohowkidar appointed to take cure of the traders goods on the Sasser.

The favour of an acknowledgment is requested.

Yours truly,

British Joint Commissioner Ladakh.

Appendix-5

Proposal to Stop Trade between Ladakh and Lhasa, Disapproved. Some of the Extracts from the British Joint Commissioner, Ladakh during 1890-91

GOVERNMENT OF INDIA

FOREIGN DEPARTMENT PROCEEDINGS.

SECRET F.

JANUARY 1892

(1) Proposal to stop trade between Ladak and Lhasa, disapproved. (2) Tibetan letters conveyed to Lhasa by the Lapohak Mission of 1890.

No.1. *Extract from the Diary of the British Joint Commissioner, Ladak, for April 1890.*

It will be remembered that in this office latter No. 187 of 20th June 1889 it was represented that the British province of Spiti paid a small annual tribute to Ladak. The Government of India, in paragraph (III) of letter No. 1345 F., dated 24th August 1880, directed that the Wazir of Ladak and the ex-Raja of Ladak must renounce all intercourse of such a nature with Spiti. I have now received word from Leh that in March last these orders were received by the Wazir, and communicated to the ex-Raja.

No.2. *Extract paragraph 18 of the Diary of the British Joint Commissioner, Ladak, for the period 11th to 20 th June 1890.*

18 th—The Wazir told me that he had received a petition from Ghulam Muhammad, the son of Haji Hyder Shah, the leading merchant of Ladak, regarding the conduct of the Lhassa officials. *Haji Hyder Shah,* with other relatives, has for many years carried on a trade with Lhasa and his son has a

house and family both at Lhasa and Leh. Ghulam Mahammad says that the officials regard him as a British spy, and that last time he went to Lhasa, all his bales of goods, and the persons of himself and followers, were searched, with a view to seeing if he had any secret papers with him. No such papers were found, and he was therefore allowed to go his way, but he says, he had to spend as much as Rs. *1,000 in bribing the Lhasa* officials not to molest him. He has, therefore, addressed a petition of the Wazir of Ladak, asking him to send a *murasilah by the hand of this year's Lapebak leader to the Lhasa* officials, asking them not to interfere with Ghulam Muhammad or other Ladak traders. The Wazir asked me how he should act, and said he would also refer to the Council for orders. As explained in paragraph 13 (*e*) of my demi-official dated 23rd June 1889 (a copy of which was forwarded to the Government of India, by the Resisdent in Kashmir with his latter No. 776, dated 1st July 1889), and also in paragraph XV of the Ladak Trade Report for 1888-89, the trade between Leh and Lhasa might, with advantage, be brought to an end. The petition of Ghulam Muhammad affords an opportunity for the dispatch of a letter to Lhasa saying that, as it has been ascertained that Ladak traders are molested at Lhasa it has been resolved to stop all trade between Ladak and Lhasa, that therefore though this year's Lapehak will be sent as usual, in future, no traders will be allowed to enter Ladak from Lhasa, while any traders who go from Ladak to Lhassa will do so at their own risk. The Lhasa trade (connected, as it is, with "beygar" politics and China tea) should be put a stop to if possible, but the trade of Changthang (in wool and pasham) should be encouraged. It would be quite possible to kill the former while fostering the latter. The trump cards are in our own hands, for so long as we are in a position to move troops from Almera and Kaladandah, *via* the Niti Pass, to the Mansurwar country—the Lhasas people dare not make any military movement against Ladak. If the Lhasa officials are to be addressed, whether in this sense, or in accordance with Ghulam Muhammad's petition, the question remains as to whether the murasilah should be issued by a Kashmir State official or an officer of the Government of India.

No. 3. No. 1208, dated the 8th August 1890.

From—Colonel R. Parry Nisbet, C.I.E., Resident in Kashmir,

To—The secretary to the Government of India, Foreign Department.

I have the honour to submit copy of a letter No. 177, dated 25th ultimo, from the British Joint Commissioner, Ladak on the subject of the trade between Leh and Lhasa, and to solicit early orders.

2. I am unable to concur in Captain Ramsay's idea that the trade should be put a stop to at any rate until the Lhasa Government has been courteously addressed by the Kasmir Darbar, requesting them to abstain from molesting traders whether Kashmir or British subjects coming from Ladak. At the same time without discouraging traders I would let them know that, though the Lhasa Government have been desired not to interfere with them, trade between Ladak and Lhasa must be carried on at their own risk and responsibility Hereafter, when opportunity offers on the part of the British Government, the Lhasa officials might be recommended not to act in any way in restraint of trade between the two countries.

No. 4. No. 177, dated the 25th July 1890.

From—The British Joint Commissioner, Ladak,

To—The Resident in Kashmir.

With reference to this office diary for 18th June 1890, I have the honour to report that the Kashmir Council have sent orders to the Wazir to act in accordance with my advice.

2. The wazir would like to address the Lhasa Government warning them to abstain from annoying our subjects, but I have told him to do nothing at present.

8. The matter is hardly one in which I should act without orders from the Government of India, and I have therefore the honour to request that you will refer the matter to the Government of India for orders. If a communication of any sort is to be addressed to the Lhasa Government, I would request that I may receive an early reply as the Lapohak starts in some twenty-nine day's time.

No. 5. No. 1651-F, dated Fort William, the 11th December 1890.

From—W.J. Cuninghan, Esq. Officisting Secretary to the Government of India.

Foreign Department,

To—The Resident in Kashmir.

I am directed to acknowledge the receipt of Colonel Nisbet's letter No. 2 1208 of the 8th August 1890, forwarding a copy of Captain Ramsay's No. 177 dated the 25th July, regarding the trade between Ladak and Tibet.

2. In reply I am to say that the Government of India concur in Colonel Nisbet's opinion that it would not be expedient to adopt the measure suggested by Captain Ramsay of putting a stop to all trade between Ladak and Lhasa, ostensibly on account of the alleged improper treatment of Ghulam Muhammad. The correspondence was not received in time to deal, before the Lapchak Mission started, with the suggestion, that a remonstrance should be made to the Lhasa Government in respect in interference with British subjects carrying on trade to that place; but I am to inquire if you can obtain and forward to the Government of India a copy of any letters that may have been conveyed to Lhasa this year by the Lapchak Mission.

No. 6. No. 511, dated the 6th Februry 1891.

From—Captain W. Evans-Gordon, Resident in Kashmir, Sialkot,

To—The Secretary to the Government of India, Foreign Department.

With reference to your office letter No. 1651-F., dated the 11th December 1890, I have the honour to forward copy of a letter No. 2, dated the 28 th ultimo, received from Captain H. Ramsay, British Joint Commissioner, Ladak, intimating that he has called for copies of official letters sent to Lhasa by the hand of the leader of the Lapchak Mission of 1890.

No. 7. No. 2, dated the 28th January 1891.

From—Captain H. Ransay, British Joint Commissioner, Ladak,

To—The Resident in Kashmir.

With reference to your endorsement No. 2115, dated 24th ultimo, I have the honour to state that there will probably be no difficulty about obtaining copies of the several official letters sent to Lhasa by the hand of the leader of the Lapchak Mission of 1890.

2. I am writing—

1. to the Wazir of Ladak asking him to have copies of the different letters prepared and submitted to the Reverend F. Redslob;

2. to Mr. Redslob asking him to translate them.

No. 8. No. 3203, dated Simla, the 15th October 1891.

From—Colonel W. F. Prideaux,

Resident in Kashmir, Srinagar,

To—The Secreatary to the Government of India, Foreign Department.

In Continuation of this office latter No. 311, dated the 6th February last, I have the honour to euclose herewith, for the information of the Government of India, copy of a letter No. 01, dated the 10th ultimo, with its enclosures in original, from Captain W. Evans-Gordon, British Joint Commissioner, Ladak, forwarding sixteen copies of the original Tibetan letters which were taken to Lhasa by the leader of the Lapehak Mission of 1890.

2. I regret that I am unable to procure translations of the letters in question, but if the Government of India can arrange for translations being made, I should be obliged if four printed copies could be supplied for the use of this office.

APPENDIX-6

A Detail Imports and Exports of Ladakh from Different Area during 1869

A.

Implorts into Le from yarkand and Chanthary during 1860.

Names of Articles	Quantity in Maunds of 80lbs. Br						Rate in Le.	Value in Le.	Remarks
	Yarkand.		Chanthang.		Total				
	Mds.	s.	Mds.	s.	Mds.	s.	Rs.	Rs.	
Bhung	1,025	34	—		1,025	34	62-8 per md.	64,116	
Phshm	268	28	260	0	528	28	50 per md.	26,435	
Wool, (sheep's)	—	—	160	0	160	0	15 per md.	2,400	From Lhassa,
Coarse cloth	72	20	—	—	76	20	87-8 per md.	6,348	
Tea, brick, green	—	—	431	24	431	24	180 per md.	77,688	
Tea, Brick, black	—	—	91	8	91	8	90 per md.	8,210	
Silk	127	1	—	—	127	1	400 per md.	50,310	On expert to the Punjab, the slik has proved to be of lower value than was asked in Le–not more than Rupees 320 per maund.
Jade stone	0	28	—		0	28	— per md.	700	
Rewauchini	1	20	—		1	20	80 per md.	120	Used as a medicine, &c.
Gillar pater	6	0	—		6	0	40 per md.	240	
Thread, &c.	0	36	—		0	36	— per md.	56	Seweed, used as medicine
Soap	1	36	—		1	36	40 per md.	76	

Judwar, Zadoari	—	2	0	2	0	1,600	per md.	3,200	
Borax	—	200	0	200	0	10	per md.	2,000	
Phulli	—	140	0	140	0	1-4	per md.	175	Soda eartu.
Salt	—	10,000	0	10,000	0	1	per md.	10,000	
Sulphur	—	220	0	220	0	15	per md.	3,300	
Saltpetre	—	84	0	84	0	10	per md.	840	
Socks, &C.	15 in No.			15 in No.		—	per md.	68	
Mushru, &c.	110 thans	—		110 thans		—		372	Slik and cotton fabries.
Carpets	358 in No.	—		358 in No.		—		2,518	
Felts	3,150 in No.	—		3,159 in No.		2	cach	6,318	
Kinsan, &c.	1,870 in No.	—		1,879 in No.		1	cach	403	Coloured leathers.
Broadeloth	6 than	—		6 thans.		150	per than.	900	Russian
Tawar	1 than	—		1 than		50	per than.	50	Cina slik.
Dariai, &c.	4,046 thans.	—		4,046 thans.		—		5,496	Silk manufactures from Yarkand.
Posteen, &c.	32 in No.	—		32 in No.		—		812	Made of china and Russian furs.

Imports into Le from Yarkand and Chanthang during 1869.—(Concluded)

Names of Articles	Quantity in Maunds of 80lbs. Br						Rate in Le.		Value in Le.	Remarks
	Yarkand.		Chanthang.		Total					
	Mds.	s.	Mds.	s.	Mds.	s.	Rs.		Rs.	
Chowris	603	0	—		603	0	1-8	each	005	Yaks' tails.
Kurus, silver	338	0	—		338	0	170	each	57,460	Chinese silver coins or ingots.
Gold dust	3,160	tolas.	450	tolas.	3,610	tolas.	13	per tola.	46,930	
Jewellery, &c.	9	boxes.	1	box	10	boxes	—	.	24,200	Six boxes of turquoises: one box of coral; one box of manufactured jewellery.
Gold thread	7	bundles	—		7	boundles	—		305	Russian.
Embroidery, gold	2	thans.	—		2	thans.	25	each.	50	
Caps	55	in No.	—		55	in No.	1	each	55	
Knives, Chinese	15	in No.	—		15	in No.	2	each	30	A drug.
Mamiran-i-chini	30	tolas	—		30	tolas.	1	per tols.	30	
Musk bags	—		450	in No.	450	in No.	10	each.	4,500	
Borese	—		125	thans.	125	thans.	15	per than.	1,875	Coarse woollen cloth.
Zankos	—		75	thans.	75	thans	8	per than	600	Do. do.

Incense	—		4	boxes.	4	boxes	—		200	
Pattu	—		50	thans.	50	thans.	8	thans.	400	Strips of fine linen cloth used by the Lamas.
Kidakh	—		2,000	thans.	2,000	thans.	8 annas	per than	1,000	
Paper	—		2,000	sheets.	2,000	sheets.	20	per 100.	400	
Total	1,505	3	11,588	32	13,093	35	—		4,12,587	From Yarkand —Rupees 2,78,799 From Chanthang — Rupes 1,33,788 Total — Rupees 4,12,587

B.

Table of Imports into Ladak from the Punjab during 1860

Names of Articles	*Quantity in Maunds of 80lbs. By*								*Rate in Le.*	*Value*	*Remarks*
	Kullu		*Rampur*		*Cashmir*		*Total*				
	Mds.	*s.*	*Mds.*	*s.*	*Mds.*	*s.*	*Mds.*	*s.*	*Rs.*	*Rs.*	
Buzzazi, piece-goods	128	33	25	7	173	13	327	13	175 per md.	54,281	
Spices	137	18	10	24	101	12	249	14	40 per md.	9,973	
Sugar	286	35	8	0	18	20	313	30	40 per md.	12,550	
Lakhi, red skins	244	86	0	5	242	18	478	14	64 per md.	30,214	
Indigo	35	8	7	10	26	34	60	7	160 per md.	11,108	
Copper vessels	28	13	2	1	18	10	48	33	100 per md.	4,883	
Iron	41	21	5	34	—		47	50	30 per md.	1,421	
Tea	69	1	—		32	7	101	8	180 per md.	18,216	Kangra and China teas.
Tamarind	14	27	—		11	32	26	19	40 per md.	1,060	
Preserves, &c.	8	16	—		0	32	9	8	40 per md.	368	
Rice	12	32	—		—		12	32	5 per md.	64	
Sank, shells	9	16	—		0	27	10	3	100 per md.	1,008	
Nowsada	0	18	—		0	18	0	36	80 per md.	72	Sal ammonine.
Lao	—		—		0	12	0	12	40 per md.	12	

Haberdashery	4	17	—		3	21	10	38	150	per md.	1,642	
Senna	28	6	12	26	12	16	48	8	20	per md.	864	
Soap	1	8	—		—		1	8	40	per md.	48	
Treacle	7	1	—		—		7	1	25	per md.	176	
Majeet, red dye	0	16	—		—		0	16	20	per md.	8	
Hallela, &c.	15	32	—		—		15	32	20	per md.	316	
Drugs, &c.	10	12	—		13	24	23	36	40	per md.	956	
Otter, skins	6,797	in No.	305	in No.	1,000	in No.	8,102	in No.	4	each	32,408	
Kalgi	328	in No.	—		—		328	in No.	1	for 3	100	Heron plumes.
Broadcloth	7	thans.	2	thans.	5	thans.	14	thans.	150	per than.	1,750	
Koran, books	1,006	in No.	—		500	in No.	1,506	in No.	2	each	3,012	
Brocades	15	thans	—		10	thans.	25	thans.	100	per than.	2,500	

Table of Imports into Ladak from the Punjab during 1869—(Concluded)

Names of Articles	*Quantity in Maunds of 80lbs. By*								*Rate in Le.*		*Value*	*Remarks*
	Kullu		*Rampur*		*Cashmir*		*Total*					
	Mds.	*s.*	*Mds.*	*s.*	*Mds.*	*s.*	*Mds.*	*s.*	*Rs.*		*Rs.*	
Tawar (silks)	—		—		11	thans.	11	thans.	50	each	550	
Snuff	—		—		17	bottles	17	bottles.	3	each.	51	
Guns, rifles, &c.	11	in No.	—		50	in No.	61	in No.	—		2,330	
Powder and caps	—				80	boxes.	80	boxos.	5	each.	400	Chiefly English
Corals	4	tolas.	—		4	tolas.	4	per tola.	1.6			
Shoes	164	pairs.	24	pairs.			188	pairs.	2	each.	376	
Combs	15	scores.	—		—		15	scores	1	per score.	15	
Dyes, Aniline	10	boxes.	—		—		10	boxes.	20	per box.	200	
Total	1,085	1	71	88	649	29	1,806	28	—		1,95,957	

D

Table of Imports from Ladak to the Punjab during 1860

Names of Articles	Quantity in Maunds of 80lbs. By								Rate in Le.	Value in Le.	Remarks
	Kullu		Rampur		Cashmir		Total				
	Mds.	s.	Mds.	s.	Mds.	s.	Mds.	s.	Rs.	Rs.	
Bhung	1,337	12	89	0	168	6	1,594	18	62.8 per md.	99,654	
Pushm, wool	93	10	—		56	0	149	10	50 per md.	7,463	
Slik	61	13	—		49	22	110	35	400 per md.	44,350	
Opium	—		—		53	12	53	13	600 per md.	31,990*	*Formerly sent to Ladak and now returned.
Phulli, soda earth	70	36	—		—		70	36	1.4 per md.	89	
Gillar patar	4	16	—		—		4	16	40 per md.	176	Soda earth
Coarse cloth	0	28	—		—		0	28	87.8 per md.	60	Sea-weed, used as a medicino
Dried currants	0	17	—		—		0	17	15 per md.	6	
Jade stone	0	17	—		—		0	17	—	400	
Silver	—		—		0	20	0	20	3,200 per md.	1,600	Broken silver from Yarkand.
Numda, felts	1,608	in No.	96	in No.	25	in No.	1,729	in No.	2 each.	3,458	
Carpets	323	in No.	8	in No.	5	in No.	336	in No.	—	2,838	
Darini, &c.	451	thans.	—		3,335	thans.	3,786	thans.	—	4,561	Silk fabrics

Mushru and chakman	44	thans	50	thans	7	thans	101	thans	—		396	Silk and cotton fabrics
Posteen	8	in No.	—		—		8	in No.	100	per md.	800	Russian and Chinese furs.
Chowris	525	in No.	—		44	in No.	569	per md.	1-8	per md.	85 †	† Yaks' tails.
Kurus, silver	200	in No.	—		172	in No.	827	in No.	170	each	63,240	
Gold dust	1,458	tolas	—		1,550	tolas	3,003	tolas.	13	per tols.	39,039	
Gold thread	5	bundles	—		—		5	bundles	50	each.	250	
Turquoise	1	box.	—		1	box.	2	boxex	800	per box	1,600	
Jewellary	40	articles.	—		—		40	articles	350	each	14,000	
Chinese knives	—		—		18	in No.	18	in No.	2	each	36	
Total	1,568	29	89	0	327	21	1,085	10	—		3,16,860	

C.

Exports from Ladak to Yarkand and Chanthang during 1809

Names of Articles	*Quantity in Maunds of 80lbs. to*						*Rate in Le.*		*Value in Le.*	*Remarks.*
	Yarkand.		*Chanthang*		*Total*					
	Mds.	*s.*	*Mds.*	*s.*	*Mds.*	*s.*	*Rs.*		*Rs.*	
Buzzazi (piece-goods)	323	12	15	0	338	12	175	per md.	59,202	English calicos, &c, from the Punjab.
Coarse cloth	—		25	0	25	0	87.8	per md.	2,188	
Spices	408	9	15	0	418	0	40	per md.	16,729	
Sugar	180	13	15	0	195	13	40	per md.	7,813	
Lakhi, red skin	438	17	6	0	444	17	62.8	per md.	27,777	
Tea	132	17	—		132	17	180	per md.	23,836	Kangra and China teas.
Indigo	77	33	4	20	82	13	160	per md.	13,172	
Copper vessels	1	20	2	0	3	20	100	per md.	350	
Tin	3	0	—		3	0	125	per md.	375	
Drugs, &c.	10	32	—		10	32	40	per md.	792	
Anola	1	20	—		1	20	20	per md.	30	A drug.
Haberdashery	6	0	2	0	8	0	150	per md.	1,200	Needles, thread, &c, &c.
Currants, dried			25	0	25	0	15	per md.	375	From Skardo.
Apricots, dried	—		100	0	100	0	5	per md.	500	

Dates, &c, died	—	2	0	2	0	40	per md.	80	
Saffron	—	1	16	1	16	1,600	per md.	2,240	From Cashmir.
Do. leaves	—	1	0	1	0	160	per md.	160	
Iron, &c.	—	2	0	2	0	80	per md.	60	
Majeet, red dye	—	16	0	16	0	20	per md.	320	From Skardo
Rice	—	150	0	150	0	5	per md.	750	
Barley, &c,	—	1,430	0	1,430	0	1.4	per md.	1,788	From Cashmir and Ladak.
Flour, &c.	—	1,880	0	1,880	0	1.8	per md.	1,995	
Ghee	—	56	0	56	0	20	per md.	1,120	
Silver	—	1	0	1	0	3,200	per md.	3,200	English rupees.
Otter skins	8,853 in No.	19	in No.	8,863	in No.	4	each.	35,452	
Fox skins	375 in No.	—		375	in No.	1	each	375	
Felts	—	2,650	in No.	2,650	in No.	2	each	5,300	
Carpets	—	151	in No.	151	in No.	—		850	Imported from Yarkand.
Turquoises and corals	—	8	boxes.	8	boxes.	—		6,800	

Exports from Ladak to Yarkand and Chanthang during 1869—(Concluded)

Names of Articles	Quantity in Maunds of 80lbs. to			Rate in Le.	Value in Le.	Remarks.
	Yarkand.	Chanthang	Total			
	Mds. s.	Mds. s.	Mds. s.	Rs.	Rs.	
Koran, books	2,000 in No.	—	2,000 in No.	2 each.	4,000	
Guns, rifles, &c.	70 in No.	—	70 in No.	—	3730	The guns and rifles chiefly of English make
Powder and caps	80 boxes	—	80 boxes	5 each.	400	English.
Aniline dyes	15 0	—	15 0	20 each	300	
Brocade	31 thans.	10 thans.	41 thans	100 each	4,100	
Merino, &c.	12 thans	10 thans	22 thans	50 thans	1,100	
Broadcloth	5 thans	7 thans	12 thans	150 thans	1,800	English.
Cashmir Pushmina	18 pairs.	10 pairs.	28 pairs.	100 pairs	2,800	Pushmina chadars, sheets.
Balti chadars	—	15 pairs.	15 pairs.	40 pairs.	600	
Embroidered cloth	—	8 thans.	3 thans.	25 each.	75	

Dariai	—		45 thans.	45 thans.	6	each.	270	Slik manufactures from Yarkand.
Wooden slates	—		75 in No.	75 in No.	1	each.	75	From Cashmir.
Do. boxes	—		75 in No.	75 in No.	2	each.	150	
Shoes	—		85 pairs	85 pairs	1	each.	85	
Kimsan, &c.	—		205 pieces.	295 pieces.	—		73	Coloured leather
Puttu chadars	—		55 pieces.	55 pieces	5	each.	275	
Kurus, silver	—		115 in No.	115 in No.	170	each.	19,550	From Yarkand.
Total	1,587	18	3,198 36	4,786 9	—		2,54,212	To Yarkand Rs. 1,96,323 To Chanthang Rs. 57,889 Total Rs. 2,54,212

E.

Imports into Ladak from Cashmir territories during 1860

Names of Articles	*Quantity in Maunds of 80lbs. from*						*Rate in Le.*	*Value in Le.*	*Remarks.*
	Cashmir.		*Skardo*		*Total*				
	Mds.	*s.*	*Mds.*	*s.*	*Mds.*	*s.*	*Rs.*	*Rs.*	
Iron	10	10	—		10	10	30 per md.	308	
Honey	14	32	—		14	32	25 per md.	371	
Tobacco	48	34	—		48	34	20 per md.	975	
Rice	341	0	—		341	0	5 per md.	1,705	
Snap	4	30	—		4	30	40 per md.	100	
Majeet	—		13	37	13	37	20 per md.	260	Red dye.
Satlron	1	38	—		1	38	1,000 per md.	2,120	
Ditto leves	1	0	—		1	0	160 per md.	160	
Silver	5	9	—		5	9	3,200 per md.	16,720	English rupees.
Lakhi, red skins	75	26	—		75	26	62-8 per md.	4,728	Prepared in Cashmir.
Anola, Hallela	12	0	—		12	0	20 per md.	240	Medicinal drugs.
Oil	3	0	—		3	0	25 per md.	75	
Currants, dried	—		15	0	15	0	15 per md.	225	
Apricots, ditto	—		85	0	85	0	5 per md.	425	

Butter	—		46	0	46	0	20	per md.	920	
Chadars, Pashmina	35	pairs.	93	pairs	128	0	—		5,288	
Puttu, &c.	30	thans.	—		89	thans.	—		246	
Miseeln, combs, paper, & c.	591	in No.	—		591	in No.	—		602	
Embroidered cloth	16	thans.	—		16	thans.	8	each.	128	
Kajri, horse trappings	7	in No.	—		7	in No.	8	each	56	
Swords, guns, & c.	15	in No.	—		15	in No.	—		425	Of Cashmir manufacture.
Shoes, &c.	8,204	pairs	—		8,204	pairs	—		3,185	
Chogas, cloth	2	in No.	—		2	in No.	80	each.	160	Embroidered robes.
Hashia (borders of shawls)	250	yards.	—		250	yds.	1	per yd.	250	
Wooden slates	64	in No.	—		64	in No.	1	each.	64	Takhta mashk used in Lhassa.
Sultak, wooden boxes	65	in No.	—		65	in No.	2	each.	130	Used for carrying flour.
Stone vessels	—		35	in No.	35	in No.	1	each	35	
Total	518	19	159	37	678	16	—		40,002	

F.

Imports from Ladak to Cashmir territories during 1860

Names of Articles	Quantity in Maunds of 80lbs. To						Rate in Le.		Value in Le.	Remarks
	Casmir.		Skardo		Total					
	Mds.	s.	Mds.	s.	Mds.	s.	Rs.		Rs.	
Pushm, white	614	0	8	34	622	84	50	per md.	31,143	From Yarkand and Chanthang.
Ditto, black	92	39	—		92	39	25	per md.	2,325	Ditto
Bhung	11	0	8	37	19	37	62.8	per md.	1,236	Ditto
Tea, brick, green	158	25	3	0	160	25	180	per md.	28,912	Brick tea from Lhassa.
Buzzazi, piece-goods	—		18	18	18	18	175	per md.	2,228	English goods imported from the Punjab.
Coarse cloth	—		1	13	1	13	87.8	per md.	116	From the Punjab.
Sugar	—		1	15	1	15	40	per md.	55	Ditto.
Borax	15	14	—		15	14	10	per md.	154	
Phulli, soda earth	25	24	—		25	24	1-4	per md.	33	
Copper vessels	—		21	15	21	15	100	per md.	2,138	Ditto.
Iron	—		4	14	4	14	80	per md.	132	
Silk	—		0	2	0	2	400	per md.	20	From Yarkand.
Jade stones	0	7	—		0	7	—		200	Ditto
Pushmina thread	2	9	—		2	9	320	per md.	712	Thread spun in Ladak.

Dried apricots	0	16	—		0	16	5	per md.	2	From Skardo
Cotton	0	8	—		0	8	40	per md.	8	From Yarkand
Namda, felts	751	in No.	54	in No.	805	in No.	2	each	1,610	Ditto
Carpets	25	0	—		25	in No.	—		172	Ditto
Pushmina enadars	12	pairs	—		12	pairs.	—		240	From Bultistan
Puttu	19	in No.	—		19	in No.	—		152	Made in Ladak
Pusteen	2	in No.	—		2	in No.	12	each.	24	Made of Ladak lamb-skins
Shoes	—		7	pairs.	7	pairs	1	each.	7	Made in Sirinnggur
Guns and swords	—		4	in No.	4	in No.	—		70	Of Indian make
Koran, copies of	—				6	in No.	2	each	12	From the Punjab
Chowries, Yaks' tails	5	in No.	—		5	in No.	1-4	each	6	From Yarkand
Gold thread, false	1	bundle	—		1	bundle.	5	each	5	Russian, brought from Yarkand
Dariai	14	thans	—		14	thans	6	each.	84	Silk fabrics from Yarkand
Mushru	6	thans.	—		6	thans	4	each	24	Slik and cotton ditto
Silks, Chinese	2	thans	—		2	thans	50	each	100	From Yarkand
Total	920	22	66	30	937	12	—		71,910	

Bibliography

PRIMARY SOURCES

1. Interviews

Interviews conducted by the author over the period 2003 to 2004 in connection with the research topic. Monks are from Lamayuru, Rigzong, Likir, Spituk, Thiksay and Disket monasteries in Ladakh and all of them were been Tibet for their monastic education.

(1) Abul Gahni Shaik. Leh, 25 July 2003.

(2) Dorje Phuntsog. Lamayuru, Leh, 7 August 2004.

(3) Nawang Tsering Shakspo, Leh, 25 July 2003.

(4) Nawang Tsering. Choklamsar, Leh, 24 July 2003.

(5) Phuntsog Rabtan. Lamayuru, Leh, 7 August 2004.

(6) Sonam Phuntsog. Choklamsar, Leh, 24 July 2003.

(7) Ven Konchok Tsultim, Lamayuru, Leh, 7 August 2004.

(8) Ven. Chamba Norup. Spituk, Leh, 4 July 2004.

(9) Ven. Chamba Thakpa. Spituk, Leh, 3 July 2004.

(10) Ven. Eshay Shesrab. Spituk, Leh, 4 July 2004.

(11) Ven. Eshey Angchok. Spituk, Leh, 3 July 2004.

(12) Ven. Eshey Wangchok. Spituk, Leh, 14 June 2004.

(13) Ven. Konchok Chokdrop. Lamayuru, Leh, 6 August 2004.

(14) Ven. Konchok Namgyal. Choklamsar, Leh, 11 June 2004.

(15) Ven. Konchok Norbu. Lamayuru, Leh, 6 August 2004.

(16) Ven. Konchok Rigzin. Choklamsar, Leh, 11 June 2004.

(17) Ven. Konchok Rigzin. Lamayuru, Leh, 7 August 2004.

(18) Ven. Konchok Stanzin. Lamayuru, Leh, 7 August 2004.

(19) Ven. Konchok Stanzin. Lamayuru. Leh, 7 August 2004.

(20) Ven. Konchok Tagspa. Lamayuru, Leh, 6 August 2004.
(21) Ven. Konchok Tharpa, Lamayuru, Leh, 6 August 2004.
(22) Ven. Konchok Tsering. Lamayuru, Leh, August 7 2004.
(23) Ven. Konchok Yangyal. Lamayuru, Leh, 6 August 2004.
(24) Ven. Lhundup Rabstan. Spituk, Leh, 3 July 2004.
(25) Ven. Lobsan Chotak. Thiksay, Leh, 15 June 2004.
(26) Ven. Lobsang Dorje. Likir, Leh, 5 August 2004.
(27) Ven. Lobsang Gyalson. Spituk, Leh, 4 July 2004.
(28) Ven. Lobsang Gyalson. Thiksay, Leh, 16 June 2004.
(29) Ven. Lobsang Namgyal. Nubra, Leh, 14 august 2004.
(30) Ven. Lobsang Norbu. Spituk, Leh, 3 July 2004.
(31) Ven. Lobsang Paljor. Thiksay, Leh, 15 June 2004.
(32) Ven. Lobsang Phunchok. Nubra, Leh, 14 August 2004.
(33) Ven. Lobsang Phuntsog. Thiksay, Leh, 16 June 2004.
(34) Ven. Lobsang Rigzin. Nubra, Leh, 13 August 2004.
(35) Ven. Lobsang Sabtan. Thiksay, Leh, 16 June 2004.
(36) Ven. Lobsang Shesrab. Thiksay, Leh, 15 June 2004.
(37) Ven. Lobsang Stanzin. Likir, Leh, 5 August 2004.
(38) Ven. Lobsang Stanzin. Nubra, Leh, 13 August 2004.
(39) Ven. Lobsang Stobgais. Likir, Leh, 5 August 2004.
(40) Ven. Lobsang Thakmat. Spituk, Leh, 4 July 2004.
(41) Ven. Lobsang Tharchin, Nubra, Leh, 13 August 2004.
(42) Ven. Lobsang Tharchin. Likir, Leh, 5 August 2004.
(43) Ven. Lobsang Thinlas. Spituk, Leh, 4 July 2004.
(44) Ven. Lobsang Thupstan. Spituk, Leh, 14 June 2004.
(45) Ven. Lobsang Thupstan. Spituk, Leh, 3 July 2004.
(46) Ven. Lobsang Tonba. Thiksay, Leh, 16 June 2004.
(47) Ven. Lobsang Tsering. Spituk, Leh, 4 July 2004.
(48) Ven. Lobsang Tsundus. Nubra, Leh, 14 august 2004.
(49) Ven. Lobsang Tundup. Nubra, Leh, 14 August 2004.

(50) Ven. Nawang Gelek. Likir, Leh, 5 August 2004.

(51) Ven. Nawang Lobsang. Spituk, Leh, 4 July 2004.

(52) Ven. Nawang Rinchen. Spituk, Leh, 4 July 2004.

(53) Ven. Nawang Stanba. Likir, Leh, 5 August 2004.

(54) Ven. Nawang Tsering. Spituk, Leh, 4 July 2004.

(55) Ven. Padma Jugskyob. Lamayuru, Leh, 7 August 2004.

(56) Ven. Phuntsog Namgyal. Lamayuru, Leh, 7 August 2004.

(57) Ven. Rabsang Norbu. Nubra, Leh, 13 August 2004.

(58) Ven. Sonam Jorphel. Lamayuru, Leh, 7 August 2004.

(59) Ven. Tashi Phuntsog. Lamayuru, Leh, 6 August 2004.

(60) Ven. Tashi Phuntsog. Lamayuru, Leh, 7 August 2004.

(61) Ven. Thpstan Shesneu. Spituk, Leh, 14 June 2004.

(62) Ven. Tsering Stobgais. Spituk, Leh, 3 July 2004.

(63) Ven. Tsewang Namgyal. Nubra, Leh, 14 August 2004.

(64) Ven. Tsreing Morup. Lamayuru, Leh, 7 August 2004.

(65) Ven. Tsultim Angdu. Rigzong, Leh, 5 June 2004.

(66) Ven. Tundup Palzang. Nubra, Leh, 14 August 2004.

(67) Ven. Yeshes Jamyang. Leh, 7 July 2004.

2. Archival Materials

(I) National Archives of India, New Delhi

Official records of the foreign department, political, Financial and Secret branch, government of India from 1838 to 1940. Following series have been consulted:

Asylum to exiled Raja. Foreign, Courts of Directors, India political dispatch, 1838, 5 and 10.

Dr. Caley's Report Relating to Trade of Ladakh. Department Foreign, Branch Political. A, Consultation October 1868, Nos. 140-141.

Dr. Caley's Report on the State of Trade. Department Foreign, Branch Political. A, Consultation November 1868, Nos. 31-32.

Department Foreign, Branch Political. A, Consultation November 1868, Nos. 316-317.

Department Foreign, Branch Political. A, Consultation November 1868, Nos. 109-110.

Department Foreign, Branch Political. A, Consultation September 1869, Nos. 67-71.

Department Foreign, Branch Political. A, Consultation September 1869, Nos. 232-234.

Department Foreign, Branch S. I, Consultation September 1869, Nos. 354-355.

Department Foreign, Branch Political. A, Consultation May 1870, Nos. 286-291.

Department Foreign, Branch Political. A, Consultation June 1870, Nos. 311.

Department Foreign, Branch Political. A, Consultation May 1871, Nos. 68-69.

Department Foreign, Branch Political. A, Consultation June 1871, Nos. 560-597.

Department Foreign, Branch Political. A, Consultation March 1871, Nos. 202-203.

Department Foreign, Branch Political. A, Consultation April 1871, Nos. 31-32.

Department Foreign, Branch Fin. B, Consultation February 1872, Nos. 77-79.

Department Foreign, Branch Fin. B, Consultation August 1872, Nos. 55-56.

Department Foreign, Branch Political. A, Consultation April 1872, Nos. 651-652.

Department Foreign, Branch Fin. B, Consultation May 1872, Nos.121-124.

Department Foreign, Branch Political. A, Consultation May 1872, Nos. 126-130.

Department Foreign, Branch Genl. B, Consultation November 1872, 61-62.

Department Foreign, Branch Political. A, Consultation January 1873, Nos. 484-487.

Department Foreign, Branch Political. A, Consultation August 1873, Nos. 146-176.

Department Foreign, Branch Political. A, Consultation November 1973, Nos. 26-29.

Department Foreign, Branch Political. A, Consultation February 1874, Nos. 151-153.

Department Foreign, Branch Political. A, Consultation March 1874, Nos. 297-299.

Department Foreign, Branch Political. A, Consultation April 1874, Nos. 9-10.

Department Foreign, Branch Political. A, Consultation May 1874, Nos. 131-132.

Department Foreign, Branch Political. A, Consultation June 1874, Nos. 190-192.

Department Foreign, Branch Political. A, Consultation July 1874, Nos. 107-108.

Department Foreign, Branch Political. A, Consultation 1874, Nos. 214-216.

Department Foreign, Branch Political. A, Consultation August 1874, Nos. 102-103.

Department Foreign, Branch Political. A, Consultation September 1874, Nos. 293-294.

Department Foreign, Branch Political. A, Consultation September 1874, Nos. 390-392.

Department Foreign, Branch Political. A, Consultation November 1874, 220-221.

Department Foreign, Branch Political. A, Consultation December 1874, Nos. 99-100.

Department Foreign, Branch Political. A, Consultation January 1875, Ncs. 304-308.

Department Foreign, Branch Political. A, Consultation February 1875, Nos. 1-2.

Department Foreign, Branch Political. A, Consultation March 1875, Nos. 466-467.

Department Foreign, Branch Political. A, Consultation May 1875, Nos. 293-294.

Department Foreign, Branch Political. A, Consultation May 1875, Nos. 295-296.

Department Foreign, Branch Political. A, Consultation July 1875, Nos. 249-241.

Department Foreign, Branch Political. A, Consultation August 1875, Nos. 203-205.

Department Foreign, Branch Political. A, Consultation September 1875, Nos. 21-24.

Department Foreign, Branch Political. A, Consultation January 1875, Nos. 306-307.

Department Foreign, Branch Political. A, Consultation October 1875, 342-343.

Department Foreign, Branch Political. A, Consultation October 1875, Nos. 344-345.

Department Foreign, Branch Political. A, Consultation December 1875, Nos.19-222.

Department Foreign, Branch Political. A, Consultation July 1876, Nos. 339-341.

Department Foreign, Branch S.I, Consultation 1876, Nos. 8-11.

Department Foreign, Branch Secret. F, Consultation December 1891, Nos. 49-53.

Department Foreign, Branch Secret. F, Consultation January 1892, Nos. 1-9.

Department Foreign, Branch Secret. F, September 1892, Nos. 491-495.

Department Foreign, Branch Secret. F, Consultation September 1893, Nos. 425-495.

Department Foreign, Branch Secret. F, Consultation July1894, Nos. 613-619.

Department Foreign, Branch Secret. F, Consultation September 1895, Nos. 374-383.

Department Foreign, Branch Frontr. Consultation April 1898, Nos. 1-11.

(II) Archive, Jammu

Persian Record, File no. 3, Year 1868 A. D, Tibeto-Kashmir (Traders) patta dated 7th Ramzan 1166 A. D, from the Emperor of Ajam, regarding continuence of the payment of 'Zaket' by the Tibeto-Kashmir Traders and fixation of the quantity of shawl to be imported by them every year 1868 A. D.

Persian Record, File no. 635, Year 1874, copy of a government of India (department of commerce and Industries) Notification dated 8th August, Year 1874, regarding Ladakh Trade Report for 1873.

Brief Summary of the State, Ladakh, Gilgit and Skardu territories.

Administration Report, Persian Record, File no. 551-52, Year 1883 A. D.

Lapchak (Lhasa) deputation of Lapchak to Lhasa with specification –articles for sale in conformity with custom. Persian Record, File. no. 980-C, Year 1886 A.D.

Persian Record, File no. 88, Year 1899, copy of the treaty entered into between Lhasa and Kashmir Darbar.

C. S. Old Record, File no. 115/F-53, Year 1900, proposed establishment of customs post at Leh, Gilget and notes by the Governor of Kashmir and British Joint Commissioner for on the subject.

C. S. Old Record, File no. 10/A-11, arrival of Dr. Sven Hedin Swidish explorer and travelers at Leh and arrangements made by the Darbar for him, year 1901.

Treaty high Road, transport difficulties on Srinager-Leh and consequent advance of Rs. 7,500 to villagers of Ladakh for supply of ponies. Persian Record, File no. 121/A-6, Year 1908.

C. S. Old Record, File no. 271/17-C, Year 1916, Grand permission to leave Ladakh for Lhasa in favour of certain lamas, year 1916.

Persian Report, File No. 361, Year 1924, latter dated 6th Chet, 1924, governing the purchase and sale of pasmina (wool) in Kashmir.

Persian Record, File no. 803-B, Year 1936, Collection of correspondence for S. 1936, from Mr. W. H. Johnson regarding administration of Ladakh and travelers reports relating to Yarkand.

Persian Record, File no. 1209, Year 1839-40, Ladakh to Lhasa, statement of the stages on the road from Ladakh to Ladakh Lhasa.

Persian Records, File no. 1113, Year 1949, orders dated 18th Basiakh, 1949, to the Wazir Wazarat Ladakh, regarding continuance by him of the formal reception and presentation of Dalis etc., to the British Joint Commissioner of Ladakh, Year 1949.

(III) District Archive Leh, Ladakh

Letter regarding some trade goods from Yarkand, from Choudhri Khushi Mohammed, Wazir Wazarat Ladakh, Leh to British Joint Commissioner Ladakh, File No. 298/ 63, dated 19th March 1909.

Letter regarding the pay of the chowkider appointed near Sasser from Captain D. G, Oliver, the British Joint Commissioner Ladakh to the Wazir Wazarat Ladakh, Leh, File no. 8/38, dated 2nd January 1909.

Letter about the British Joint Commissioner travel to Rudokh, from Lieutenant Colonel Adelbert Talbort, Resident in Kashmir to the vice-president of the Jammu and Kashmir State Council, File no. 2109, dated 14th July 1900.

Latter regarding the export of grain from Ladakh to the Tibetan territory, from Khan Bahadur Ahemed Khan, Revenue Member of the State Council to the vice-President of State Council, Srinagar, dated 10th September 1900.

3. Government Sources

Census of India-Series 8-Jammu and Kashmir, 1981.

Gazetteer of Kashmir and Ladakh, compiled under the direction of the quarter master General of India, in the intelligence Branch, (Calcutta: n/d, 1890; Delhi: Vivek Publishing House, 1974).

SECONDARY SOURCES

1. Travelogues

Cunningham. A, Ladakh, Physical, Statistical and Historical, (London: n/d, 1854; reprinted. New Delhi: Sagar Publications, 1970).

Drew, F, The Northern Barrier of India, (Jammu: Light and Life Publishers, 1971).

———, The Jummoo and Kashmir Territories: A Geographical account, (Delhi: Oriental Publishers, 1971).

Fraser, David, The marches of Hindustan (London: n/d 1906; reprinted as Tran-Himalayas Unveiled, New Delhi: Cosmo Publications, 1987).

Hedin Sven, Central Asia and Tibet. Towards to the Holy City of Lhasa, (London: Hurst and Blackett, 1903).

Trans-Himalaya Discoveries and Adventures in Tibet, Volume *I* (London: Macmillan And Co; Limited, 1909).

_______, Tans-Himalaya, Discoveries and Adventures in Tibet, Vol. III (London: Macmillan, 1913).

Moorcroft, W. and George Trebeck, Travels in the Himalayan Provinces on Hindustan and Punjab; in Ladakh and Kashmir; in Pashawar, Kabul, Kunduz and Bokhara, from 1819-182, Vol. 1 (London: John Murray, 1841; New Delhi: Sagar Publications, 1971, and Karachi: Oxford University Press, 1979).

Tucci, G, Travels of Tibetan Pilgrims in the Swat Valley (Calcutta: n/d 1940).

Thomason Thomas Western Himalaya and Tibet; A narrative Journey through the Mountains of Northern India during the year 1897-98 (Kadmandu: Ratna Pustak, 1978).

Vigne, G.T, Travels in Kashmir, Ladakh, Iskardo and the Countries Adjoining the Mountain-course of the Indus, and the Himalayan North of Punjab, 2 vols. (London: Henry Colburn, 1842; Reprinted, New Delhi: Sagar Publications 1981).

Younghusband, Francis, The Heart of a Continent (London: John Murray, 1896; Repr. Hongkong: Oxford University Press, 1984).

2. Tibetan Texts

Francke A. H, "La dvags rgyal rabs" text published in his book, Antiquities of Indian Tibet (New Delhi: S. Chand & Co. (Pvt.) Ltd., 1926), pp. 19-59.

Gergan, Joseph, Bla dvags rgyal rabs C'I gter (New Delhi: n/d, 1976).

Paldan Thupstan, Chags rabs gnand don kun tsan: An introduction to Monastery, Castle and Buddhism in Ladakh (Leh-Ladakh: n/d, 1976).

Phuntsog Sonam, La dvags dep thir sheys chey zegs ma (Delhi: n/d, 2002).

Rabgais Tashi, Maryul La dvags kyi Snon rabs kun gsal melon Zhes bya ba zugso (Leh- Ladakh: n/d, 1984).

3. Books

Bell Charles, The people of Tibet (New Delhi: Asian Educational Service, 1928; rep. 1991).

Choudhury, Deba Prasad, Trade and politics in the Himalaya-Karakoram Boderlands (Hyderabad: Orient Longman, 1996).

Christoph Von Furer- Haimendrof, Himalayan Traders (London: John Murray, 1975).

Crook, John H and Henry A. Osmanston (eds), Himalayan Buddhist Village: Environment, Resources, Society and Religion life in Zanskar- Ladakh (Bristol and New Delhi: n/d, 1994).

Das Sarat Chandra, Journey to Lhasa and Central Tibet; edited by W.W Rockhill (New Delhi: Manjushri Pub. House, 1970).

_______________, The Religious and History of Tibet (New Delhi: Cosmo Pub., 1988).

Datta, C.L. Ladakh and Western Himalayan Politics 1819-1948 (New Delhi: Munshiram Manoharlal Publishers Pvt. Ltd. 1973).

Detlef Ingo Lauf, Tibetan Sacred Arts (Berkeley and London: Shambhala Publications, 1976).

Francke, A, History, Folklore and Culture of Tibet (New Delhi: ESS ESS Pub., 1979).

_______, Antiquities of Indian Tibet, Volume one (Calcutta: n/d, 1915).

_______, Antiquities of Indian Tibet: The Chronicles of Ladakh and Minor Chronicles, (Eds.) A. W. Thomas (New Delhi: S. Chand & Co. (Pvt.) Ltd., 1926).

_______, Ladakh: A Mysterious Land, the History of Western Tibet (London: n/d, 1907, reprinted; New Delhi: Cosmo publication, 1978).

Franz. Michael, Rule by Incarnation: Tibetan Buddhism and Its Role in Society and State (Boulder, COLO: Westview Press, 1982).

Fraser David, Trans-Himalayan Unveiled (New Delhi: Cosmo Publications, 1986).

Genoud, Charles, Buddhist Wall Paintings of Ladakh (Geneve: Edition Olizane, 1982).

Goodman Michael Harris, The Last Dalai Lama (New Delhi: Rupa and Co., 1986).

Grunfeld Tom, The Making of Modern Tibet (Bombay: Oxford University Press India, 1987).

James F. Fisher (ed) Himalayan Anthropology (The Hague: n/d, 1978).

Jogesh Chunder Dutt, The Rajatarangini of Jonaraja, (Delhi: Gyan Publishing House, 1986),

Lamb, A, Sino-Indian border in Ladakh (Canbera: Australian. National University Press, 1973).

________, Britain And Chinese Central Asia; The Road to Lhasa 1768 to 1905 (London: Routledge and Kegan Paul, 1960).

MacDonald David, Cultural Heritage of Tibet (New Delhi: Light and Life Publishers, 1978).

Miller Robert James, Monasteries and Culture Changes in Inner Mongolia (Wiesbaden: Otto Harrassonwitz, 1959).

Norbeg, Hodge Helena, Ancient Futures: Learning from Ladakh (San Francisco: Sierra Club Books, 1991).

Norbu Dawa, Red Star Over Tibet (New Delhi: Sterling Publishers Pvt. Ltd., 1987).

_________, China's Tibet Policy (Great Britain: Curzon, 2001).

Paldan Thupstan, The Guide to the Buddhist Monasteries and Royal Castles of Ladakh (New Deslhi: n/d, 1997).

Peissel, Michel, Mustang: A lost Tibetan Kingdom (London: Colline and Harvill Press, 1968).

________, Zanskar: the Hidden Kingdom (London: Collins and Harvill, 1979).

Goodman Michael Harris, The Last Dalai Lama (New Delhi: Rupa and Co., 1986).

———, L., A Study on the Chronicles of Ladakh (Calcutta: n/d, 1939).

Pirie, Fernanda, The impermanence of power: village politics in Ladakh, Nepal and Tibet, unpublished paper, presented at the 10th Colloquium of the International Association of Ladakh Studies, Mansfield College, Oxford, 7-10 September, 2001.

Radhu, Abdul Wahid, Caravane Tibetaine (Paris: n/d, 1981).

Rahul Ram, Himalayan as a Frontier (New Delhi: Vikas, 1978).

Rizvi Janet, Ladakh: Cross-roads of High Asia (Delhi: Oxford University Press, 1983).

___________, Trans-Himalayan Caravan: Merchant, Princes and Peasant in Ladakh (New Delhi: Oxford University Press, 1999).

Roerich George, Tibetan Paintings (Paris: Librairie Orientaliste, Paul Geuthner, 1925).

Shakspo Nawang Tsering, An Insight.into Ladakh (Leh: n/d, 1993).

Smil Schlagintweit, Buddhism in Tibet (Delhi: Book Faith India, 1999).

Snellgrove David L. and Richardson, The Cultural History of Tibet (London: The Trinity Press, 1968).

Snellgrove David L. and Tadeusz Skorupski, The Cultural Heritage of Ladakh, Vol. 1 (Warmister, England: Aris & Phillips Ltd., 1977).

____________, The Cultural Heritage Of Ladakh, Vol. 2 (New Delhi: Vikas Publishing House Pvt. Ltd., 1980).

Stein, R.A, Tibetan Civilization (London: Faber and Faber, 1972).

Tsering Nawang, Buddhism in Ladakh (New Delhi: Sterling Publishers Pvt. Ltd., 1979).

The Dalai Lama, My land and My people (New York: Potala Corporation, 1976).

—Tucci, G, Tibetan Painted Scroll, 2 Vols. (Rome: La Libreria Dello Stato, 1949).

Vanessa Boeye and Clare Marullu, The Last Forbidden Kingdom, Mustang, Land of Tibetans Buddhims, forwarded by His Holiness the Dalai Lama, (London: Thomas and Hudson Ltd., 1995).

Vohra, Rohit, An anthropology: the Buddhist Dards of Ladakh (Luxembourg: Skydie Brown International, S. A, 1989).

Waddell, L, A, The Buddhism of Tibet or Lamaism, with its mystic cult, symbolism and mythology and in its relation to Indian Buddhism, 2nd edition (Cambridge: W. Heffer & Sons, Limited, 1959).

Walter R. Lowremce, The Valley of Kashmir, (Srinagar: Gulshan Books, 2007),

Warikoo, K, Jammu Kashmir and Ladakh, Linguistic Predicament, P. N. Pushp (edited) (New Delhi: Har-Anand Publications, 1996).

_______, Jammu, Kashmir and Ladakh: a classified and comprehensive bibliography, (New Delhi: Sterling, 1976).

_______, Central Asia and Kashmir: a study in the context of Anglo-Russian Riverly (New Delhi: Gian Publishing House, 1989).

Wessels, C Early Jesuit t:avelers in Central Asia 1603-1721 (New Delhi: Asian Educational Services, 1992).

Zain-ul-Aabedin Aabedi, Emergence of Islam in Ladakh, (New Delhi: Atlantic Publishers & Distributers (P) Ltd., 2009),

4. Articles/Journals

Abdul Gani Sheikh Ladakhi Culture Over the centuries, *New Hope*, Volume 3, No. 1, January-February, 2002

Bray John, "The Lapchak Mission from Ladakh to Lhasa and the Government of India's Foreign policy in the Second Half of the Nineteenth Century" Tibet Journal 15, No. 4, 1990, pp. 75-96.

Crook John, "Ecology and Culture in the Adaptive, Radiation of Tibetan speaking people in the Himalaya" in Osmaston & Denwood (eds.), Recent research on Ladakh, Vol. 4 & 5, (Bristol 1989 & London: SOAS Studies, 1992), pp. 19 - 37.

Crook John and Tsering Shakya, "Monastic Communities In Zanskar: Location, Function and Oraganisation" in J. H. Crook and A. Henry Osmaston (eds.), Himalayan Buddhist Village: Enviroment, Resources, Society and Religion Life in Zanskar-Ladakh (New Delhi: Motilal Banarasidass, Bristol: University of Bristol, 1994), pp. 601-629.

Crowden, James, "Butter-trading Down the Zanskar Gorge: the Winter Journey" in John Crook and Henry Osmaston, (eds). Himalayan Buddhist Villages: Environment, Resources, Society and Religious Life in Zanskar, Ladakh (Delhi: Motilal Banarsidass and Bristol: University of Bristol, 1994).

Cunningham, A. "Journal of a Trip Though Kullu and Lahul, to the Chu Mureri Lake, in Ladakh, During the month of August and September 1846" Journal of the Asiatic Society of Bengal, Vol. XVII, part. I, 1848.

Denwood Philip, "The Tibetanisation of Ladakh: the Linguistic evidence" Osmaston and Denwood (eds.) Recent Research on Ladakh, Vol. 4 & 5 (Bristol 1989 & London: SOAS Studies, 1992), pp. 281-287.

Dutt Srikant, "A brief study of the Bhutan–Tibet Relations" Tibetan Review, November 1998, pp. 12-15.

Gyaltsan Jamyang, "Monkas of Mangtro Gonpa" Osmasten Henry, and Philip Denwood, (eds.) Recent reasech of Ladakh Vol. 4 & 5 (Bristol 1989 & London: SOAS Studies, 1992), pp. 55-59.

Hayward, George W. "Journey from Leh to Yarkand and Kashgar." Journal of the Royal Geographical Society, 40:33-166, 1870.

John Bray, The Lapchak Mission From Ladakh to Lhasa in British India Foreign Policy, *Tibet Journal, 15 (4), 1990*

Khan Gohlam Hyder, "Journal about Moorcroft's journey to Ladakh, Kashmir, Balkh and Bokhara, 1819-1825"; (eds.) Hearsey, Asiatic Journal, Vols. XVII, 1834 and XVIII, 1835

Koros, A. Csoma de. "Geographical Notice of Tibet", Journal of Asiatic Society of Bengal, Vol. I, 1832.

Lattimore, Owen, "Caravan Routes of Inner Asia" Geographical Journal, Vol. LXXII, no. 6, December 1928.

Mann. R.S, "Role of Monasteries in Ladakhi Life and Culture" Indian Anthropologist, 15(1) 1985 (Jan.), pp. 33-50.

Mark, Karl, "Three documents relating to the History of Ladakh," Journal of Asiatic Society of Bengal, New series, pt. I, 1891.

Meinertzhager, R., "Ladakh, with special reference to its Natural History" Geographical Journal, Vol. LXX, pt. II, 1927.

Michael Carrigiom, "Tibet's architectural influence in Ladakh and Bhutan" Tibetan Review, 34 (1), 1999(Nov), pp. 14-18.

Mishra, Tara Nanda, "The archaeological research in the high mountains of Mustang district" Ancient Nepal, 134, Kathmandu, 1984, pp. 147-161.

Norbu Dawa, "Indo- Tibetan Cultural Relations through the Ages" Tibet House Bulletin, Vol. 13, New Delhi, May, 1998.

———————, "Chinese Strategic thinking on Tibet and the Himalayan Religion" Strategic Analysis, Vol. xii, no.4, New Delhi, July 1988.

———————, "Cultural Preconditions for Development: Some Asian experience" South Asian Survey, Vol. 1, no. 2, July-December, 1994.

———————, "Is Tibetan Culture Congruent with Modernity? Some clues from Asian experience" Tibetan Review, 32(2) 1999(feb.) pp. 8-14.

Pascale Dollfus, The History of Muslims in Central Ladakh, *Tibet Journal (Autumn, 1995)*,

. Peissel, Michel, "Mustang, Remote Realm in Nepal" National Geographic Magazine, CXXVIII, 4, Washington, DC 1965, pp. 578-604.

Ramble Charles, "How Buddhists are Buddhist Communities. The construction of tradition in two Lamaist Villages" Journal of the Anthropological Society of Oxford, Vol. XXI, No 2. Oxford, 1990, pp. 185-197.

________, "The Founding of a Tibetan Village, the Popular Transformation of History" Kailash, a Journal of Himalayan Studies, Vol. X, No 3-4, Kathmandu, 1983.

Shah Murray Ahmad, "Route from Kahmir via Ladakh to Yarkand" Journal of the Royal Asiatic Society of Great Britain and Irland, Vol. XII, 1850.

Shakspo Nawang Tsering, "The significance of Khuksho in the cultural history of Ladakh" Osmaston and Denwood (eds.), Recent Research on Ladakh, Vol. 4 & 5 (Bristol 1989 & London: SOAS Studies, 1992), pp.181-287.

Shakya Tsering, Tashi Rabgyas and John Crook, "Monastic Economics in Zanslar" in Crook, J.H. and Henry, A. Osmaston (eds.), Himalayan Buddhist Village: Environment, Resources, Society and Religion Life in Zanskar-Ladakh (New Delhi: Motilal Banarasidass and Bristol: University of Bristol, 1994), pp. 559-599.

Singh Harjit, "Territorial Organization of Gonpas in Ladakh" Colloques Internationaux du C. N. R. S, No. 268- Ecologie Et Geologie De Himalaya, Paris, 7-10 December, 1976,

Southwell, C. A. P., "The Nobra Valley-Ladakh Karakoram" Journal of the Royal Asian Society, Vol. XXXVI, 1942.

Stobdan, P, "Tibet and the institution of Dalai Lama" Strategic Analysis, 20(5) 1996 (August), pp. 699-715.

Trotter, Sir Henry, "Account of the Pundit's journey in Great Tibet from Leh in Ladakh to Lhasa, and of his return to India via Assam" Journal of the Royal Geographical Society, Vol. XLVII, 1877.

Tsering Nawang, "The fate of Traditional Education in Ladakh" Osmaston and Denwood (eds.) Recent research on Laadakh, Vol. 4 & 5 (Bristol 1989 & London: SOAS Studies, 1992), pp. 19-37.

Vohra Rohit , "Early History of Ladakh: Mythic lore and fabulation" Osmaston and Denwood (eds.) Recent research on Ladakh, vol. 4 & 5, (Bristol 1989 & London: SOAS Studies, 1992), pp. 215-233.

5. Unpublished Thesis

Denwood Philip, Ladakhi dialects in their regional prospective, unpublished paper, presented at the 10th Colloquium of the International Association for Ladakh Studies, Mensfield College, Oxford, 7-10 September, 2001.

Hira Paul Gangnagi, Lo Tsa Ba Rinchen Bzang Po and Sarma School, unpublished thesis, Delhi University, 1994.

Singh, Harjit Ladakh: Problems of Regional Development in the Context of Growth Point Strategy, unpublished dissertation, JNU, 1978.

News Papers

Daily Excelsior, Jammu.
Hindustan Times, New Delhi.
The Hindu, Delhi.
Times of India, New Delhi.

Index

U

V